EU ENLARGEMENT AND THE CONSTITUTIONS OF CENTRAL AND EASTERN EUROPE

ANNELI ALBI
University of Kent

CAMBRIDGE
UNIVERSITY PRESS

CAMBRIDGE UNIVERSITY PRESS
Cambridge, New York, Melbourne, Madrid, Cape Town, Singapore, São Paulo

Cambridge University Press
The Edinburgh Building, Cambridge CB2 2RU, UK

Published in the United States of America by Cambridge University Press, New York

www.cambridge.org
Information on this title: www.cambridge.org/9780521607360

First published 2005

Printed in the United Kingdom at the University Press, Cambridge

A catalogue record for this book is available from the British Library

ISBN-13 978-0-521-84541-0 hardback
ISBN-10 0-521-84541-6 hardback
ISBN-13 978-0-521-60736-0 paperback
ISBN-10 0-521-60736-1 paperback

EU ENLARGEMENT AND THE CONSTITUTIONS OF CENTRAL AND EASTERN EUROPE

CAMBRIDGE STUDIES IN EUROPEAN LAW AND POLICY

This series aims to produce original works which contain a critical analysis of the state of the law in particular areas of European Law and set out different perspectives and suggestions for its future development. It also aims to encourage a range of work on law, legal institutions and legal phenomena in Europe, including 'law in context' approaches. The titles in the series will be of interest to academics; policymakers; policy formers who are interested in European legal, commercial, and political affairs; practising lawyers including the judiciary; and advanced law students and researchers.

Books in the series

EU Enlargement and the Constitutions of Central and Eastern Europe
Anneli Albi

Market Freedom and Social Rights in the European Economic Constitution
Stefano Giubboni

CONTENTS

TABLES

SERIES EDITORS' PREFACE

The enlargement of the European Union on 1 May 2004 to bring in ten new Member States, eight of which are in Central and Eastern Europe, marked a historical shift in the EU. No longer could it be seen as primarily a creature of Western Europe (plus elements of Southern Europe). On the contrary, the tumultuous events which accompanied the ending of the Cold War, including the break-up of several federations (Soviet Union, Yugoslavia and Czechoslovakia) opened the way for the EU to become something much closer to a pan-European polity.

Accession involves constitutional change, both on the part of the EU and on the part of the acceding state or states. This study by Anneli Albi comprises the first full length study of the impact of accession upon the constitutions of the acceding states. Although the perspective is primarily a bottom-up one, looking at the constitutional change in terms of what were essentially 'new' and relatively 'closed' constitutions of the post-Communist era, Albi also brings in constitutional change – EU-style – in the form of the Constitutional Treaty signed in Rome on 29 October 2004, and due in turn for ratification in each of the twenty-five Member States. It is clear that change and adjustment, including formal constitutional amendment but also involving the role of numerous judicial actors, especially constitutional courts, will continue for the foreseeable future as the EU enters the critical post-enlargement stage.

This book is the first in a new CUP series, Cambridge Studies in European Law and Policy, edited by Laurence Gormley of the Rijksuniversiteit Groningen and Jo Shaw of the University of Edinburgh. Albi's study responds amply to the series' aims, namely to produce original works in English which contain a critical analysis of the state of the law in a particular area of European Law understood in its widest sense and set out the perspectives and suggestions for its future development, and to encourage a range of work on law, legal institutions and legal phenomena in Europe, including 'law in context' work as well as more doctrinally focused expository work. Of critical importance to Albi's study are the key political markers of sovereignty and democracy, in the latter case in the form of the referendums which were held on accession in each of the new Member States. Albi's approach – like many on the EU – is to treat it as a *sui generis* polity, which cannot simply be assimilated to national or international models. However, the interest of the book lies in the unavoidable challenge of statist concepts and ideas, and whether they continue to have an important role to play in post-enlargement Europe and in an increasingly globalised and interconnected world.

Laurence Gormley
Jo Shaw
4 March 2005

ACKNOWLEDGEMENTS

I am grateful to the publishers for their kind permission to incorporate material from the following articles:

Hart Publishing Ltd for sections from A. Albi, 'Post-modern Versus Retrospective Sovereignty: Two Different Sovereignty Discourses in the EU and Candidate Countries?' in N. Walker (ed.), *Sovereignty in Transition* (Hart, Oxford, 2003), pp. 401–22, and A. Albi, 'Referendums in the CEE Candidate Countries: Impact on EU Treaty Amendment Procedure' in C. Hillion (ed.), *EU Enlargement: A Legal Approach* (Hart, Oxford, 2004), pp. 57–76.

Sweet and Maxwell Ltd for sections from A. Albi and P. Van Elsuwege, 'EU Constitution, National Constitutions and Sovereignty: An Assessment of a "European Constitutional Order"' (2004) *European Law Review* (forthcoming).

Kluwer Law International for sections from A. Albi '"Europe" Articles in the Constitutions of Central and Eastern European Countries' (2005) *Common Market Law Review* pp. 399–423.

CASES

European Court of Justice

Permanent Court of International Justice

Bulgaria

Czech Republic

Denmark

Estonia

France

Germany

Hungary

Ireland

Italy

Latvia

Lithuania

Poland

Supreme Court, Decision of 27 April 1995, on free movement of doctors under Europe Agreement 43
Antimonopoly Court, Case XVII Amr 65/96, 1997.01.08 wyrok s. antym. XVII Amr 65/96 Wokanda 1998/1/60, on public transport tickets 53
Constitutional Tribunal, Case K. 15/97, 29.09.1997 wyrok TK U K 15/97 OTK 1997/34/37, on different retirement age for men and women 53
Constitutional Tribunal, Case VII Anna 39/97, 1997.10.08 wyrok s antynom VII Ama 39/97 Wokanda 1998/9/48, on Antimonopoly Office 43
High Administrative Court, Case NSA I SA/Ld 777/97. 1999.09.09 wyrok NSA I SA/Ld 777/97 Pr.Gosp. 1999/I/40, on customs tax 43
Supreme Court, Case SN N I CKN 1217/98, 2001.05.29 wyrok SN N I CKN 1217/98 OSNAP 2002/1/13, on Polish Bar 42, 53
High Administrative Court, Case NSA I SA/Po 3057/98. 1999.12.29 wyrok NSA U N I SA/Po 3057/98 ONSA 2001/1/34, on Protocol No. 4 of the Europe Agreement 42, 43
Constitutional Tribunal, Case K.27/99, 2000.03.28 wyrok TK U K 27/99 OTK 2000/2/62, on different retirement age for men and women 53
Constitutional Tribunal, Decision of 27 May 2003, on referendum turnout 152

Romania

Constitutional Court, Decision No. 356, September 2003 107
Constitutional Court, Decision of 23 October 2003, on constitutional amendment referendum 156

Slovakia

Constitutional Court, Decision No. 26/97, II. US 31/97, summary in English at www.concourt.sk/A/a.index.htm
Constitutional Court, Decision No. 95/99, on the Protection of the Right Guaranteed by an International Treaty, II. US 91/99, summary in English at www.concourt.sk/A/a.index.htm 172

Slovenia

Constitutional Court, Decision No. RM-1/97, 5 June 1997, Uradni list RS, No. 40/97, on Europe Agreement, in English at www.us-rs.si/en 73, 74, 116, 172, 173

TREATIES, LAWS AND OTHER INSTRUMENTS

European Union

International treaties and instruments

Constitutions

Other national Acts

ABBREVIATIONS

Bull.	Bulletin
CMLR	Common Market Law Reports
CEE	Central and Eastern Europe
EA	Europe Agreement
EC	European Community
ECHR	European Convention on Human Rights and Fundamental Freedoms
ECJ	European Court of Justice
ECR	European Court Reports
ECSC	European Coal and Steel Community
EEA	European Economic Area
EEC	European Economic Community
EFTA	European Free Trade Area
EMU	Economic and Monetary Union
EU	European Union
EUI	European University Institute
GNA	Grand National Assembly (in Bulgaria)
IGC	Intergovernmental Conference
IR	Irish Reports
NATO	North Atlantic Treaty Organisation
OJ	Official Journal of the European Communities
OSCE	Organisation for Security and Co-operation in Europe
QMV	qualified majority voting
Ser.	Series
TEU	Treaty on European Union
UN	United Nations
WTO	World Trade Organisation

INTRODUCTION

On 1 May 2004, the European Union embarked on a historic and in many respects unprecedented expansion. It admitted ten new countries, predominantly from Central and Eastern Europe (CEE) which, for half a century, had been separated by the Iron Curtain. One of many aspects that make this enlargement special is that the acceding countries regained their sovereignty only a little more than a decade ago. In response to a painful past, the new constitutions of Central and Eastern Europe accord a prominent status to sovereignty and independence, and were notably closed to the transfer of powers to international organisations. In order to join the European Union (EU), these constitutions therefore needed to be 'opened up', and the countries engaged into a major process of constitutional revision to enable the transfer of a part of their sovereignty to a highly integrated supranational organisation. This proved to be a sensitive and controversial exercise, not least because unlike previous enlargements, these countries joined at a time when the EU has been engaged in a major constitutional reform involving on occasions federal undertones. This book explores the amendments against the background of comparative experience and theory of sovereignty, as well as in the context of political sensitivities, such as rising euroscepticism ahead of accession referendums. It also undertakes a broader inquiry into the role and rationale of the national constitutions in the process of European integration, as well as exploring the implications of the European Constitution.

The book is divided into ten chapters. It starts by outlining the background of the enlargement process. Chapter 2 explores the experience of the 'old' Member States in adapting their constitutions to the demands of EU membership, in order to provide a point of reference to the developments in the accession countries. Chapter 3 highlights some idiosyncrasies of the new constitutions of Central and Eastern Europe: their protective stance towards sovereignty, and their detailed and up-to-date character and prominent role in CEE legal orders. These features set the context for the discussion of constitutional developments regarding European integration in the subsequent chapters. In chapter 4, the pre-accession adaptations, which usually have been addressed in terms of technicalities of harmonisation and negotiations, will be explored through the broader lens of sovereignty and legitimacy. Showing that the legislative activity of CEE countries in the preceding years has largely been dominated by taking over EU legislation, the chapter draws attention to the paradox that the candidate countries appeared to regain some of their sovereignty upon accession, as they started to participate in the EU's decision-making process. Of particular interest to chapter 4 will be the Europe Agreement Decision of the Hungarian Constitutional Court, where judicial harmonisation during the pre-accession period was found to require a prior constitutional amendment.

The centre of gravity of the book lies in chapter 5, which explores the constitutional amendment debates in individual countries. In order to get a full feel of the factors that influenced the outcome of the amendment process, this chapter should be read together with chapter 7, which discusses the sensitivities surrounding the then imminent accession referendums. These included the popular sentiments about the delegation of sovereignty, widespread euroscepticism in a number of candidate countries and previous experience with invalid referendums resulting from insufficient turnout rates. In order to avoid exacerbating the situation, it was important to keep the constitutional amendments to a minimum, as a wider range of amendments pertaining to the EU's effects upon sovereign governance could have become a dangerous tool in the hands of eurosceptic movements. Besides the shadow of accession referendums, the amendments were also influenced by the constitutional theory in the region, which is explored in chapter 6. That chapter shows that the constitutional theory in Central and Eastern Europe has been underpinned by the traditional paradigm of sovereign nation-state, and the EU has until recently been portrayed as an international organisation. Concluding that as a result of the above factors, the amendments in the CEE constitutions remained relatively minimal, the final part of chapter 5 discusses how this relates to the rationale of constitutions, in the light of the debate about a 'European deficit' in the constitutions of the 'old' Member States.

In chapter 8, the focus turns to the constitutional aspects regarding membership in other international organisations. This will complement the overall discussion of EU membership by offering a point of comparison with constitutional experiences in organisations of more traditional nature, such as NATO.

The penultimate chapter thereafter explores the role of the constitutional courts of the accession countries. Given that constitutional challenges to the supremacy of EU law have mainly originated from those countries that have a constitutional court, the chapter assesses how the advent of new 'activist' constitutional courts may affect the old dispute over who is the ultimate judicial arbiter in the EU – the European Court of Justice (ECJ) or the national constitutional courts.

The final chapter undertakes an analysis of the broader implications of the European Constitution for national constitutions and sovereignty. The European Constitution will be assessed in the light of constitutional boundaries set to European integration by the highest national courts, especially by the German Constitutional Court in the *Maastricht* decision. Taking a post-national approach to the notion of constitution, the chapter contends that the new basic document has a constitutional nature, and, combined with previous steps of integration, it appears to strengthen the case for revising the concept of sovereignty.

The text in principle covers events occurring up to the day of accession, 1 May 2004, but on occasions some subsequent developments will be mentioned, including the final changes to the European Constitution made by the Intergovernmental Conference in June 2004. It should be noted at the outset that the book deals with the eight accession countries of Central and Eastern Europe – Poland, Hungary, the Czech Republic, Slovakia, Slovenia, Estonia, Latvia and Lithuania. In addition, it will include Romania and Bulgaria, the two candidate countries which started accession negotiations simultaneously with the other applicants but are expected to join in 2007 at the earliest. The two remaining accession countries, Malta and Cyprus, are not dealt with in this book due to their different constitutional background.

The book is based on the author's doctoral thesis, which was defended at the European University Institute in Florence in 2003. I would like to express my gratitude to everyone who has provided me insightful comments, general guidance and/or information in different phases of my research for this book. In particular, I am grateful (in alphabetical order) to Ruxandra Adam, Giuliano Amato, Rainer Arnold, Miriam Aziz, Esmeralda Balode, Stanislaw Biernat, Neil Brennan, Maja Brkan, Arnis Buka, Grainne De Burca, Per Cramer, Jeno Czuczai, Victor Duculescu, Peter Van Elsuwege, Mark Jeavons, Michael Gallagher, Daniela Gregr, Solvita Harbacevica, Christophe Hillion, Irmantas Jarukaitis, Alfred Kellermann, Juhani Kortteinen, Julia Laffranque, Susan Millns, Andrea

EU membership was not a self-evident path, and alternative relationships, such as forming an economic area or a loose form of confederation, were offered by the EU's leaders, the CEE countries insisted on the prospect of full membership in order to avoid remaining in a geopolitical 'grey zone'. The prospect of enlargement was ultimately opened in the Copenhagen Summit of the European Council in June 1993. In that summit, a threefold set of criteria, widely known as the 'Copenhagen Criteria', were defined for membership.[4] The first criterion is a political one, requiring demonstration of stability of institutions that guarantee democracy, rule of law, human rights and the protection of minorities. Secondly, there is the economic criterion, under which a country must be a functioning market economy, able to cope with competitive pressures and market forces within the EU. The third was a legal criterion, according to which the country must be able to take on the obligations of membership, that is harmonise its national law with more than 80,000 pages of the so-called *acquis*, the entire body of Community law. The possibility of accession was further defined in Article O of the Maastricht Treaty (TEU), which provides that 'any European State may apply to become a member of the Union'.

Based on Article O TEU, Hungary and Poland opened the chain of submitting accession applications in the spring of 1994, followed in the next couple of years by the other countries. The preparations for accession started with a comprehensive 'screening' of the national legislation with regard to its compatibility with EU *acquis*. This was followed by a gigantic task of harmonisation (sometimes termed approximation) of national law with EU law. A set of 'pre-accession instruments' or so-called 'conditionality documents', including the White Paper and the Accession Partnerships, were developed by the EU to assist the countries in their adaptations, providing at the same time a basis for the Commission's supervision over the meeting of the obligations. Since 1997, the Commission regularly assessed the process of harmonisation in its annual Progress Reports. It is interesting to note that the pre-accession strategies were specifically designed for the eastward enlargement. According to the Commission, these are unnecessary should, for instance, Switzerland or Norway want to become EU members, since they 'already meet all of the membership criteria'.[5]

[4] Bull. EC 6–1993, Pt I.12–13.

[5] See European Commission, 1999 Composite Paper, Reports on Progress Towards Accession by Each of the Candidate Countries, COM (1999)500 final, 13 October 1999, p. 2, cited in M. Maresceau, 'Pre-Accession' in Cremona, *Enlargement of the European Union*, p. 11.

The central basis of the relationships between the EU and the CEE candidate countries in the pre-accession period has lain in the Association Agreements or so-called Europe Agreements.[6] These Agreements established an association between the EU and individual countries, and aimed to help the countries to achieve their goal of EU membership. Initially designed by the Commission as an alternative to accession, the Europe Agreements gradually evolved towards the main vehicle for accession. The Agreements, alongside the pre-accession instruments and the complex process of legal adaptations, will be explored in more detail in chapter 4.

In July 1997, the Commission recommended in its Opinions attached to the *Agenda 2000* to commence accession negotiations with five CEE countries – Hungary, Poland, the Czech Republic, Slovenia and Estonia – as well as with Cyprus. Although none of the Central and Eastern European applicants were found to fully satisfy the Copenhagen Criteria, the Commission was of the view that the selected countries would be able to meet the conditions in the medium term. The invitation was confirmed by the Luxembourg European Council, after which the negotiations were formally opened on 30 March 1998 under the UK Presidency. The second round of countries were invited to join the accession negotiations in December 1999 in the Helsinki European Council; the negotiations were opened in February 2000. This group consisted of Slovakia, Latvia, Lithuania, Romania and Bulgaria, as well as Malta. In the course of accession negotiations, which were structured along thirty-one so-called 'negotiation chapters', the terms of adoption, implementation and enforcement of the *acquis* were agreed, as well as exceptions and transition periods.

In October 2002, the European Commission recommended to admit to the EU eight candidate countries from CEE, plus Cyprus and Malta. Bulgaria and Romania were expected to achieve their EU-readiness as of 2007 onwards. Following Ireland's approval of the Nice Treaty in the notorious second referendum in October 2002, the European Council announced in its Brussels Summit the biggest enlargement in the EU's history. The Accession Treaties were signed on 16 April 2003 in the European Council Summit in Athens, and were then submitted to the Member States and to the candidate countries for ratification. In the latter, the ratification

[6] Europe Agreement with Hungary (OJ 1993, L347/1), Poland (OJ 1993, L348/1), Romania (OJ 1994, L357/1), Bulgaria (OJ 1994, L358/1), Slovakia (OJ 1994, L359/1), the Czech Republic (OJ 1994, L360/1), Latvia (OJ 1998, L26), Lithuania (OJ 1998, L51), Estonia (OJ 1998, L68) and Slovenia (OJ 1999, L51).

involved the adaptation of national constitutions and the holding of accession referendums, which will be the key topic of this book.

As already mentioned, the process of expansion is set to continue. Romania and Bulgaria are continuing negotiations, and are expected to enter the EU from 2007 onwards. These two countries have been joined by Croatia, which submitted its application for accession in February 2003, and has completed the so-called 'screening process'. Turkey continues on the waiting list, although its Association Agreement was concluded already in 1963, and it formally applied for EC membership in 1987. In the Helsinki European Council of 1999, Turkey was finally granted the status of a candidate country; however, negotiations will not be opened until the country is found to meet the political criteria for accession. The controversies surrounding Turkey's membership notoriously include it being an Islamic (albeit a secular) country; its territory being partly in Europe but predominantly in Asia; its size – with almost 68 million people it would be the second biggest country after Germany; and a troublesome albeit improving record of human rights protection.

Last but not least, it should be noted that enlargement has motivated political and economic change not just in the candidate countries: the incentive of potential future membership has equally proved a powerful tool for economic and political reforms in the neighbouring countries.[7] This is especially the case with the troubled region of the Western Balkans.

[7] See in more detail M. A. Vachudova, 'Strategies for Democratization and European Integration in the Balkans' in Cremona, *Enlargement of the European Union*, pp. 141–60, and K. Smith, 'The Evolution and Application of EU Membership Conditionality' in Cremona, *Enlargement of the European Union*, pp. 105–40.

2

Constitutional adaptations in the 'old' Member States

Transfer of sovereign powers: main models

The cornerstone of national constitutions is the idea that sovereignty is vested in the people. Accordingly, national constitutions establish the *pouvoir constituant*'s agreement as to how sovereign powers are distributed and exercised in the state, and embody the idea that no supreme power can be imposed outside the constitutionally established mechanisms. The first exception to this principle was the application of international law in internal legal orders: the Permanent Court of International Justice established in its *Wimbledon* decision of 1923 that obligations undertaken by states under international treaties do not harm sovereignty but are its attribute.[1] In 1951, a number of European countries decided to yield sovereign powers to supranational institutions by creating the European Coal and Steel Community. To legitimise such a step, France, Germany and Italy relied on the provisions permitting limitations of sovereignty or the transfer of sovereign powers to international organisations, which had been introduced in the post-War constitutions. The Benelux countries introduced similar provisions some years after entering into ECSC or EEC.[2] As new treaties were concluded and more countries joined, the picture of constitutional authorisation for European integration became more diverse. In particular, the Maastricht Treaty led in many countries to the introduction of provisions on transfer of powers to the EU, and to amendments concerning various specific aspects of EU membership. Since a number of comprehensive and insightful accounts about the adjustment of the constitutions for EU membership in individual

[1] *S. S. Wimbledon*, PCIJ, Ser. A No. 1 (1923) 25.

[2] The Netherlands amended the Constitution in this respect in 1953, Luxembourg in 1956 and Belgium in 1970. See in more detail on the original six Member States, B. De Witte, 'Constitutional Aspects of European Union Membership in the Original Six Member States: Model Solutions for the Applicant Countries?' in A. Kellermann, J. De Zwaan and J. Czuczai (eds.), *EU Enlargement: The Constitutional Impact at EU and National Level* (Asser Press, The Hague, 2001), p. 65 *et seq.*

Member States are available elsewhere,[3] this chapter seeks to chart some overarching trends and developments. It will first explore the way in which the delegation of sovereign powers has been accommodated, coming then to amendments pertaining to various specific aspects of EU membership.[4]

Although the experience amongst the 'old' Member States is rather diverse, four broader models for accommodating EU integration in the national constitutions could be distinguished:[5]

- constitutions which contain an explicit provision on delegating powers to the European Union and, in addition, have been comprehensively revised in respect of various specific aspects of EU membership (Germany, France, Austria, Portugal);
- constitutions which contain an explicit provision on delegating powers to the European Union, and some other provisions concerning EU membership (Ireland, Sweden, Greece);
- constitutions where EU membership has been accommodated under a broader clause on international organisations, but some amendments have been made concerning specific aspects of EU membership (Finland, Belgium, Italy, Spain);
- constitutions that are silent on the European Union, accommodating its membership under provisions on international organisations (Denmark, Luxembourg, the Netherlands).

The first and second groups consist of those constitutions which contain explicit provisions on the delegation or transfer of powers to the European Union, the difference lying in the level of comprehensiveness of EU regulation in these constitutions. France, Germany and Portugal

[3] See for the constitutional adaptations in individual countries, e.g. J. Rideau (ed.), *États Membres de l'Union Européenne: Adaptations, mutations, résistances* (LGDJ, Paris, 1997), and Kellermann, De Zwaan and Czuczai, *EU Enlargement*. For a comparative overview see A. Jüränki, 'Transferring Powers of a Nation-State to International Organisations: The Doctrine of Sovereignty Revisited' in A. Jüränki (ed.), *National Constitutions in the Era of Integration* (Kluwer Law International, The Hague, 1999), pp. 61–85; P. Mabaka, 'L'Europe dans le droit constitutionnel positif des Etats' in J. Ziller (ed.), *L'européanisation des droits constitutionnels à la lumière de la Constitution pour l'Europe* (L'Harmattan, Paris, 2003), pp. 25–38.

[4] Updated English versions of the constitutions are available at the website 'Consolidating European Public Law', European University Institute, Florence, www.iue.it/OnlineProjects/LAW/conseulaw/

[5] See also, for a broadly similar typology, F. Jacobs, 'The Constitutional Impact of the Forthcoming Enlargement of the EU: What Can Be Learnt from the Experience of the Existing Member States?' in Kellermann, De Zwaan and Czuczai, *EU Enlargement*, p. 189.

amended their constitutions in this respect during the process of ratifying the Maastricht Treaty.[6] In Ireland, Austria and Sweden, the constitutions were amended on the countries' entry into the EC/EU, and Greece introduced the amendments in 2001. The former group of countries, as well as Austria, have in a detailed manner regulated various aspects of membership in their constitutions, doing so in a special chapter (France, Austria) or throughout the constitution (Germany, Portugal). Other countries have limited the EU-related constitutional revision to one or two issues; we will come to these in the next section. To give an example of the delegation clauses, article 88(1) of the French Constitution, which forms part of a new title XV on the European Union, provides that France shall participate 'in the European Union constituted by States that have freely chosen . . . to exercise some of their powers in common'.[7] Article 23(1) of the German Constitution provides for participation in the EU to 'realise a unified Europe', and allows the country to 'delegate sovereign powers' for this purpose. It should be noted that although in the Austrian Constitution, the delegation clause is addressed to 'intergovernmental organisations' rather than expressly to the EU, the symbolic importance of placing an extensive section on the 'European Union' into the very first chapter of the Constitution (Chapter 1B, articles 23a–23f) justifies its inclusion into this group.[8] The Irish Constitution uses a different formula, providing that Ireland may become a member of the European Communities (article 29(4)). Following the *Crotty* decision[9] concerning the ratification of the Single European Act, the Irish Constitution has subsequently been amended to provide an express authorisation for the ratification of each new treaty. In Greece, article 28 providing that powers may be vested in international organisations, was complemented in 2001 by a so-called 'interpretative clause', according to which the provisions of article 28 equally constitute the foundation for participation in the European integration process.

[6] In the two former countries, the constitutional courts had to assess the constitutional implications of the Maastricht Treaty in the famous *Maastricht* decisions, which will be examined in chapter 10.

[7] See for France, e.g. A. Bonnie, 'The Constitutionality of Transfers of Sovereignty: the French Approach' (1998) 4 *European Public Law* 517.

[8] See for Austria's comprehensive constitutional revision, e.g. S. Griller, 'Introduction to the Problems in the Austrian, the Finnish and Swedish Constitutional Order' in Kellermann, De Zwaan and Czuczai, *EU Enlargement*, pp. 147–63.

[9] *Crotty* v. *An Taoiseach* [1987] IR 713, reported in G. Hogan, 'Ireland and the European Union: Constitutional Law and Practice' in Kellermann, De Zwaan and Czuczai, *EU Enlargement*, p. 91 *et seq*.

The third and fourth groups are formed by those constitutions where EU integration has been accommodated under a general clause on international organisations, instead of making an express reference to the EU. While those of the third group contain some amendments pertaining to a few specific aspects of EU membership, the constitutions of the fourth group are still effectively silent on EU membership in 2004. In fact, the constitutional landscape was dominated by the last group until 2000–2001 – the constitutions of Denmark, Luxembourg, the Netherlands, Italy and Greece did not give to a reader any signs of the country's membership of the EU. However, Greece introduced in 2001 the afore-mentioned 'interpretative clause', and Italy introduced in the same year a provision (article 117) on the impact of EU law on the regions, which complements article 11 on the 'limitations of sovereignty', although the latter continues to be regarded as the main basis for EU membership. Finland adopted in 2000 a new constitution, which addresses some specific aspects of EU membership, especially the redivision of powers of state institutions with regard to representing the country in EU affairs. The new constitution replaced the previous one, which, albeit making references to the participation of the Parliament in EU affairs, did not contain any express basis for the delegation of powers. The accession took place by means of the so-called 'system of exceptive amendment', under which the Parliament may ratify, by a special majority, treaties which conflict with the constitution. This system was deployed by the Constitutional Law Commission of the Parliament (an authoritative body for interpreting the constitution) to reconcile the incompatibility of EU accession with articles 1 and 2 (sovereignty and division of powers) of the then Finnish Constitution.[10] The Constitution of Spain does not expressly mention the EU, but it falls into the third group due to the amendment of article 13(2), whereby the right of the citizens of other states to vote and stand in the elections, on the conditions provided in the treaties, was introduced prior to the ratification of the Maastricht Treaty. The Belgian Constitution also falls into the third group due to a similar provision, combined with some other references to the EU.

As concerns the issue of how the delegation or transfer of competences is formulated in the constitutions, no standard formulation appears to be available. On the contrary, a plethora of formulations appears to be

[10] M. Scheinin and T. Ojanen, 'Finland' in Rideau, *États Membres*, pp. 185–8, 191; A. Rosas, 'Finland's Accession to the European Union: Constitutional Aspects' (1995) 1 *European Public Law* 166.

in use, such as 'delegation', 'transfer', 'vesting in' or 'attribution', of 'powers' or 'sovereign rights', and 'limitation' or 'restriction' of '(exercise) of sovereignty'. As a matter of fact, different formulations can even be found within the same constitution. For instance, the constitutions of Germany and France both use as many as four expressions. The German Constitution speaks about participation (article 23(1)), delegation (article 23(1)), transfer (article 24(1)) and limitation of sovereignty (article 24(2)). The French Constitution speaks about participation (article 88(1)), limitation of sovereignty (Preamble to the 1946 Constitution), transfer (article 88(1)) and common exercise of sovereignty (article 88(1)).

Considering the EU's ever-intensifying presence in the formerly sovereign areas of governance, it may be interesting to consider reasons why the transfer of powers to the EU has not been explicitly stated in many constitutions. With regard to the Benelux countries, it has been commented that the provisions on international organisations were adopted during the 1950–1970s with a view to EC membership, and amendment has not been on the agenda because these countries have traditionally been European integration-friendly, and no constitutional conflicts have arisen. This is also largely the case with Italy, whose integration provision was introduced with a view to joining the United Nations, and was later also applied in respect of EC membership. Luxembourg's clause on 'temporary' transfer of sovereignty (article 49*bis*) has been explained by the smallness of the population, and the resulting scarcity of legal discussion. Italy embarked in the second half of the 1990s on a major constitutional revision, which would also have introduced the EU provisions, but the whole plan collapsed in 1998 for political reasons;[11] eventually, the provision on regions in the context of EU law was adopted in 2001.

There also appears to be an interesting correlation that most constitutions that lack a provision on the transfer of powers to the EU share a more difficult amendment procedure. While the constitutions of the first two groups can be amended by a relatively simple parliamentary procedure, except for Ireland where a referendum is required, the constitutions of the two latter groups require for amendment either the dissolution of Parliament, approval by two consecutive Parliaments, or a referendum. Parliament has to be dissolved in Belgium, Luxembourg and, when amending the fundamental provisions, in Spain, where additionally a referendum is required. The approval of two Parliament memberships is required in Greece (note the relatively late introduction of EU amendments in 2001),

[11] See De Witte, 'Constitutional Aspects', pp. 73–4.

the Netherlands and Finland (in Finland, urgent amendments may also be adopted by a five-sixths majority of the Parliament membership). In Denmark, a referendum or a five-sixths majority of the Parliament membership is required for amendments. Another amendment-related factor plays a role in Finland and the Netherlands, where treaties that conflict with the constitution may be approved by Parliament by a special majority.

Other EU amendments

Having looked at the provisions on the delegation of sovereignty, we will now come to those issues that have led to amendments concerning specific aspects of EU membership. There is a wide variety of such issues, depending on the content of individual constitutions and constitutional traditions in individual countries. Amongst these, three issues could be discerned which have triggered amendments in a substantial number of constitutions.

First, eight countries have deemed it necessary to secure in the constitution the control of national Parliaments over governments in the EU decision-making process. This normally includes the Parliaments' right to information about proposals for legislative acts in the EU, and to issue positions to national governments in their decision-making activity in the Council. Such provisions can be found in the constitutions of Germany (articles 23(2–3), 52(3a)), Finland (articles 93(2), 96–7, 50(3)), Portugal (articles 161n, 163f and 197(1i)), Austria (article 23e), Sweden (Parliament Act Chapter 10), France (article 88(4)), Belgium (article 168) and Greece (article 70(8)). The reasons for such amendments are well known: the decision-making process in the EU is heavily dominated by the executive branch, coupled with an increasing erosion of the Parliaments' supreme power to legislate due to successive delegations of powers to the EU.

The second commonly regulated issue is the EU citizens' right to vote and stand in the elections of local municipalities in another Member State. It has necessitated an amendment in Germany (article 28(1)), France (article 88(3)), Portugal (article 15(5)), Austria (articles 23a and 117(2)), Spain (article 13(2)) and Belgium (article 8(3)). Besides this, the Portuguese and Austrian constitutions also stipulate the EU citizens' right to stand and vote in the elections of the European Parliament. The reasons for such amendments lie in the traditional constitutional view that voting rights belong to citizens due to their inextricable bond with a nation-state, and many constitutions express this principle in some form.

These provisions necessitated a revision following the introduction by the Maastricht Treaty of the active and passive voting rights of EU citizens in such elections, should they be resident in another Member State (Article 19(1) EC). In France, this was preceded by the Constitutional Council's finding in the *Maastricht* decision[12] that EU citizens' electoral rights in local elections go against article 3 of the Constitution, which provides that national sovereignty belongs to the people, who exercise it through their representatives or by way of referendum, and that only French nationals form the electorate.

The third group of amendments is related to Economic and Monetary Union (EMU).[13] Of the twelve participating countries, provisions to this effect are found in the constitutions of Germany, France, Portugal and Greece. Associated with a state's authority and national identity, the control over national currency has traditionally formed another core area of sovereignty,[14] and it is regulated in some form in most constitutions. In comparison with many other policy areas where the Member States have delegated to the EU just some prerogatives, the entrance into EMU means a complete, albeit progressive, surrender of monetary competences.[15] As with the issue of voting rights of EU citizens, the French Conseil Constitutionnel spelled out in the *Maastricht* decision that EMU harms the 'essential conditions of exercise of national sovereignty', and therefore necessitates a constitutional amendment prior to ratifying the Treaty. The new article 88(2) of the French Constitution provides that 'France consents to the transfers of competences necessary for the establishment of the Economic and Monetary Union'. In Germany, the ratification of the Maastricht Treaty was likewise preceded by an amendment in this respect. The amended article 88 provides that the Federal Bank's 'tasks and powers can . . . be transferred to the European Central Bank which is independent and primarily bound by the purpose of securing the stability of prices'. The Portuguese Constitution was amended in this respect on two

[12] Decision No. 92–308 DC, 9 April 1992, available at www.conseil-constitutionnel.fr/decision/1992/92308dc.htm. See for comment, e.g. J.-P. Jacque, 'Commentaire de la décision du Conseil constitutionnel n 92–308 DC du 9 avril 1992: Traité sur l'Union européenne 1992' (1992) *Revue Trimestrielle du Droit Européen* 251; L. Dubois, 'France' in Rideau, *États Membres*, pp. 217–21; Bonnie, 'Constitutionality of Transfers', pp. 517–32.

[13] See on this issue in more detail, A. Albi, 'Common Currency and National Constitutions' in C. Zilioli and F. Torres (eds.), *Governing EMU: Legal, Political, Economic and Historical Aspects* (European University Institute, Florence, forthcoming 2004).

[14] A. Chirico, *La soveranita monetaria tra ordine giuridico e processo economico* (CEDAM, Padova, 2003), p. 139.

[15] Chirico, *La soveranita monetaria*, p. 144.

occasions, in 1992 and 1997. In the aftermath of the 1997 amendment, article 102 provides that the Bank of Portugal 'shall carry out its functions in accordance with the law and with the international rules to which the Portuguese State is bound'.[16] In Greece, article 80(2) provides that the law regulates the regime of currency emission. As part of the 2001 package of amendments, a clause was added, which provides that this paragraph does not obstruct the participation of Greece in Economic and Monetary Union. Notwithstanding similar debates in other EMU states, no specific steps to legitimise membership of EMU have been undertaken. For instance, in the Netherlands, some authors have found the attribution of monetary competences to the Community institutions to contradict article 106, which provides in a general mode that the law regulates the monetary system,[17] and it has been commented that this provision has lost most of its meaningfulness since the Maastricht Treaty.[18]

Besides the above, some issues have led to an amendment in two or three countries. These are the participation of the federal subdivisions, autonomous regions and/or local municipalities in EU affairs;[19] the prohibition of parallel powers in the European Parliament and in state institutions;[20] and national procedures for nomination of EU officials.[21] It should be noted that only the Irish Constitution expressly establishes the supremacy of Community law (article 29(4)). In other constitutions, this important issue is accommodated under the provisions on the application of international law, which in some cases were introduced in view of the application of EC law (e.g. in the Netherlands).

In addition to the above amendments, there are a variety of further issues that have brought about an amendment in individual Member States. For example, Austria has introduced amendments concerning some organisational issues pertaining to the work and elections of European Parliament members (articles 10(1), 23b, 30(3), 151(11), 141). The Belgian Constitution has a provision on the election date of the European Parliament (article 117(2)). The Constitution of Finland assigns EU issues to the government's competence, while representation in foreign

[16] See C. Botelho Moniz, 'The Portuguese Constitution and the Participation of the Republic of Portugal in the European Union' (1998) 4 *European Public Law* 468.

[17] Reported in B. De Witte, 'Pays-Bas' in Rideau, *États Membres*, p. 368.

[18] L. Besselink, 'The Separation of Powers under Netherlands Constitutional Law and European Integration' (1997) 3 *European Public Law* 314.

[19] Constitutions of Germany, Austria, Belgium and Portugal.

[20] Constitutions of Italy, Finland and Austria.

[21] Constitutions of Austria and Portugal.

affairs has usually fallen under the President's responsibility (article 93). The constitutions of Austria (article 23c) and Portugal (article 164p) regulate the national nomination of EU officials, and Austria has an amendment on the participation in the Common Foreign and Security Policy (article 23f). The French Constitution contains a provision on the free movement of persons, with a reference to the Amsterdam Treaty. The German Constitution contains a provision on the right of asylum concerning EC countries (article 16a), and on the administration of EC taxes at the federal level (article 108(1)). Germany has recently amended article 12a of the Constitution, to permit the access of women to military service, in response to the *Tanja Kreil* case in the European Court of Justice.[22]

Overall, the picture amongst the 'old' Member States is thus rather diverse, and no standard solution appears to be available for the new accession countries. On the contrary, a broad range of solutions can find support in comparative experience. However, a trend can be discerned towards a wider reflection of EU issues in the national constitutions as integration has progressed. Indeed, while in the early years of integration, EC membership was accommodated under provisions on international cooperation, the ratification of the Maastricht Treaty caused a broader wave of amendments, and the period of 2000–2001 witnessed a wider recognition of EU membership in three other countries.

[22] Case C-285/98, *Tanja Kreil* v. *Germany* [2000] ECR I-69.

3

Some idiosyncrasies of CEE constitutions

Constitutional history of CEE countries

Before exploring the adaptation of CEE constitutions for EU membership, it is instructive to outline the constitutional background of these countries, in order to better understand some characteristic features of their constitutions. In broad outline, the constitutional history of the ten Central and East European countries could be divided into four major periods:[1]

- the adoption of the first constitutions in most countries as a result of establishing independent republics between the two World Wars;
- the putting into place of the Communist constitutions in the aftermath of the Soviet takeover in the 1940s;
- the adoption of the new constitutions or comprehensive revision of the Communist constitutions after the regime change in the early 1990s; and

[1] See for historical background and overview of the contents of the CEE constitutions e.g. I. Dick and A. E. Howard (eds.), *Constitution Making in Eastern Europe* (Woodrow Wilson Centre Press, Washington, 1993); J. Zielonka and A. Pravda (eds.), *Democratic Consolidation in Eastern Europe*, vol. I, *Institutional Engineering* (Oxford University Press, 2001); R. Müllerson, M. Fitzmaurice and M. Andenas (eds.), *Constitutional Reform and International Law in Central and Eastern Europe* (Kluwer Law International, The Hague, 1998); T. Verheiren, *Constitutional Pillars for New Democracies: The Cases of Bulgaria and Romania* (PSWO Press Leiden University, Leiden, 1995); S. Bartole, *Riforme costituzionali nell'Europa centro-orientale* (Bologna, 1993); R. Ludwikowski, *Constitution-Making in the Region of Former Soviet Dominance* (Duke University Press, Durham and London, 1996); C. Taube, *Constitutionalism in Estonia, Latvia and Lithuania: A Study in Comparative Constitutional Law* (Iustus Förlag, Uppsala, 2001); D. A. Loeber, 'Regaining Independence: Constitutional Aspects: Estonia, Latvia, Lithuania' (1998) 24 *Review of Central and East European Law* 5; A. Racz, 'Major Phases of Constitutional Development' in A. Harmathy (ed.), *Introduction to Hungarian Law* (Kluwer Law International, The Hague, 1998); K. Merusk and R. Narits, *Constitutional Law: Estonia* (Kluwer Law International, The Hague, 1999).

- subsequent constitutional adjustments, including the 'opening up' of the constitutions for transfer of powers to international organisations and to the EU.

Amongst the countries in question, Poland, Bulgaria and Romania have long-standing traditions of statehood and constitutions. In fact, Poland was the first country in Europe, and the second in the world, to adopt a constitution in 1791. Bulgaria and Romania adopted their first constitutions respectively in 1879 and 1866, having gained their independence from the Ottoman Empire. In other CEE countries, the constitutional history commenced with gaining independence in 1918, as a result of the Versailles Peace Conference following the First World War: Czechoslovakia and Hungary emerged from the dissolution of the Habsburg Empire, while the Baltic countries separated from Russia. Czechoslovakia and Estonia adopted constitutions in 1920, and Latvia and Lithuania in 1922. Poland and Romania adopted new constitutions in 1921 and 1923 respectively. Hungary had no written constitution until 1949 due to its system of customary constitutional law. In terms of form of governance, Hungary, Romania and Bulgaria were monarchies until 1946; the other countries chose the republican form with a parliamentary system of government. In the 1930s, in line with the authoritarian tendencies in the rest of Central Europe, presidential powers were strengthened across the region in a wave of amendments and new constitutions.

After the Second World War, Central and Eastern Europe was surrendered into the Soviet sphere of influence. The Baltic states had been occupied by and annexed to the USSR already in 1940, in the aftermath of the Molotov-Ribbentrop Secret Pact by which the future spheres of influence had been determined between Hitler and Stalin. In the Central European countries, the factual Soviet takeover occurred in the second half of the 1940s, when the USSR-sponsored Communist parties won the elections by fraud and coercion. Popular uprisings against Moscow's rule in 1956 in Hungary and in 1968 in the Czechoslovakia were suppressed by brutal force. The Soviet regime introduced new constitutions, modelled closely on the 1936 Stalinist Constitution.[2] Czechoslovakia adopted it in 1948 (new constitution in 1960, amended in 1968); Poland adopted

[2] The first Communist constitutions are available in English in J. F. Triska (ed.), *Constitutions of the Communist Party-States* (The Hoover Institution on War, Revolution and Peace, Stanford University, 1986), and the second wave of the Communist constitutions in W. B. Simons (ed.), *The Constitutions of the Communist World* (Sijthoff & Noordhoff, Alphen, 1980).

the Provisional Constitution in 1947 and the Communist Constitution in 1952 (amended seventeen times up to 1989, with far-reaching amendments in 1976); Romania in 1948 (new constitutions in 1952 and 1965); Hungary in 1949 (amended in 1960 and 1972); Bulgaria in 1947 (new constitution in 1971). The Stalinist constitutions were also introduced in the Baltic countries that had been annexed to the USSR. Central to these constitutions was the proclamation of the principal Communist ideals: leadership of the Marxist-Leninist Party in society; state-owned means of production; centrally planned state economy; state monopoly in foreign trade; limited right to personal property, etc. The working class was declared to be society's leading class, and the countries were renamed as 'Socialist People's Republics', where the power belongs to 'the working people'. Even though the constitutions proclaimed human rights and freedoms, the rights were merely declaratory in the reality of a repressive, totalitarian regime. The constitutions were regarded as political rather than legal documents.

At the end of the 1980s, the Gorbachev period of *perestroika* and *glasnost* brought about the overturn of the Communist regimes in Central and South-Eastern Europe, as well as the restitution of the independence of the Baltic countries. In Poland, Hungary, Czechoslovakia, Bulgaria and Romania, the regime change was carried out during the autumn-winter period of 1989. In the Baltic states, the public demonstrations of 1988–1989, commemorating the Molotov-Ribbentrop Secret Pact, paved the way to their independence in 1991, which *de jure* had not ceased to exist. Slovenia as a new state emerged on the map as a result of its separation from the Yugoslav Federation in 1991. In 1993, the dissolution of the Czechoslovak Federation produced two other nation-states, the Czech Republic and Slovakia. The regime change took place in most countries by peaceful constitutional means, as with, for example, the so-called 'velvet revolution' in Czechoslovakia and 'the singing revolution' in the Baltic countries. However, Slovenia's independence was preceded by a liberation war; Romania experienced a dramatic, bloodstained regime change not based on the existing power structures, and in Lithuania, a few civilians were killed by the Soviet army.

Among the constitutional documents of the transformation period, the following pattern can be distinguished: the new or restored states adopted new constitutions, whereas the Central European countries, whose independence had not been suspended, opted for a successive amendment of their Communist constitutions. For instance, Hungary maintained the 1949 Soviet Constitution, although revising it fundamentally in 1989 and introducing nine further amendments in 1990, to the extent that the Constitutional Court has stated that, in the aftermath of the amendments, 'a new Constitution came into effect which differs fundamentally from the former state, legal and political order'.[3] Even though the Preamble to the amended Constitution regards the amendments as interim 'pending the adoption of a new Constitution', more than a decade later the 1949 Constitution continues to be in place. In Czechoslovakia, the Communist Constitution of 1960, which underwent fundamental revision in 1989–90, was formally retained in force until the dissolution of the Federation. A new Czechoslovak Constitution had been debated in 1990–92. However, after the separation of the Czech Republic and Slovakia in 1992, both countries adopted new constitutions. In Poland, the 1952 Communist Constitution was fundamentally amended in 1989 and 1990, although remaining in force. In December 1992, the so-called 'Small Constitution' was adopted, which kept in force a part of the 1952 Constitution, including the chapters on citizens' rights. Even though drafts for a new constitution existed from 1991 onwards, the lack of political consensus over the choice of a parliamentary or presidential model delayed the adoption of the new constitution until 1997.

Unlike Central European countries, the South-East European and two Baltic countries opted for entirely new constitutions, adopted in three of them by the *pouvoir constituant* in referendums. The Romanian Constitution was adopted by referendum in 1991, and the Bulgarian Constitution by the Grand National Assembly in the same year. In the Baltic states, the (re)adoption of the constitutions was preceded by certain constitutional steps that paved the way for re-establishing their *de jure* valid but *de facto* suspended sovereignty. These started with the adoption of the Declarations of Sovereignty in 1988–1989, whereby applicability of the federal laws of the USSR was subjected to prior ratification by the local Supreme Soviets (highest local governing bodies of the federal Republics of the USSR). This was followed by the introduction of the constitutional documents, which prepared the modalities for leaving the USSR, leading to the independence referendums in 1991. Based on an overwhelming approval of independence in these referendums,[4] the countries adopted the Declarations of Independence and started work towards new constitutions.

[3] Decision No. 11/92 (III.5) *AB hatarozat* No. 23, 5 March 1992, at 933, cited in I. Pogany, 'Constitutional Reform in Central and Eastern Europe: Hungary's Transition to Democracy' (1993) 42 *International and Comparative Law Quarterly* 340.

[4] In Lithuania, 90 per cent voted for, with a turnout of 84 per cent; in Estonia the figures were respectively 77 per cent and 82 per cent, and in Latvia 73 per cent and 88 per cent.

Estonia and Lithuania adopted their new constitutions in referendums in 1992,[5] whereas Latvia re-instated its 1922 Constitution, as a symbolic demonstration of the legal continuity of Latvia's statehood. Although the adoption of a new constitution had been envisaged in the 1990 Declaration 'On the Renewal of the Independence of the Republic of Latvia', it has never been implemented. Slovenia's path to independence was marked by similar constitutional steps. In 1988, the country reinforced its autonomy by constitutional amendments, and declared in 1990 the pre-eminence of the Republic's laws over the federal laws. This was followed by suspension of the federal laws and adoption of the modalities to leave the Federation in February 1991. In June 1991, the Basic Constitutional Charter on the Independence and Sovereignty of the Republic of Slovenia was adopted, following the independence referendum in December 1990.[6] The new constitution was adopted in December 1991. The dates and modalities of revising the Communist constitutions and of adopting the new constitutions are available in Table 3.1.

Prominence of the constitutions in CEE legal orders

The new post-Communist constitutions mark in many ways a complete departure from the totalitarian past. As a reaction to the Soviet system, all these constitutions proclaim the fundamental principles of liberal democracy, such as political pluralism; protection of civil and political rights and freedoms; free elections; a rule-of-law-based state; separation and balance of legislative, executive and judicial powers; economic freedom; private ownership; free press. They removed all references to Communist values, and ascribed the supreme power to the nation instead of the 'working class'. For the purposes of our study, two features conditioned by the painful Communist past are of special interest.

The first of these is that in contrast to the propagandist and political nature of the Soviet constitutions, in which the mechanisms for exercising power and guarantees against state intervention remained illusory, the new constitutions are regarded as legal rather than political documents. Being new or comprehensively revised, they establish with detail and precision the mechanisms of and procedures for exercising power and the inter-relationship between governing institutions; the observance of the constitutions is safeguarded by powerful constitutional adjudicating

[5] In Estonia, 91 per cent voted in favour, with a turnout of 67 per cent; in Lithuania these figures were respectively 75 per cent and 74 per cent.

[6] 88 per cent voted in favour of independence, with the turnout of 93 per cent.

Table 3.1 *Adoption of new constitutions*[a]

Constitutional solution	Country	Adoption date		Means of adoption
Re-establishment of the previous constitution	Latvia	Readopted 21.8.1991	Original 1922	Assembly
Revision of the existing constitutions		Amendments	Original	
	Hungary	23.10.1989	1949	Assembly
	Czechoslovakia until 1992	1989, 1991	1960	Assembly
Revision of the existing constitution		Amendments	Original	
	Poland	7.4.1989 29.12.1989 17.10.1992	1952	Assembly
	New Constitution 1997			Referendum
New constitutions	Slovenia	25.6.1991		Assembly
	Bulgaria	12.7.1991		Grand National Assembly
	Romania	8.12.1991		Referendum
	Estonia	28.6.1992		Referendum
	Slovakia	1.9.1992		Assembly
	Czech Republic	16.12.1992		Assembly
	Lithuania	25.10.1992		Referendum

[a] This table, with some adjustments and additions, is based on the author's translation from M. Lesage, 'Introduction: Transition vers la démocratie et l'Etat de droit et changement constitutionnel' in M. Lesage (ed.), *Constitutions d'Europe Centrale, Orientale et Balte* (La documentation Française, Paris, 1995), p. 14.

bodies. The new post-Communist constitutions express the countries' 'will to get rid of the past and to enter a new era – and of their eagerness to establish a firm basis for new constitutional systems based upon principles of democracy and the rule of law'.[7] It has been commented that it is typical of the constitutions of transition countries or newly established democracies to attempt to regulate every societal need or ideal in the text of

[7] E. Smith, 'The Constitution as an Instrument of Change: Introduction' in E. Smith (ed.), *The Constitution as an Instrument of Change* (SNS Förlag, Stockholm, 2003), p. 15.

the constitution, as epitomised by the length of the 1976 Portuguese Constitution (close to 300 articles), adopted just after the definitive fall of the Salazar regime.[8] Overall, due to past experience and the above-described elements, the constitutions of Central and Eastern Europe appear to enjoy a more prominent position in the legal orders of their countries than perhaps their counterparts in many Western European countries; they seem to be taken more 'seriously'. Indeed, it has been commented that in Western European tradition, constitutions are not infrequently conceived of as 'one of the main symbols of what has already been achieved (Norway) or as a compilation of texts solemnly describing . . . how the polity regards itself as governed (Sweden)'.[9]

In line with this, CEE constitutions have undergone amendments to reflect changes in the mode of exercise of state powers, or in the interrelationship between institutions of governance. We will outline these amendments in chapter 5; a list of these amendments as well as of major unsuccessful amendment proposals is available in Table A2 in the Appendix. Amongst the amendments across the region, two trends in particular have emerged within the past decade. First, most constitutions have by now been amended in respect of the transfer of powers to the EU and international organisations, as well as with regard to other international obligations, such as those arising from the Europe Agreements and membership of NATO. The second common tendency is the strengthening of presidential powers, which has been subject to a lively debate in a number of CEE countries, albeit with little success to date. Generally, the constitutional drafters have chosen a parliamentarian rather than a presidential system, with the exception of a semi-presidential system in Romania, and have now found it preferable to strengthen the presidential powers in some respects, or to introduce direct presidential elections. In the latter respect, Lithuania's rather troubled impeachment process of its directly elected President Rolandas Paksas, ahead of the country's accession to the EU and NATO, should provide valuable food for thought.

'Souverainist' character

Another characteristic feature of the post-Communist constitutions of Central and Eastern Europe is that they are distinctly more protective of sovereignty than most constitutions in Western Europe. Five decades

[8] E. Smith, 'The Constitution between Politics and Law' in Smith, *Constitution as an Instrument of Change*, p. 34.

[9] Smith, 'Constitution as an Instrument of Change: Introduction', p. 15.

of forced subordination to the USSR, with detrimental consequences for the culture, economy and social life of these countries, and to nationhood in the Baltic countries, has left a deep imprint into the constitutions. This finds in particular expression in four features common to CEE constitutions, which justify their characterisation as 'souverainist' constitutions.[10] These features are as follows:

- nine constitutions out of the ten CEE constitutions distinguish between *independence* (external sovereignty) and *sovereignty* (internal sovereignty), a distinction less common in Western European constitutions;
- the provisions of sovereignty are protected by numerous safeguards, such as a prohibition on limiting sovereignty, and the obligation of state institutions to safeguard sovereignty and independence;
- there were no provisions on transfer of powers to international organisations until recently in nine out of the ten constitutions;
- in some countries, the amendment of sovereignty is prohibited, and in some others such amendment must or may undergo a referendum.

We will explore each of these features in more detail. First, the importance of sovereignty in the constitutions of Central and East Europe is apparent from the number and complexity of the provisions on sovereignty, which are presented in Table 3.2 and explained in the subsequent sections. All except the Slovak Constitution distinguish between *sovereignty* and *independence.* The former implies internal sovereignty, referring to a state's power competences; the latter denotes external sovereignty, bearing the connotation of independent statehood in the international arena. The former derives from constitutional law; the latter is primarily meaningful under international law. In comparison, six constitutions amongst the fourteen written constitutions of the 'old' Member States do not mention sovereignty at all, declaring simply that the people constitute the source of power.[11] Another four use a one-sentence formula that sovereignty belongs to the people,[12] regarding external and internal sovereignty as a unified phenomenon. Only three constitutions draw a distinction between sovereignty and independence: those of Luxembourg

[10] This argument draws on A. Albi, 'Post-modern Versus Retrospective Sovereignty: Two Different Sovereignty Discourses in the EU and Candidate Countries?' in N. Walker (ed.), *Sovereignty in Transition* (Hart, Oxford, 2003), p. 401 *et seq.*

[11] The constitutions of Germany, Belgium, Sweden, Austria, the Netherlands and Denmark.

[12] The constitutions of Italy, France, Spain and Greece. The Finnish Constitution contains two separate sentences in this regard.

Table 3.2 *Provisions on sovereignty and independence and their safeguards (emphasis added)*[a]

Estonia	Preamble: established on the inextinguishable right of the people of Estonia to *national self-determination* . . . 1. Estonia is an *independent* and *sovereign* democratic republic, wherein the *supreme power of state is vested in the people.* 1.2. The *independence* and *sovereignty* of Estonia are *timeless and inalienable.* 54. An Estonian citizen has a duty . . . to defend the *independence* of Estonia.
Lithuania	Preamble: having for centuries defended its . . . *independence* . . .; embodying the inborn right of each person and the People to live and create freely in . . . the *independent State* of Lithuania. 1. The State of Lithuania shall be an *independent* and democratic republic. 2. *Sovereignty* shall be *vested in the People.* 3(1). No one may limit or restrict the *sovereignty of the People* or make claims to the *sovereign powers of the People.* 3(2). The People and each citizen shall have the right to oppose anyone who encroaches on the *independence* . . . of Lithuania by force. 4. The People shall exercise the *supreme sovereign power* vested in them either directly or through their democratically elected representatives. 135(1). In conducting foreign policy, the Republic of Lithuania . . . shall strive to *safeguard* . . . *independence* . . . 136. The Republic of Lithuania shall participate in international organizations provided that they do not contradict the . . . *independence* of the State.
Latvia	1. Latvia is an *independent* democratic Republic. 2. The *sovereign power* of the State of Latvia is vested in the *people of Latvia.*
Romania	1(1). Romania is a *sovereign, independent, unitary and indivisible National State.* 2(1). *National sovereignty* resides with the Romanian people . . . 2(2). No group or person may exercise *sovereignty* in one's own name.

Table 3.2 (*cont.*)

	4(1). The State foundation is laid on the *unity of the Romanian people.* 8(2). Political parties . . . contribute to the definition and expression of the political will of the citizens, while observing *national sovereignty* . . . 37(2). Any political parties or organizations which . . . militate against . . . the *sovereignty, integrity,* or *independence* of Romania shall be unconstitutional. 80(1.1). The President . . . is the safeguard of the *national independence* . . . 82(2) and 103. [The oath given by the President, Prime Minister and other Ministers:] 'I solemnly swear . . . to defend . . . Romania's *sovereignty, independence* . . .' 117(1). The Army shall . . . guarantee the *sovereignty, independence* . . . of the State. 148(1). The provisions of this Constitution with regard to the *national, independent, unitary* and *indivisible character of the Romanian State* . . . shall not be subject to revision.
Hungary	2(1). The Republic of Hungary shall be an *independent,* democratic state under the rule of law. 2(2). In the Republic of Hungary all *power is vested in the people,* who exercise their *sovereignty* through elected representatives and directly. 5. The State of the Republic of Hungary shall defend . . . *power of the people,* the *independence* . . . of the country. 6(1). The Republic of Hungary . . . shall refrain from the use of force and the threat thereof against the *independence* . . . of other states. 19(2). Exercising its rights flowing from the *sovereignty of the people,* the Parliament shall ensure the constitutional order of society . . . 51(1). The Chief Prosecutor and the Office of the Public Prosecutor . . . shall steadfastly prosecute any act which violates or endangers the . . . *independence* of the country. 68(1). The national and ethnic minorities living in the Republic of Hungary participate in the *sovereign power of the people* . . . they represent a constituent factor of the State.

(*cont.*)

Table 3.2 (*cont.*)

Czech Republic	Preamble: at the time of the renewal of an *independent* Czech state . . . 1. The Czech Republic is a *sovereign*, unified, and democratic law-observing state . . . 2(1). All *state power* derives from the people . . . 9(2). Any change of fundamental attributes of the democratic law-observing state is inadmissible.
Slovakia	Preamble: proceeding from the natural right of nations to *self-determination* . . . 1. The Slovak Republic is a *sovereign*, democratic, and law-governed state. 2(1). *State power* is derived from citizens . . . 34(3). The exercise of the rights of citizens belonging to national minorities and ethnic groups . . . must not be conducive to jeopardizing the *sovereignty* . . . of the Slovak Republic . . . 106. The National Council of the Slovak Republic can recall the president from his post if the president is engaged in activity directed against the *sovereignty* . . .
Bulgaria	Preamble: in awareness of our irrevocable duty to guard the *national and state integrity* of Bulgaria . . . 1(2). The entire *power of the state* shall derive from the people. 1(3). No part of the people, no political party nor any other organisation, state institution, or individual shall usurp the expression of the *popular sovereignty.* 9. The armed forces shall guarantee the *sovereignty* . . . and *independence* of the county . . . 44(2). No organization shall act to the detriment of the country's *sovereignty* and *national integrity*, or the *unity of the nation* . . . 18(2) and (3). The state shall exercise *sovereign rights* . . . 24(2). The foreign policy of . . . Bulgaria shall have as its uppermost objective the . . . *independence* of the country . . .
Slovenia	Preamble: Proceeding from the Basic Constitutional Charter on *Independence* and *Sovereignty* of the Republic of Slovenia . . . and the fundamental and permanent right of the Slovene nation to *self-determination* . . .

Table 3.2 (*cont.*)

	3(1). Slovenia is a state of all its citizens and is founded on the *permanent* and *inalienable* right of the Slovene nation to *self-determination*. 3(2). In Slovenia power is vested in the people.
Poland	Preamble: Homeland, which recovered . . . the possibility of a *sovereign* and democratic determination of its fate . . . 4(1). *Supreme power* in the Republic of Poland shall be vested in the Nation. 5. The Republic of Poland shall safeguard the *independence* and integrity of its territory . . . 26. The Armed Forces of the Republic of Poland shall safeguard the *independence* . . . of the State . . . 104(2). Deputies' oath: 'I do solemnly swear . . . to safeguard the *sovereignty* . . . of the State. . .' 126(2). The President of the Republic shall . . . safeguard the *sovereignty* . . . of the State . . . 130. President's oath: '. . . I pledge that I shall steadfastly safeguard . . . the *independence* . . . of the State . . .'

[a] This table is a somewhat modified version of a table published in A. Albi, 'Post-modern Versus Retrospective Sovereignty: Two Different Sovereignty Discourses in the EU and Candidate Countries?' in N. Walker (ed.), *Sovereignty in Transition* (Hart, Oxford, 2003), pp. 404–6.

(articles 1 and 32), Portugal (Preamble, articles 1, 2, 3(1) and 7(1)) and Ireland (Preamble and article 5).

The widely entrenched distinction between sovereignty and independence in Central and Eastern Europe has, in the author's view, particular historic reasons. In Western Europe, the different history of statehood and decades of integration have rendered this distinction less common, whereas in Central and Eastern Europe, these terms form a precondition for explaining the earlier situation with regard to sovereignty. In the case of the Central and South-East European countries, the USSR controlled *de facto* their internal sovereignty – the content of the law-making activity – while they formally retained independent statehood (external sovereignty). Although the Baltic states and Slovenia possessed neither internal nor external sovereignty, their process of liberation underwent distinct stages, first achieving sovereignty and then independence. Their liberation movements were initiated with the Declarations of Sovereignty, according to which the federal laws were only applicable subject to a prior ratification by the local Parliaments. This was shortly followed by the Declarations of Independence, which manifested the (re)appearance of the independent states on the international scene. The issue of sovereignty remains sensitive due to the geopolitical situation of the Central and Eastern European countries, especially of the three Baltic countries.

Besides the distinction between sovereignty and independence, the CEE constitutions add to these provisions a variety of safeguards. The most protectionist group is formed by the Baltic constitutions, which, prompted by an oppressive history and (re)adopted at the beginning of the 1990s when troops of the Soviet occupation were still in the countries, reflect the primary quest to assert the Republics' independence from Russia. As examples of safeguards on sovereignty (for detailed provisions see Table 3.2), the Estonian Constitution declares that sovereignty and independence are eternal and inalienable. This provision was originally meant to prevent Estonia's capitulation in a potential conflict with Russia, so as to avoid repetition of the historical precedent where the then President of Estonia permitted the invasion of USSR troops in 1940. The constitution also mentions the inextinguishable right of the Estonian people to self-determination, and the citizens' duty to protect the country's independence. The Lithuanian Constitution prohibits limitation of and claims to the sovereign power of the people, and foreign policy must safeguard Lithuania's independence. In both countries, as well as in Latvia, the provisions of sovereignty may only be amended by means of a referendum.

The Romanian Constitution is likewise highly protective towards sovereignty. It declares that Romania is a sovereign, independent, unitary and indivisible nation-state, and prohibits amendment of these characteristics. Further, political organisations have to respect, and the President and the army have to safeguard, the sovereignty and independence of the state; sovereignty may not be exercised in the name of any group or person. The President, Prime Minister and other ministers have to give an oath pledging to defend Romania's sovereignty and independence. In the constitution of neighbouring Bulgaria, foreign policy and the army have to protect and all organisations have to respect the country's sovereignty, independence and national integrity. The constitution prohibits the usurpation of popular sovereignty, recalls the irrevocable duty to guard Bulgaria's national and state integrity, and emphasises the national character of the Bulgarian state.

Amongst the constitutions with less numerous safeguards, the Hungarian Constitution obliges the state to defend sovereignty and independence, and the Prosecutor's Office is to prosecute acts against Hungary's independence. Sovereignty is further mentioned in connection with the Parliament's exercise of rights, and the participation of national minorities in the sovereign power of the people. The Czech Constitution prohibits the amendment of the provisions related to 'the fundamental attributes of the democratic law-observing state', which according to Czech legal theory includes the principles of popular sovereignty and democracy, rule of law and division of powers.[13] The Slovene Constitution recalls sovereignty and independence in its Preamble and, Slovenia being a new state, the constitution also underlines the permanence and inalienability of the right to self-determination. The Slovak Constitution provides that the President is to be recalled for activities against sovereignty, and that national minorities may not jeopardise Slovakia's sovereignty.

At the liberal end towards international cooperation we find the new 1997 Polish Constitution, which replaced the previous constitutional documents. Unlike other CEE constitutions at the time, the new Polish Constitution is open for delegation of powers to international organisations, and it is remarkable also for the reason that it begins with the principle of the rule of law, and with a declaration about the common good being the objective of the state. However, it contains clauses providing that Poland and its armed forces have to safeguard the country's independence, and the deputies and the President have to give an oath to safeguard the sovereignty/independence of the state. In addition, the previous constitutional documents had equally been closed towards international cooperation.

Besides complex safeguards for sovereignty, nine constitutions amongst the ten Central and East European candidate countries did not initially contain provisions on transferring powers to international organisations. In the words of Miroslaw Wyrzykowski, 'it is characteristic that Eastern European constitutions, although promulgated during the period when Western Europe's constitutions were adapted to accommodate the Treaty of Maastricht, neither have any provisions authorizing the "constitutional" process of European integration, nor any open integration clauses'.[14] However, this is in contrast with their remarkably open

[13] K. Vodicka, 'Unaufhebbare Grundprinzipien der tschechischen Verfassungsordnung' (1996) 42 *Osteuropa Recht* 225.

[14] M. Wyrzykowski, 'The Constitutions of the Eastern European Countries in the Structure of European Constitutionalism' in R. Bieber and P. Widmer (eds.), *L'Espace Constitutionnel Européen* (Schulthess Polygraphischer Verlag, Zürich, 1995), p. 161.

stance towards international law: many of them expressly provide for direct applicability and supremacy of treaties, and have been acclaimed for their 'internationalised'[15] or 'international law-friendly'[16] character in the comparative European context.[17]

Initially, only the Lithuanian Constitution included a special provision that permitted Lithuania's participation in international organisations, 'provided that they do not contradict the interests and *independence* of the State' (emphasis added) (article 136). The Lithuanian 'Founding Fathers' have reconciled the quest for Western cooperation and the sensitivity towards the East by explicitly prohibiting Lithuania's participation in the organisations based on the former USSR (article 150). The Slovak Constitution authorises the entrance into a 'state alliance' (article 7), but this provision was, according to most authors, aimed at a closer relationship with the Czech Republic instead of a delegation of powers to international organisations.[18] The Estonian and Bulgarian Constitutions contained a clause authorising the Parliaments to ratify, *inter alia*, treaties concerning the participation in international organisations (articles 121 and 85 respectively), but there were no explicit provisions authorising the delegation of state powers to international organisations. In fact, the *travaux préparatoires* of the Estonian Constitution in the Constitutional Assembly made it clear that on the basis of article 1, Estonia's entrance into political, economic and military associations of states would require a prior constitutional amendment and a referendum.[19] Some constitutions declared a general will for international cooperation. For instance, the Hungarian Constitution provides that Hungary 'seeks to cooperate with all the nations and countries of the world' (article 6(2)). The Romanian Constitution declares that the country 'fosters and develops peaceful relations with all states, and in this context, good neighbourly relations, based on

[15] E. Stein, 'International Law in Internal Law: Toward Internationalization of Central-Eastern European Constitutions?' (1994) 88 *American Journal of International Law* 427.

[16] K. Korkelia, 'New Trends regarding the Relationship between International and National Law (with a Special View Towards the States of Eastern Europe)' (1997) 23 *Review of Central and East European Law* 227. See for a similar view also V. S. Vereshchetin, 'New Constitutions and the Old Problem of the Relationship between International Law and National Law' (1996) 7 *European Journal of International Law* 29.

[17] The position of international law in domestic law will be addressed in chapter 5.

[18] M. Hoskova, 'Legal Aspects of the Integration of the Czech Republic and Slovakia into European Security and Economic Structures' (1994) 37 *German Yearbook of International Law* 91; Stein, 'International Law', p. 443.

[19] *Põhiseadus ja Põhiseaduse Assamblee* [Constitution and Constitutional Assembly] (Õigusteabe AS Juura, Tallinn, 1996), p. 530.

the principles and other generally recognised provisions of international law' (article 10). However, EU integration triggered a major wave of 'opening up' of the constitutions for explicit delegation of powers, which will be explored in chapter 5.

It should be noted that during the drafting process of the new constitutions, foreign experts in several countries did recommend the inclusion of provisions on transferring powers to international organisations. For instance, in the Czech Republic, the draft of the constitution contained an article to this effect,[20] and it was pointed out that without such a provision, the Republic would most likely not be in a position to accede to the European Union. The omission of such a provision from the final constitution was regarded as curious by foreign advisers.[21] Provisions on integration into international and European organisations had also been recommended by foreign experts in Estonia during the deliberations in the Constitutional Assembly. Altogether, the choice to omit provisions on delegation of powers to international organisations, while at the same time introducing provisions about the status of international law, probably reflects the gradual nature of the move away from the total absence of an international dimension in the Communist constitutions. The Communist constitutions did not contain provisions on the position and applicability of international treaties; these had to be ratified and transposed by national law according to the dualist concept governing in the Socialist sphere.[22] The issue of relationship between international law and domestic law did not play any role in the policy of Central and Eastern European states during the Communist period, and scholarly publications and research on the topic were relatively rare.[23]

Besides the above safeguards for sovereignty, and the absence of delegation clauses, there are additional safeguards regarding the amendment

[20] Stein, 'International Law', pp. 440–1. [21] Stein, 'International Law', p. 441.

[22] T. Schweisfurth and R. Alleweldt, 'The Position of International Law in the Central and Eastern European Countries' (1997) 40 *German Yearbook of International Law* 165, with reference to Stein, 'International Law', p. 432. See also with regard to Poland, W. Czaplinski, 'The Relationship between International Law and Polish Municipal Law in the Light of the 1997 Constitution and Jurisprudence' (1999) *Droit Polonais Contemporain* 19, and with regard to Bulgaria, E. Evtimov, 'Die Bulgarische Verfassung und das Europarecht: Spannungsfelder und Lösungsansätze' (2001) 47 *Osteuropa Recht* 397 and E. Konstantinov, 'The Implementation of International Treaty Obligations in the National Legal Order: The Answer of the Bulgarian Constitution' (1995) 2 *Journal of Constitutional Law in Eastern and Central Europe* 63.

[23] Czaplinski, 'Relationship between International Law and Polish Municipal Law', pp. 19–20.

of sovereignty in some constitutions. First, some CEE constitutions, as already mentioned, simply prohibit the amendment of the fundamental constitutional provisions (Romania and the Czech Republic), or declare certain principles timeless and inalienable (Estonia – sovereignty and independence; Slovenia – the right to national self-determination). In four constitutions, amendment of the provisions on sovereignty requires a referendum, and it is optional in three others, whereas, in comparison, referendums generally have an unimportant role in the constitutional amendment procedures of the 'old' Member States, with six of them not holding referendums at all.[24] In Romania, the constitution requires a referendum for any constitutional amendments; this mirrors the Constitutional Assembly's intention to make the basic law of the land 'carved in stone'.[25] The constitutions of Estonia, Latvia and Lithuania require a referendum for amending the fundamental provisions proclaimed in the first chapters, including sovereignty. In Latvia and Estonia, the ordinary provisions may also optionally be subject to a referendum. Poland provides an optional referendum specially for amending the fundamental provisions of Chapter I, and for entry into international organisations. The Slovene Constitution provides a referendum for any constitutional amendments, where so required by thirty deputies. In Bulgaria, constitutional amendments may not be submitted to a referendum, but the Grand National Assembly has to be specially elected in order to amend fundamental issues.[26] It should also be noted that the possibility of holding a referendum is envisaged in the recent EU amendments for the entrance into international organisations or the EU in the Czech Republic, Slovenia and Latvia. Referendums, as will be seen in chapter 7, require a rather high minimum turnout (usually 50 per cent, and three-quarters of all the citizens who have voting rights when amending article 1 in Lithuania), and may not be re-initiated during a certain period in the event of a failure. Finally, the amendment of the constitutional amendment procedure requires a referendum in Estonia, Latvia, Lithuania and Romania. In Poland, an optional referendum is specially provided for in this case, and in Bulgaria, the Grand National Assembly is to be elected.

[24] Germany, Luxembourg, Belgium, Greece and, until the forthcoming referendum on the European Constitution, Spain and the Netherlands.

[25] A. Ciobanu-Dordea, 'Constitutional Problems of Accession in Romania' in A. Kellermann, J. De Zwaan and J. Czuczai (eds.), *EU Enlargement: The Constitutional Impact at EU and National Level* (Asser Press, The Hague, 2001), p. 311.

[26] See for amendment procedures in individual countries chapter 5, and Table A2 in the Appendix.

Constitutions have been portrayed as a reflection of society's soul: 'the constitution is who we *are*',[27] that is 'a characteristic way of life, the national character of a people, their ethos or fundamental nature as a people, a product of their particular history and social conditions'.[28] In the context of the constitutions of Central and Eastern Europe, this has usually been associated with the definition of who can be citizens, and efforts to identify the common fundamental values of a community.[29] However, the discussion in this chapter has shown that there is something even more fundamental entrenched in the CEE constitutions regarding the 'product of . . . particular history' or 'who we are'. It is the strong historical quest for liberation and sovereignty which, finally re-established, is entrenched with a complex set of provisions of sovereignty, a variety of safeguards, apprehensiveness towards international organisations and rigid amendment procedures. In the words of Katharina Mathernova, '[p]eoples of Central Europe characteristically pay much attention to historical events; they carry a "backpack full of history" on their shoulders'.[30] On the basis of the above, it could be said that this is true also at the constitutional level. It is in this light that the following chapters discuss European integration of the CEE countries. The next chapter assesses the legitimacy of the pre-accession adaptations, and the subsequent chapters discuss the constitutional implications of EU membership.

[27] W. Sadurski, 'Conclusions: On the Relevance of Institutions and the Centrality of Constitutions in Post-Communist Transitions' in Zielonka and Pravda, *Democratic Consolidation*, p. 461.

[28] H. Fenichel Pitkin, 'The Idea of a Constitution' (1987) 37 *Journal of Legal Education* 167, cited in Sadurski, 'Conclusions', p. 462.

[29] e.g. Sadurski, 'Conclusions', pp. 462–3.

[30] K. Mathernova, 'Czecho?Slovakia: Constitutional Disappointments' in Dick and Howard, *Constitution Making*, p. 58.

4

Constitutional issues in the pre-accession period

Europe Agreements in CEE legal orders

The main legal basis for the relationship between the EU and CEE has lain in the Europe Agreements,[1] which created an association between the EU and each individual country. The Europe Agreements established a free trade area in industrial goods, provided a general framework for political dialogue, and established the basis for cooperation in various other fields, such as industry, environment, technology, science and education. They also provided a framework for the EU's financial and technical assistance to these countries. Central to the Agreements was the obligation to harmonise the countries' legislation with EC law; the Agreements specified the areas of priority, which mainly lay in internal market and competition. The Europe Agreements were first concluded with the Vishegrad countries – Poland, Hungary and the Czechoslovak Federation in 1991 – followed in 1993 by Romania, Bulgaria and, after the dissolution of the Czechoslovak Federation, Slovakia and the Czech Republic. The Europe Agreements with Estonia, Latvia and Lithuania were signed in 1995, and with Slovenia in 1996. For the eight CEE accession countries, the Europe Agreements ceased to exist as of 1 May 2004, but they continue to be in force with regard to Romania and Bulgaria.

This section explores in hindsight the position and application of the Europe Agreements in CEE legal orders, as this experience continues to be of relevance for current and future candidate countries. We will start with a discussion on the direct effect of the Europe Agreements, and on the application of the Europe Agreements in CEE courts. The subsequent sections then turn to consider some broader issues pertaining to the legitimacy of harmonisation under the Europe Agreements.

The European Court of Justice (ECJ) has encountered on several occasions the issue of whether the Europe Agreements' provisions possess

[1] See, for the publication details of the Europe Agreements, chapter 1, note 6.

direct effect, that is whether they are formulated sufficiently clearly and precisely, and confer concrete subjective rights to natural or legal persons. The cases of *Barkoci and Malik*,[2] *Gloszczuk*,[3] *Kondova*[4] and *Jany*[5] concerned the direct applicability of the right of self-employment, and the issue of whether this right took the same scope as that provided in Article 43 of the EC Treaty.[6] The provisions on equal treatment of self-employed persons were virtually identical in all the Europe Agreements. For instance, Article 44(3) of the Polish Association Agreement provided that '[e]ach Member State shall grant . . . a treatment no less favourable than that accorded to its own companies and nationals for the establishment of Polish companies and nationals as defined in article 48 and shall grant in the operation of Polish companies and nationals established in its territory a treatment no less favourable than that accorded to its own companies and nationals'. The fourth paragraph of this article defined the terminology used in this provision, adding that the rights did not extend to seeking or taking up employment in the labour market. These provisions did not require the adoption of implementing provisions.

[2] Case C-257/99, *Barkoci and Malik* [2001] ECR I-6557. The case concerned two Czech citizens of Roma origin, who failed to be granted asylum in the United Kingdom and applied then for entry on the basis of the right of non-discrimination of self-employed persons under the Europe Agreement. They contested the legality of the UK Immigration Rules, which required the acquisition of leave for entry into the United Kingdom in the country of origin. They invoked the analogy with the right of self-establishment in EC law, under which the rights of entry and residence form part of the right to self-employment.

[3] Case C-63/99, *Gloszczuk* [2001] ECR I-6369. Mr Gloszczuk was a Polish national who had entered the United Kingdom under a visiting visa, took up a building activity as a self-employed person and stayed longer than permitted. He sought recognition of his right of establishment under the Polish Europe Agreement, claiming that the right existed independently of his status of entry. His wife was also an 'over-stayer', her rights depending on those of her husband.

[4] Case C-235/99, *Kondova* [2001] ECR I-6437. Ms Kondova, a Bulgarian national, entered the United Kingdom under a holiday-work visa. She then applied for asylum and, after a negative result, married a Mauritian who had an indefinite leave to stay in the United Kingdom. As her application to stay was turned down, she invoked Article 45 of the Bulgarian Europe Agreement to stay as a self-employed cleaner.

[5] Case C-268/99, *Jany* [2001] ECR I-8615. The case concerned two Polish and four Czech nationals, who contested the decisions whereby they were refused residence permits for working as self-employed prostitutes.

[6] See for overview C. Hillion, 'Cases C-63/99 *Gloszczuk*; C-235/99 *Kondova*; C-257/99 *Barkoci and Malik*; Case C-268/99 *Jany*, Case C-162/00 *Pokrzeptowicz-Meyer*' (2003) 40 *Common Market Law Review* 465; K. Inglis, 'The Europe Agreements Compared in the Light of their Pre-accession Reorientation' (2000) 37 *Common Market Law Review* 1201; M. Hofmann, 'The Right to Establishment for Nationals of the European Union Associated Countries in the Recent Jurisprudence of the European Court of Justice' (2001) 44 *German Yearbook of International Law* 471.

As with the earlier Association Agreements, the ECJ proceeded from its well-established formula, according to which '[a] provision in an agreement concluded by the Community with non-member countries must be regarded as being directly applicable when, regard being had to its wording and the purpose and nature of the agreement itself, the provision contains a clear and precise obligation which is not subject, in its implementation or effects, to the adoption of any subsequent measure'.[7] In all four cases, the ECJ found that the establishment provisions, such as Article 44(3) of the Polish Association Agreement in the *Gloszczuk* case, had direct effect. The Court's justification was as follows:

> Article 44(3) lays down, in clear, precise and unconditional terms, a prohibition preventing Member States from discriminating, on grounds of their nationality, against, *inter alia*, Polish nationals wishing to pursue, within the territory of those States, economic activities as self-employed persons or to set up and manage undertakings there which they would effectively control. This rule of equal treatment lays down a precise obligation to produce a specific result and, by its nature, can be relied on by an individual before a national court to request it to set aside the discriminatory provisions of a Member State's legislation making the establishment of a Polish national subject to a condition which is not imposed on that Member State's own nationals, without any further implementing measures being required for that purpose.[8]

However, the Court continued that although the rights of entry and residence formed corollaries of the right of establishment, those rights are not absolute privileges because, under Article 58(1) of the Polish Europe Agreement, the host Member State was entitled to limit these rights by its rules on entry, stay and establishment. These national rules could provide a system of prior control, such as subjecting the leave of entry to the condition that the applicant would show a genuine intention of taking up an activity as a self-employed person, possess sufficient financial resources, have reasonable chances of success and would not at the same time enter into employment. Since in the three former cases the applications for the leave of entry had been submitted at a time of illegal residence in the host country, and false information had been presented to the authorities about the purpose of the leave of entry, these claims were ultimately rejected.

[7] Case 12/86, *Demirel* [1987] ECR 3719, para. 14, and Case C-262/96, *Sürül* [1999] ECR I-2685, para. 60.

[8] Case C-63/99, *Gloszczuk* [2001] ECR I-6369, paras. 33–4.

In the *Jany* case, the ECJ equally reiterated that the rules of entry for pursuing a self-employed activity were governed by the national regime. In this case, the Court additionally had to clarify the extent of the permissible activity. It found that the 'economic activities as self-employed persons' under the Europe Agreements had the same meaning and scope as Article 43 of the EC Treaty, and hence included the activity of prostitution.

The direct effect of the provisions on equal treatment of legally employed workers has been addressed in the *Meyer* case.[9] It concerned Article 37(1) of the Polish Europe Agreement, which provided that '[s]ubject to the conditions and modalities applicable in each Member State[,] the treatment accorded to workers of Polish nationality legally employed in the territory of a Member State shall be free from any discrimination based on nationality, as regards working conditions, remuneration or dismissal, as compared to its own nationals'. The ECJ held that this provision had direct effect because it laid down in clear, precise and unconditional terms a prohibition of discrimination with regard to the conditions of employment, remuneration and dismissal. This interpretation was not found to be affected by the proviso 'subject to the conditions and modalities applicable in each Member State' because a Member State cannot subject the principle of non-discrimination to conditions or discretionary limitations, without rendering this provision meaningless and depriving it of practical effect. Furthermore, the ECJ extended the application of its case law under Article 39 EC to this provision, to the extent that it concerns non-discrimination of Community nationals in the use of fixed-term contracts.

In contrast to the above-discussed provisions, the provisions on the supply of services[10] were expressly subject to the implementing measures, to be adopted by the Association Council, and therefore appeared

[9] Case C-162/00, *Pokrzeptowicz-Meyer* [2002] ECR I-1049. Mrs Pokrzeptowicz-Meyer was a Polish national who had been working since 1992 under a fixed-term contract as a foreign language teacher in a part-time post in Germany. Upon the expiry of her contract in 1996, she applied for a declaration that her contract would not be terminated. She claimed that the national law that allowed the use of fixed-term contracts for foreign-language assistants, whereas their use for other teaching staff performing special duties had to be individually justified by an objective reason, was incompatible with Community law, on the grounds that ECJ case law prohibited discrimination against Community nationals, and this would extend under the Polish Europe Agreement to Polish nationals.

[10] e.g. Article 55 of the Polish Europe Agreement; Article 51 of the Estonian Europe Agreement.

not to possess direct effect. Similarly, direct effect of the provisions on social security for the Europe Agreements' nationals[11] appears to be excluded due to the express requirement for further implementing measures, as well as due to the use of a general, programmatic formulation 'with a view to coordinating', rather than conferring a concrete individual right. It has been commented that this type of formulation in the Europe Agreements results from a reaction to the *Kziber* case,[12] where the ECJ found a similar clause in the EC-Morocco Cooperation Agreement to be laid down in clear, precise and unconditional terms, so as to prohibit nationality-based discrimination in unemployment allowances by Belgian authorities. This made the Member States cautious, and they decided not to use the same formulation in subsequent analogous agreements.[13] The Europe Agreements' provisions on competition[14] were equally unlikely to meet the criteria for direct effect because of containing an explicit clause on the necessity of further implementation by the Association Council.[15] As regards the provisions on free movement of goods, the Europe Agreements' provisions on abolition of customs duties and quantitative restrictions on export and import between the associated country and the EU[16] reproduced in substance the provisions on free movement of goods in the EC Treaty. However, in the EU, several cases decided by the ECJ[17] indicate that, based on the test of purpose and nature of the treaty, the Europe Agreements' afore-mentioned provisions would not necessarily have been given the same interpretation as those of the EC Treaty. This is because, unlike the EC Treaty which creates a common market, the Europe Agreements established an association,

[11] e.g. Articles 38–9 of the Polish Europe Agreement; Articles 39–40 of the Romanian Europe Agreement; Articles 37–8 of the Estonian Europe Agreement.

[12] Case 18/90, *Kziber* [1991] ECR I-199.

[13] See M. Maresceau, '"Europe Agreements": A New Form of Cooperation between the European Community and Central and Eastern Europe' in P. C. Müller-Graff (ed.), *East-Central European States and the EC: Legal Adaptations to the Market Economy* (Nomos, Baden-Baden, 1993), pp. 228–9.

[14] e.g. Article 63 of the Polish Europe Agreement; Article 64 of the Estonian Europe Agreement; Article 63 of the Romanian Europe Agreement.

[15] Also M. Ojala, *The Competition Law of Central and Eastern Europe* (Sweet & Maxwell, London, 1999), p. 65; J. Gomula, 'Dispute Settlement under Association Agreements with Central and Eastern European States' (1995–1996) 22 *Polish Yearbook of International Law* 126.

[16] e.g. Article 7 *et seq.* of the Polish Europe Agreement; Article 8 *et seq.* of the Romanian Europe Agreement; Articles 10–14 of the Estonian Europe Agreement.

[17] e.g. Opinion 1/91, *EEA* [1991] ECR I-6079, at 6101 *et seq.*; Case 270/80, *Polydor* [1982] ECR 329, para. 18.

and unlike the EC Treaty's character as a constitutional document of the Community, the Europe Agreements merely formed international treaties for the EC.[18]

These decisions indicate that the Europe Agreements were also capable of entailing directly effective rights in the candidate countries.[19] This, however, was subject to the direct applicability of treaties in the individual country, that is whether the constitutional system of the country allowed the courts to apply treaties, and individuals to rely on them *vis-à-vis* the national authorities, without the need for further national legislation. As was already mentioned in chapter 3, the new CEE constitutions are generally considered to be favourable towards international law, as according to many of them ratified treaties form part of national law, and take precedence in case of conflict with domestic norms. The position of international law in CEE countries will be outlined later in chapter 5. Suffice it to say here that the Europe Agreements, as ratified and published treaties which had entered into force in all ten countries in question, were capable of being directly applied in the constitutional systems of Lithuania,[20] Bulgaria,[21] Poland, Estonia and Slovenia.[22] In Latvia, the so-called system of reference is applied to international treaties, including the Europe Agreement. The Czech Republic, Slovakia and Romania were previously dualist countries where only human rights treaties took precedence. Hence, only those Europe Agreement provisions which concerned human rights, such as non-discrimination of workers, enjoyed a privileged position. Other provisions were subject to domestic approval through a

[18] See in this respect also S. Peers, 'An Ever Closer Waiting Room? The Case for Eastern European Accession to the European Economic Area' (1995) 32 *Common Market Law Review* 206 at pp. 209–10; Ojala, *Competition Law*, p. 65.

[19] See also A. Evans, *The Integration of the European Community and Third States in Europe* (Clarendon Press, Oxford, 1996), p. 353.

[20] See for comment, 'Republic of Lithuania Constitutional Law on the Amendment of Articles 136 and 138 of the Constitution of the Republic of Lithuania: Draft of the Working Group established under the Seimas Chancellery' in *Stojimas I Europos Sajunga Ir Konstitucija. Seminaro Medziaga 29–30.06.1999* (Eugrimas, Vilnius, 2000), p. 138; J. Masiokas, 'Status of Lithuanian and European Union Nationals under the Association Agreement' (1998) 11 *Revue Baltique* 32.

[21] See for comment, E. Evtimov, 'Die Bulgarische Verfassung und das Europarecht: Spannungsfelder und Lösungsansätze' (2001) 47 *Osteuropa Recht* 401.

[22] See for more detailed country reports on the application of the Europe Agreements, F. Hoffmeister, E. Evtimov, V. Tyc *et al.*, 'International Agreements in the Legal Orders of the Candidate Countries' in A. Ott and K. Inglis (eds.), *Handbook on European Enlargement* (T. M. C. Asser Press, The Hague, 2002), pp. 209–348.

statute.[23] This changed in the Czech Republic and Slovakia with the introduction of the monist approach as part of the 2001 EU amendments, and in Romania as part of the 2003 amendments, to be discussed in chapter 5. Hungary continues to take a dualist approach towards the application of treaties.

There was relatively little case law in CEE on the direct application of the Europe Agreements' provisions. Where these were invoked, it was more in terms of supporting the argument rather than as a main ground for deciding. The courts more often made recourse to the 'harmonisation provisions' of the Europe Agreements, using them as a ground for indirect application of EC primary and secondary law; we will come to this so-called phenomenon of 'judicial harmonisation' in the third section of this chapter. Poland was amongst the few countries where the Europe Agreement's provisions as such were directly applied in a number of cases. For instance, the High Administrative Court found in a judgment of 1998 that, as an international agreement ratified upon prior consent granted by a statute, the Europe Agreement constituted part of the domestic legal order, was directly applicable and took precedence over statutes in case of a conflict.[24] The Supreme Court, in a case concerning the application of competition law to the activities of the Polish Bar, relied on the Europe Agreement's definition of 'economic activities' in Article 44(4), in order to include the activities of the professions. On this ground, it rejected the Bar's argument that barristers were not involved in 'economic activities' and that they thereby did not constitute undertakings for the purpose of competition law.[25] The High Administrative Court, in a customs tax

[23] R. Arnold and M. Nedelka, 'Different Models of Adjusting to European Integration with a View to the Implementation and Enforcement of the Europe Agreements' in P. C. Müller-Graff (ed.), *East Central Europe and the European Union: From Europe Agreements to a Member Status* (Nomos, Baden-Baden, 1997), p. 365; M. Hoskova, 'Legal Aspects of the Integration of the Czech Republic and Slovakia into European Security and Economic Structures' (1994) 37 *German Yearbook of International Law* 90; V. Kunova, 'Constitutional Aspects of the Accession of the Slovak Republic to European Union' in A. Kellermann, J. De Zwaan and J. Czuczai (eds.), *EU Enlargement. The Constitutional Impact at EU and National Level* (Asser Press, The Hague, 2001), p. 329.

[24] Case SA/Po 3057/98 1999.12.29 wyrok NSA U N I SA/Po 3057/98 ONSA 2001/1/34, reported in A. Kellermann, 'Constitutional Aspects for Bulgaria of the Integration Process to the EU: Pre-accession Effect of Association Agreement?', paper presented at seminar 'The Impact of (Future) Accession to the European Union on the National Legal Systems', organised by T. M. C. Asser Instituut and Centre for the Study of Democracy, Sofia, 16–17 April 2004, p. 12 *et seq.*

[25] Case SN N I CKN 1217/98 2001.05.29 wyrok SN N I CKN 1217/98 OSNAP 2002/1/13, reported in Kellermann, 'Constitutional Aspects for Bulgaria', p. 12 *et seq.*

case, applied directly Article 27 of Protocol No. 4 to the Europe Agreement, interpreting the notion of 'products originating in the Community' to mean that the results of verification of the certificate of origin were binding upon the Customs Office of the importing state.[26] In addition to direct application, the Polish courts also used the Europe Agreement in a supportive capacity. For example, in a case concerning the prohibition by the Antimonopoly Office of a merger with a Dutch company that could have dominated the Polish market after taking over a local company, such a prohibition was not found to be justified. This was partly for the reason that restricting EU investors' access to the Polish market would not contribute to the realisation of the objectives of the Europe Agreements. These objectives were set out in Article 1 (promotion of the expansion of trade between Poland and the Community), Article 7 (establishment of a free trade area) and Article 65 (ensuring that competition is not distorted).[27] An example of a rejection of the Europe Agreement can be found in a case in the Polish Supreme Court, where the Court found that since the Agreement's provisions on equal national treatment did not apply to the free movement of workers, there was no ground for proceedings with regard to national restrictions on EU citizens who wanted to practise as doctors in Poland.[28] In another case, a Polish court did not apply provisions amending Protocol No. 4 to the Europe Agreement, for the reason that the Protocol was not published in the Polish *Journal of Laws*. Such publication is decisive for rendering an international agreement a part of the national legal system.[29] In other countries, the courts applied the Europe Agreements in terms of judicial harmonisation to EU law, to which we come in the third section of this chapter.

The application of the Europe Agreements has additionally brought up the issue of direct applicability and rank of the Association Council decisions in CEE legal orders. These decisions divided into three groups: decisions which modified the Europe Agreements, decisions of interpretation and decisions concerning discords between the parties on the application of the Agreements. Within the EC legal order, the ECJ has established,

[26] Case NSA I SA/Ld 777/97 1999.09.09 wyrok NSA I SA/Ld 777/97 Pr.Gosp. 1999/1/40, reported in Kellermann, 'Constitutional Aspects for Bulgaria', p. 12 *et seq*.

[27] Case VII Ama 39/97 1997.10.08 wyrok s antymon VII Ama 39/97 Wokanda 1998/9/48, reported in Kellermann, 'Constitutional Aspects for Bulgaria', p. 12 *et seq*.

[28] Polish Supreme Court, Decision of 27 April 1995, reported in Kellermann, 'Constitutional Aspects for Bulgaria', p. 12 *et seq*.

[29] Case NSA I SA/Po 3057/98 1999.12.29 wyrok NSA U N I SA/Po 3057/98 ONSA 2001/1/34, reported in Kellermann, 'Constitutional Aspects for Bulgaria', p. 12 *et seq*.

in respect of a decision of the Turkey-EU Association Council, that such decisions can have direct effect, 'when, regard being had to their wording and their purpose and nature, as well as to those of the association agreement, they contain a clear and precise obligation which is not subject, in its implementation or effects, to the adoption of any subsequent measure'.[30] However, in CEE constitutional systems, only duly ratified and promulgated treaties are capable of being directly applicable, and take precedence over domestic acts. The Association Council decisions, meanwhile, fell into the category of executive agreements, which were usually concluded by the governments and did not undergo a parliamentary ratification. Such decisions were obligatorily published only by the European Union in the *Official Journal*; publication in the national official gazettes was left to the discretion of the governments or, as in Poland, took place in an official gazette of a lower level.[31] In Bulgaria, it was commented that the Constitutional Court's decision of 1992 raises doubts about whether Association Council decisions, which are neither ratified nor published, are at all binding for Bulgarian state bodies.[32] Similarly, in Lithuania, the Constitutional Court has declared unconstitutional a legislative provision that had granted immediate effect to unratified treaties, as these need to be implemented in the internal legal system.[33] In terms of the hierarchic position of the Association Council decisions, it corresponded, as a rule, to the domestic act of reception, usually a government's decree. The Association Council decisions needed domestic implementation and could not be invoked directly by the individuals *vis-à-vis* the courts and other state bodies in the CEE legal orders.

Extent of harmonisation and adoption of EU obligations

At the heart of the Europe Agreements lay the obligation to harmonise the candidate countries' laws with EU law. While the process, procedure and institutional set-up of harmonisation and of accession negotiations

[30] Case C-192/89, *Sevince* [1990] ECR I-3461, para. 2.

[31] Reported in W. Czaplinski, 'L'Intégration européenne dans la constitution polonaise de 1997' (2000) *Revue du Marché Commun et de l'Union Européenne* 169. However, Czaplinski finds that at least some of the Association Council decisions should have a position corresponding to that of the Europe Agreement in the Polish legal order.

[32] Decision No. 7, 2 July 1992, on the interpretation of articles 85(3) and 149(1.4) of the constitution, published in *Durzhaven Vestnik* 56/92, cited in Evtimov, 'Die Bulgarische Verfassung', pp. 400, 402. See on this decision in more detail chapter 5, n. 130.

[33] Decision No. 8/95 on the constitutionality of the Law on International Treaties (1997) 4 *East European Case Reporter of Constitutional Law* 255.

have extensively been researched elsewhere,[34] this and subsequent sections will assess the process of harmonisation rather through the lens of the afore-mentioned protective approach to sovereignty in the constitutions of Central and Eastern Europe.

According to a standard clause in all Europe Agreements, approximation of the candidate countries' existing and future legislation to that of the Community constituted the main precondition for their economic integration into the Community, and the countries were to use 'best endeavours to ensure that future legislation is compatible with Community legislation'.[35] This was complemented by a list of priority areas for harmonisation, comprising primarily those which concerned the functioning of the internal market, such as customs law, company law, banking law, intellectual property, financial services, competition and technical rules and standards. Besides these priority areas, the extent of harmonisation should be considered together with the so-called conditionality documents. These included, first, the above-mentioned Copenhagen Criteria, which defined the legal, economic and political criteria for membership. In 1995, the Commission issued a White Paper,[36] which defined the measures of approximation in internal market areas, as well as the priorities of harmonisation. In 1997, the European Commission published *Agenda 2000*,[37] to which it attached the Commission's Opinions on the individual countries concerning their progress in meeting the Copenhagen Criteria. *Agenda 2000* specified that the ability to take on the obligations of membership denoted the adoption of 80,000 pages of the *acquis communautaire*, including the Treaties and secondary legislation, but also ECJ case law, soft law and international agreements. Since 1998, the European Commission issued the Accession Partnerships,[38] where the harmonisation deadlines and priorities were set out, coupled with articulation

[34] See for individual countries e.g. P. Desny, 'The Harmonisation of the Legislation of the Czech Republic with European Union Law' (1997) 8 *Perspectives* 45; H. Pisuke, 'Estonia and the European Union: European Integration in Estonia' (1996) *Juridica International, Law Review of Tartu University* 2; A. Lazowski, *Adaptation of the Polish Legal System to European Union Law: Selected Aspects* (Sussex European Institute Working Paper No. 45, Brighton, 2001).

[35] e.g. Article 68 of the Polish Europe Agreement; Article 69 of the Lithuanian Europe Agreement; Article 69 of the Czech Europe Agreement.

[36] White Paper, *Preparation of the Associated Countries of Central and Eastern Europe for Integration into the Internal Market of the Union* (COM (95) 163 final).

[37] *Agenda 2000: For a Stronger and Wider Union, Bulletin of the European Communities*, Supplement 5/97, available at www.europa.eu.int/comm/enlargement/agenda 2000/

[38] Accession Partnerships with individual countries are available at the European Commission's website www.europa.eu.int/comm/enlargement

of the conditions for the EU's financial assistance, and for the Commission's supervision over meeting the demands. On the candidate countries' side, the Accession Partnerships involved the National Programmes for Adopting the Community *Acquis*, in which the countries specified legal acts, institutional and administrative reforms and human and budgetary resources they intended to deploy in each priority area. In 1997, the so-called 'Road Maps' were introduced by the Member of the Commission responsible for the internal market, to help the candidate countries take on the Community *acquis*. The candidate countries' efforts to adopt the *acquis* and to meet the political and economic criteria were assessed by the EU Commission in its annual Progress Reports.[39]

Unlike previous enlargements, the *acquis* to be adopted took in several respects a remarkably wider scope. According to the European Commission *Agenda 2000* and Council of Ministers' document on the accession principles,[40] harmonisation included institutional structures and the long-term values and goals that the EU was developing, such as the Common Foreign and Security Policy, Monetary Union and Justice and Home Affairs. These, notably, are areas traditionally associated with the core fields of state sovereignty. Indeed, the foreign policy of the candidate countries has effectively followed that of the EU, and Romania's deviation from it as concerns American citizens' immunity in respect of the International Criminal Court was forcefully deplored by the EU. Furthermore, as Heather Grabbe has pointed out, the Accession Partnerships added policy areas that have not been adopted by all Member States (Schengen, EMU), and even areas that were beyond the EU's domestic competences (judicial reform, prison conditions, reform of social security systems, pension reform, corporate governance, civil service reform, national minorities, etc.).[41] Perhaps the most costly demand beyond the

[39] See more on the conditionality documents, e.g. P. C. Müller-Graff, 'Legal Framework for Relations between the European Union and Central and Eastern Europe: General Aspects' in M. Maresceau (ed.), *Enlarging the European Union: Relations Between the EU and Central and Eastern Europe* (Longman, London and New York, 1997), pp. 27–31; M. Maresceau and E. Montaguti, 'The Relations between the European Union and Eastern Europe: A Legal Appraisal' (1995) 32 *Common Market Law Review* 1327; K. Inglis, 'The Europe Agreements Compared in the Light of their Pre-accession Reorientation' (2000) 37 *Common Market Law Review* 1173; M. Maresceau, 'Pre-Accession', in M. Cremona (ed.), *The Enlargement of the European Union* (Oxford University Press, 2003), pp. 9–42; C. Hillion, 'Enlargement of the European Union: A Legal Analysis' in T. Arnull and D. Wincott (eds.), *Accountability and Legitimacy in the European Union* (Oxford University Press, 2003), pp. 401–18.

[40] 2078th Council meeting General Affairs, Brussels, 30–31 March 1998 (ref PRES/98/96).

[41] H. Grabbe, 'A Partnership for Accession? The Implications of EU Conditionality for the Central and East European Applicants', European University Institute, Robert Schuman Center, Working Paper No. 99/12 (Florence, 1999), p. 20 *et seq.*

EU's domestic competence was the request to shut down nuclear power plants in Lithuania, the Czech Republic, Bulgaria and Slovakia. In addition, for the first time, the condition of effective implementation was added to the list of membership criteria, as of the Madrid summit in 1995; it was further emphasised in the summits of Luxembourg and Helsinki.[42] Phelon Nicolaides has drawn attention to the EU's capacity to use inadequate implementation as a pretext for demanding more concessions or even delaying enlargement, given that this is the first time that adequate implementation has been required from newcomers, and that no clear measure is available *vis-à-vis* the 'old' Member States. Another criterion which was added later was that of 'good neighbourliness': *Agenda 2000* and the Helsinki European Council in 1999 stated that before accession, applicants should make every effort to resolve any outstanding border disputes among themselves or involving third countries.[43] Altogether, by the time of accession, obligations to be adopted amounted well beyond the 80,000 pages of *acquis*, leaving very little of national law-making completely untouched by EU law. Legislative and administrative harmonisation was complemented by judicial harmonisation, which will be discussed in more detail in the next section.

The candidate countries, on their part, adopted in the early phases of integration the acts which subjected all draft laws to the control of compatibility with EU law by special government institutions, and required a clear demonstration of reasons for divergence.[44] For instance, in the former Czechoslovakia, the government's regulation of 1991 required all ministries to bear in mind the existence of EC law, and the legislator to approximate draft laws to EC standards. Specific reasons had to be demonstrated for incompatibility, and the government made it clear that drafts diverging from EC law would not receive a positive evaluation before being sent to Parliament.[45] After the dissolution of the Federation, the Czech

[42] See P. Nicolaides, 'Preparing for Accession to the European Union: How to Establish Capacity for Effective and Credible Application of EU Rules' in Cremona, *Enlargement*, p. 45.

[43] K. Smith, 'The Evolution and Application of EU Membership Conditionality' in Cremona, *Enlargement*, p. 118.

[44] See for Poland, e.g. E. Piontek, 'Towards Membership of the European Union' (1994) *Droit Polonais Contemporain* 6; Lazowski, 'Adaptation of the Polish Legal System'. For Hungary see E. Györi, 'Parliaments and the European Union: the Involvement of the Hungarian National Assembly in the Process of European Integration' in Z. Mansfeldová and M. Klíma (eds.), *The Role of the Central European Parliaments in the Process of European Integration: Proceedings of International Conference, Prague, 12–14 September 1997* (Academy of Sciences, Prague, 1998), p. 78.

[45] Desny, 'Harmonisation', p. 45; Hoskova, 'Legal Aspects', pp. 84–5.

Republic introduced the Department of Compatibility with EU Law. The Department did not recommend the government to proceed with bills where an incompatibility with EU law was found.[46]

This harmonisation in the case of CEE countries has been characterised as a 'voluntary harmonisation'[47] or 'voluntary adaptation'[48] because it differed from the obligation of harmonisation in the Member States and, unlike the EEA Agreement, the Europe Agreements proposed harmonisation as a voluntary legislative programme, with no enforcement procedures apart from national control mechanisms.[49] However, on the side of the candidate countries, for which membership was a priority, harmonisation appears to have formed an obligation. This emerges when reading the Europe Agreements together with the candidate countries' Accession Applications, and the accession criteria formulated in the above-mentioned conditionality documents, such as the Copenhagen Criteria, the Council of Ministers' Accession Principles of 1998, the White Paper and Accession Partnerships. While the first two documents declared that full harmonisation was a precondition for accession, the implementation of the White Paper and Accession Partnership formed the basis for evaluating a candidate country's readiness for accession in the European Commission's annual Reports. Non-compliance with these documents would have meant postponement or denial of EU membership, as well as suspension of financial assistance under the Accession Partnerships. Indeed, the European Commission warned the accession countries in May 2003 that it would impose punitive measures if the countries failed to implement the necessary legislation.[50] In addition, whether or not the harmonisation was ultimately a legal obligation, it constituted a far-reaching adoption of a foreign law, which may have called for a higher legitimacy from the point of view of internal constitutional law – we will come to this question in the light of the Hungarian Constitutional Court's Europe Agreement decision in the fourth section of this chapter.

At the time when the candidate countries were in the process of adopting an extensive amount of EU law, they effectively did not participate in

[46] Desny, 'Harmonisation', p. 47.

[47] A. Evans, 'Voluntary Harmonization in Integration between the European Community and Eastern Europe' (1997) 22 *European Law Review* 202.

[48] P. C. Müller-Graff, 'East Central Europe and the European Union: From Europe Agreements to a Member Status' in Müller-Graff, *East Central Europe*, p. 33.

[49] See Maresceau and Montaguti, 'Relations between the European Union and Eastern Europe', p. 1336.

[50] 'Acceding States Warned over Slow Take-up of Rules', *EU Observer*, 1 May 2003, www.euobserver.com

the creation of the *acquis*. Neither did the candidate countries of this round participate in the drafting of new EU legislation, unlike, for instance, the EEA states.[51] They also had a rather marginal say with regard to the contents of the Europe Agreements and the afore-mentioned EU conditionality documents.[52] It has even been suggested that the mechanical adoption of EU legal rules, designed for economies at a rather different stage of development and containing anomalies of specific political contexts, did not take into account the interests and the economic, political and legal situation of CEE countries, particularly of their structural economic problems.[53] For instance, several commentators suggested that in environmental and social spheres, CEE countries should not have completed the harmonisation until shortly before accession,[54] and that their economies should have been allowed substantial derogations in terms of production conditions, although the products themselves would have had to meet Single Market standards.[55] Furthermore, it has been pointed out that the EU's competences with regard to CEE countries were exercised without justifying and restraining principles such as subsidiarity, proportionality and competence, and with little involvement of restraining institutions, such as the European Parliament, national Parliaments and the ECJ.[56] In the words of Heather Grabbe, '[t]here is a paradox in EU-CEE relations: applicants are treated like Member States in the extent of their obligations under the Accession Partnerships, but as applicants they have no rights and little say in determining the substance of relations, leaving the EU as a hegemonic actor'.[57]

However, an important change in this respect took place with the opening of the EU Convention in February 2002. For the first time, the

[51] See for the EEA countries, Evans, *Integration of the European Community*, p. 257 *et seq.*

[52] U. Sedelmeier, *The European Union's Association Policy towards Central and Eastern Europe: Political and Economic Rationales in Conflict* (Sussex European Institute, Brighton, 1994), cited in Grabbe, 'A Partnership for Accession', p. 34.

[53] Evans, 'Voluntary Harmonization', p. 201 *et seq.*; S. Nello and K. Smith, *The European Union and Central and Eastern Europe: The Implications of Enlargement in Stages* (Ashgate, Aldershot, 1998), p. 18, with reference to A. Smith, P. Holmes, U. Sedelmeier, E. Smith, H. Wallace and A. Young, *The European Union and Central and Eastern Europe: Pre-Accession Strategies* (Sussex European Institute, Brighton, 1996); H. Grabbe and K. Hughes, *Eastward Enlargement of the European Union* (Royal Institute of International Affairs, London, 1998), p. 37.

[54] Nello and Smith, *The European Union*, p. 18, with reference to Smith *et al.*, *The European Union.*

[55] Grabbe and Hughes, *Eastward Enlargement*, p. 36, with reference to Smith *et al.*, *The European Union.*

[56] Grabbe, 'A Partnership for Accession', p. 24.

[57] *Ibid.*

representatives of the candidate countries officially participated in the debates of EU internal affairs – in fact, in the drafting of the future architecture of the EU. The candidates were, however, not allowed to block any consensus that could have emerged amongst the Member States. Earlier, the only means of participation available for the candidate countries was the so-called 'Structured Relationship' talking-shop of the CEE heads of states and ministers, which had taken place since 1994 in the framework of the European Council; it was replaced in 1998 by an even weaker forum, the European Conference.[58]

The accession negotiations offered no major change in this 'asymmetric power relation'. According to *Agenda 2000* and other sources, most of the *acquis* was non-negotiable for the CEE countries, which according to the statements at the time of Commission officials meant 99 per cent of it.[59] By contrast, Greece, Spain and Portugal, countries whose economic and political profile was comparable to the CEE candidates, were allowed considerable compromises and adaptations after their entry. The consolidation of democracy in these countries was expected to take place after membership, and long transition periods were allowed so as to aid economic development: for instance, more than a decade for some trade policy issues and agriculture, and five to seven years for the abolition of customs duties and the adjustment of monopolies.[60] However, in respect of the CEE countries, several EU statements indicated that the scope for bargaining was much more limited: CEE countries were not to expect derogations and long transition periods, e.g. five years instead of formerly seventeen, in well-defined spheres.[61] The Council of Ministers also made it clear that full harmonisation, with strictly limited transition opportunities, formed the principle for this and future accessions.[62] Eventually, however, some longer transition periods were granted, for instance as regards land sales to foreigners and some environmental issues. Further, unlike earlier enlargements, harmonisation had to be carried out prior to accession. The role of negotiations was also limited for the reason that the meeting of conditions was judged by the Commission under the Accession Partnerships, rather than through the official accession negotiations running in parallel.[63] The candidate countries, in turn, were in competition

[58] See in more detail Inglis, 'The Europe Agreements', pp. 1182, 1188–9.
[59] Grabbe, 'A Partnership for Accession', p. 23.
[60] See *ibid.*; Grabbe and Hughes, *Eastward Enlargement*, p. 59.
[61] Grabbe, 'A Partnership for Accession', p. 22 *et seq.*
[62] 2078th Council meeting General Affairs, Brussels, 30–31 March 1998 (ref PRES/98/96).
[63] Grabbe, 'A Partnership for Accession', p. 23.

amongst themselves concerning the speed of closing the negotiation chapters. Some smaller candidate countries, with a lower negotiating power, built the entirety of their tactics on speed rather than effective negotiation (e.g. Estonia). Only towards the final phase of the negotiations in 2001–2002 did the governments realise that the closing of the negotiation chapters at any cost did not appeal to the people, jeopardising the success of the accession referendums, and the negotiators were therefore instructed to take a tougher stance in Brussels.

It should also be pointed out that it was disputable whether the EU had on its part a legal obligation to reward harmonisation with full membership. At first, the Europe Agreements were perceived by the EU as an alternative to, rather than as a preparatory instrument for, accession; only later did the Europe Agreements become a key element in the pre-accession strategy.[64] The Preambles to the Europe Agreements formulated the goal of a country's accession vaguely, to avoid expressing the EU's promise for future membership: membership was recognised as a candidate country's ultimate objective, rather than as a mutual goal.[65] For instance, the Preamble to Estonia's Europe Agreement declared that '[r]ecognising the fact that Estonia's ultimate objective is to become a member of the European Union[, the association aims to] . . . help Estonia to achieve this objective'. According to Peter-Christian Müller-Graff, such a formulation means that '(1) one partner is aware of the intention of the other, but (2) does not incur any corresponding contractual commitment, and (3) that both partners only assess the agreement as being helpful for the achievement of the objective of one partner'.[66] The negotiating history of the first Europe Agreement states – Poland, Hungary and the Czech Republic – indicates that the EU was rather reluctant to make a reference to accession in the Agreements, and even this vague formulation was a result of a strong lobby by the Vishegrad countries.[67] However, the Copenhagen European Council made a more substantial commitment to enlargement, by declaring that membership forms a common goal, and setting forth the accession conditions. Still, the rather broad formulation

[64] Maresceau, 'Pre-Accession', p. 17.

[65] Maresceau and Montaguti, 'Relations between the European Union and Eastern Europe', p. 1332.

[66] P. C. Müller-Graff, 'East Central Europe and the European Union: From Europe Agreements to Member Status' in Müller-Graff, *East Central Europe*, p. 16, cited in Maresceau, 'Pre-Accession', p. 15.

[67] P. Van Ham, *The EC, Eastern Europe and Unity: Discord, Collaboration and Integration since 1949* (Pinter, London, 1993), p. 198.

of the Copenhagen Criteria was seen as allowing for a considerable degree of subjectivity,[68] and additionally the completion of the EU's internal reforms was established as a precondition for enlargement. As Duncan Kennedy and David Webb have put it:

> [t]hese efforts [pre-accession adaptations], . . . while significant, do not constitute a coherent and bilateral commitment to coordinate legal and regulatory policies and institutions. This perhaps represents the worst of both worlds: the Association Countries cede a level of independence at a crucial time in their democratic reform and economic restructuring programmes and receive little that is tangible in return.[69]

Judicial harmonisation

Legislative harmonisation brought about the question whether it should be accompanied by judicial harmonisation, that is whether the national courts should apply the interpretation of the European Court of Justice and take account of EU legislation when applying provisions of domestic laws or the provisions of the Europe Agreements.[70] Judicial harmonisation would have ensured the effective and uniform interpretation and application of the Europe Agreements between the EU and a candidate country, as well as between the candidate countries themselves. Unlike the EEA Agreement, the Europe Agreements contained no provisions to the effect of observing EU secondary legislation and the case law of the ECJ in the interpretation of the Agreements' provisions.[71] The experience of the EC-EFTA relations indicates that harmonisation may in soft form include judicial implementation.[72] In fact, a constitutional amendment was under consideration in the Czech Republic in order to avoid a situation where the legislative branch was harmonising, while the judicial branch could be 'disharmonising'.[73]

[68] See further Nello and Smith, *The European Union*, p. 20 *et seq.*

[69] D. Kennedy and D. E. Webb, 'The Limits of Integration: Eastern Europe and the European Communities' (1993) 32 *Common Market Law Review* 1115.

[70] See for discussion on judicial harmonisation, e.g. G. Zukova, 'Uniform Interpretation and Application of International Agreements in the European Union' in G. Zukova, *Legal Aspects of Trade in Goods between the EU and its Candidate States: The Case of Latvia* (Latvias Vestnesis, Riga, 2004), pp. 207–26; Evans, 'Voluntary Harmonization', pp. 204, 208; Gomula, 'Dispute Settlement', p. 113; Masiokas, 'Status of Lithuanian', p. 32 *et seq.*

[71] cf. Article 6 of the Agreement of the European Economic Area (OJ 1994, L001/3).

[72] See Evans, 'Voluntary Harmonization', pp. 207–8.

[73] Reported by V. Balas, 'Legal and Quasi-legal Thresholds of the Accession of the Czech Republic to the EC' in Kellermann, De Zwaan and Czuczai, *EU Enlargement*, p. 275.

The constitutional courts of the candidate countries generally gave positive signals with regard to judicial harmonisation, with some reservations. In Poland, the Constitutional Tribunal found in two cases which concerned the different age of retirement for male and female employees[74] that such a treatment was at odds with the constitution, and also referred to conflict with article 5 of Directive 207/76/EEC on equal treatment and ECJ cases such as *Marshall*.[75] Although pointing out that EU law was not binding in Poland, the Tribunal nevertheless stressed that Articles 66 and 68 of the Europe Agreement placed Poland under an obligation to 'use its best endeavours to ensure that future legislation is compatible with Community legislation'. This obligation implied that Polish courts are obliged to interpret the existing law so as to bring it into compliance with EC law. In the 'Polish Bar' case mentioned earlier,[76] the Supreme Court of Poland relied on Council Directive 77/249/EEC in reaching the conclusion that individual barristers should be considered to be 'undertakings' for the purpose of competition law. In doing so, the Court stated that Articles 68 and 69 of the Europe Agreement obliged Poland to approximate its legislation to that of the Community, and emphasised the importance of the application of the existing law in line with EC law in fulfilling this obligation. In a case concerning a refusal to supply public transport tickets by a public transport undertaking to a newsagent,[77] the Antimonopoly Court, in the absence of Polish provisions regulating this issue, referred to Article 85(3) (now 81(1)) of the EC Treaty and to relevant EC regulations granting block exemptions. It found that there was no reason why EC competition law could not be taken into account in order to fill the lacuna. Altogether, the approach of Polish courts has been characterised as a 'pro-European interpretation of laws', sometimes classified as 'soft' adaptation of law to EU standards, equivalent to the doctrine of indirect effect in EC law.[78] Academic commentators raised the question as to how much discretion the courts have in using this tool of interpretation? It has been suggested by various Polish authors that while the situation was straightforward when the approximated provisions were clear and

[74] Case K. 15/97, 29.09.1997 wyrok TK U K 15/97 OTK 1997/34/37, and Case K.27/99, 2000.03.28 wyrok TK U K 27/99 OTK 2000/2/62, both reported in Kellermann, 'Constitutional Aspects for Bulgaria', at 12 *et seq*.

[75] Case 152/84, *Marshall* [1986] ECR 723.

[76] Case SN N I CKN 1217/98 2001.05.29 wyrok SN N I CKN 1217/98 OSNAP 2002/1/13, reported in Kellermann, 'Constitutional Aspects for Bulgaria', p. 12 *et seq*.

[77] Case XVII Amr 65/96 1997.01.08 wyrok s. antym. XVII Amr 65/96 Wokanda 1998/1/60, reported in Kellermann, 'Constitutional Aspects for Bulgaria', p. 12 *et seq*.

[78] Reported by Lazowski, *Adaptation of the Polish Legal System*, p. 21.

unambiguous, problems arose where the legal act did not conform to EU law. According to some commentators, a 'pro-European' interpretation was to be applied in cases where there was some ambiguity, and there were no socio-economic obstacles to such an interpretation, given that non-conformity with EU law was permitted for economic and legal reasons during the pre-accession period.[79]

In the Czech Republic, the High Court in Olomouc[80] and the Czech Constitutional Court in the same case,[81] applied Article 86 (now 82) EC through Article 64 EA (which refers to the criteria regarding application of (ex) Articles 85, 86 and 92 EC) in a case concerning the abuse of a dominant position by the car manufacturer Skoda. The Constitutional Court additionally referred to the ECJ case *Merci Convenzionali Porto di Genova*.[82]

In Lithuania, the Constitutional Court made reference to EC Directives 90/388/ and 98/10/EEC in the 'Telecommunications' case,[83] which concerned the constitutionality of the Telecommunications Law that referred to the requirements of EU law. This reference was made in order to justify that the telecommunications market should be liberalised gradually and through the use of transitional periods. In the 'Death Penalty' case,[84] the Constitutional Court referred to the European Parliament's Resolution of 1997 on the abolition of the death penalty, where the European Parliament had called for establishing the abolition of the death penalty as a condition in all negotiations concerning the Partnership and Cooperation Agreements. In addition, the Lithuanian Constitutional Court has ordered opinions from the experts of the Government's European Law Department in cases that involved EU law.[85]

In Latvia, some Justices of the Constitutional Court stated in a dissenting opinion that Latvia's obligation to harmonise its laws under the Europe Agreement does not just mean approximation of texts. According

79 Reported in *ibid.*, p. 22.

80 Case 2A6/96, reported in V. Tyc, 'Czech Republic' in Ott and Inglis, *Handbook on European Enlargement*, p. 231.

81 Case III.US 31/97–35, 1997, reported in Tyc, 'Czech Republic', p. 231.

82 C-179/90, *Merci Convenzionali Porto di Genova* [1991] ECR I-5889.

83 Decision of 6 October 1999, in English at www.lrkt.lt/1999/n9a1006a.htm

84 Decision of 9 December 1998, in English at www.lrkt.lt/1998/n8a1209a.htm

85 e.g. Decision of 18 October 2000 on the constitutionality of the Law on the Reorganisation of the Joint-stock Petrol Companies, in English at www.lrkt.lt/2000/r001018.htm; Decision of 5 February 2002 on the constitutionality of the Law on Higher Education, in English at www.lrkt.lt/2002/r020205.htm; Decision of 14 March 2002 on the constitutionality of the Law on Pharmaceutical Activities, in English at www.lrkt.lt/2002/r020314.htm

to them, Western legal theory and legal thinking should also be adopted, because '[o]nly then the legislation, approximated on the content level, will function in the same way as in the European Union. Unified legal understanding in the European tradition and legal manner is one of the preconditions of functioning of the European Union.'[86]

In Estonia, the Constitutional Review Chamber of the National Court made a general reference to the need to consider the legal principles of the EU. According to it, '[i]n creating the general principles of law for Estonia[,] the general principles of law developed by the institutions of the Council of Europe and the European Union should be considered. These principles have their origin in the general principles of law of the highly developed legal systems of the Member States.'[87] Further, the need to assess Estonia's legal acts in the light of European law, deriving from the legal-political obligation to approximate Estonia's law with the EU *acquis* under the Europe Agreement, was underlined by the then Chief Justice Rait Maruste in his dissenting opinions. In the 1998 Decision on seamen's passports,[88] he referred to Article 48 (now 39) of the EC Treaty which establishes the freedom of movement of workers and non-discrimination on grounds of nationality. He added that equal treatment is one of the general principles of European law, and restrictions can be imposed only where justified by a real and serious threat to state policy. According to Maruste, '[t]hese are the legal-political landmarks that Estonia has to be guided by in further legal regulation of movement of labour force, including seafarers'. In another dissenting opinion, the Chief Justice Maruste referred to Case C-295/90 in the ECJ on the annulment of Council Directive 90/366/EEC of 28 June 1990 on the right of residence for students,[89] in order to justify the need for retaining the legal force of an overruled act until the correct legal grounds have been established.[90]

However, it is important to mention here that the Constitutional Court of Hungary has found that the direct applicability of EU secondary law and case law through the Association Council decisions would constitute

[86] Dissenting opinion of Justices A. Endziņš, J. Jelāgins and A. Ušacka in Case No. 2000-03-01 on the compatibility of the Parliament's Election Law with the constitution and with the International Covenant on Civil and Political Rights.

[87] Decision No. III-4/A-5/94, on the constitutionality of Property Law Enforcement Act, 30 September 1994, in English at www.nc.ee/english/

[88] Concurring opinion of R. Maruste to Decision No. 3-4-1-4-98 of the Constitutional Review Chamber, 27 May 1998, in English at www.nc.ee/english/

[89] Case C-295/90, *Parliament* v. *Council* [1992] ECR I-4193.

[90] Dissenting opinion of R. Maruste to Decision No. 3-4-1-3-97 of the Constitutional Review Chamber, 24 March 1997, in English at www.nc.ee/english/

a violation of the sovereignty provisions of the Hungarian Constitution, and therefore require an authorising constitutional amendment. We will come to this in the next section.

Pre-accession adaptations in the light of sovereignty and legitimacy

Usually, it is EU membership that is considered to affect a state's sovereignty. However, given the high level of protection of sovereignty in the CEE constitutions, the issue of sovereignty also deserves attention in the context of the pre-accession process: the above sections showed the extent of the harmonisation in CEE countries, without having a significant participation in the creation of this foreign law. Indeed, questions about the legitimacy of the pre-accession adaptations have been brought up in Hungary, Estonia and elsewhere.

In Hungary, the Constitutional Court raised the issue of sovereignty with regard to judicial harmonisation in its 'Europe Agreement' decision,[91] a judgment that elicits a broader question about the legitimacy of the overall harmonisation exercise. In this case, the applicant claimed that Article 62(2) of the Hungarian Europe Agreement and the Implementing Regulations[92] were unconstitutional because these obliged the application of certain competition rules in accordance with the application criteria of (ex) Articles 85, 86 and 92 of the EC Treaty. Reference to the application criteria of the EC Treaty, however, implied in the applicant's view direct application of EU secondary legislation and the ECJ case law, which means direct application of the rules of a foreign legal order, and thereby a transfer of Hungary's legislative power.[93] The

[91] Decision 30/1998, (VI 25) AB, *Magyar Közlöny*. See for overview J. Volkai, *The Application of the Europe Agreement and European Law in Hungary: The Judgement of an Activist Constitutional Court on Activist Notions* (Jean Monnet Working Paper No. 8/99, Harvard, 1999), available at www.law.harvard.edu/Programs/JeanMonnet/papers/99/990801.html; H. Küpper, 'Integration mit Hindernissen – Die "Europa-Entscheidung" des ungarischen Verfassungsgerichts' (1998) *Recht in Ost und West* 333; A. Tatham, 'Constitutional Judiciary in Central Europe and the Europe Agreement: Decision 30/1998 (VI.25) AB of the Hungarian Constitutional Court' (1999) 48 *International and Comparative Law Quarterly* 913.

[92] Decision 2/96 96/652 of the EC-Hungary Association Council, 6 November 1996, on the implementation of competition rules.

[93] The applicant's contentions are further elaborated in B. Berke, 'Implementation of the Association Agreement, Approximation of Laws, Eventual Accession: Some Constitutional Implications' in F. Mádl (ed.), *On the State of the EU Integration Process: Enlargement and Institutional Reforms* (ELTE University, EU Centre for Research and Documentation, Budapest, 1997), pp. 334–5.

Constitutional Court upheld this claim as regards the Implementing Regulations. It found that the Implementing Regulations indeed obliged the Hungarian competition authorities to apply directly Community competition law. Direct application of Community law, however, is a particular feature of the relationship between the Member States and the European Community, and thus a feature of a foreign autonomous legal order of another subject of international law. Therefore, the Constitutional Court found that direct application of EC law in Hungary could not be based on the application rules of Community law, but on the Hungarian Constitution. The Hungarian Constitution, however, only allows the undertaking of international obligations by means of treaties, whereas the application of Community competition law through the Europe Agreement would go beyond a treaty obligation. Although participation in international relations inevitably entails a certain encroachment upon sovereignty, such a dynamic reference to a foreign legal order would imply a transfer of sovereignty. Such transfer, however, can only take place by explicit constitutional authorisation, due to the constitutional norm that Hungary is a sovereign and independent democratic state based on the rule of law. The principles of the rule of law and popular sovereignty require that the exercise of public power be based on democratic legitimacy deriving from popular sovereignty. Therefore, the Court held that:

> According to Article 2(1) and (2) of the Constitution, the norms of public power that form the domestic law of another legal system of public power – in this case the Community – and on the creation of which the Hungarian Republic does not have any influence because Hungary is not a Member State of the European Union, cannot appear with an obligation of applicability in the jurisprudence of Hungarian law enforcement institutions. In fact, this would require an express constitutional authorisation.[94]

Hence, Hungary not being an EU Member State and not participating in the EU's law-making process, the direct applicability of EU law must be subject to a constitutional authorisation.

In addition, the Court stressed that the constitution may only be amended according to the prescribed procedure, and not in a disguised way by Parliament by means of ratifying a treaty. According to the Court, Parliament does not have an unlimited power; it may only act within the limits of powers determined by the constitution. In particular, it may not infringe paragraphs 1 and 2 of article 2 of the constitution.

[94] Para. V.3, cited in Volkai, 'Application of the Europe Agreement', p. 19.

Notwithstanding the above findings, the Court did not declare the Europe Agreement unconstitutional: it ruled that the application criteria of Article 62(2) may not be directly applied in the Hungarian legal order. As regards the Implementing Regulations, the proceedings were postponed so as to grant the legislator time to reformulate the provisions and fulfil Hungary's international obligations in a way that would conform to the constitution. The provisions of the Europe Agreement and Implementing Regulations were not left devoid of content: the Court held that EC law should be applied indirectly, when the courts and authorities interpret the state's internal law.[95]

It has rightly been pointed out that the same competition clauses, referring to the 'criteria arising from the application of the rules' of (ex) Articles 85, 86 and 92 of the EC Treaty, were contained in all the Europe Agreements.[96] Indeed, a Slovenian commentator has noted that the Slovene Constitutional Court should have equally controlled the constitutionality of Article 65(2) of the Slovenian Europe Agreement in respect to the application of EU competition rules in its 'Europe Agreement' decision.[97] In addition, the Europe Agreements contained several further provisions that referred to the application of 'Community rules', which could raise similar questions.[98]

The question of the legitimacy of the pre-accession adaptations has also been raised on several occasions in Estonia. In 2000, the leader of the Eurosceptic movement, Kalle Kulbok, addressed to various state institutions, including the President, Defence Police and Ministry of Justice, an official query about the constitutionality of the government's pre-accession activities, given that article 1 of the constitution declares Estonia's sovereignty and independence to be eternal and inalienable. For 'philological purposes', Kulbok also mentioned article 62 of the Criminal Code, according to which activities against Estonia's independence and sovereignty are sanctioned by imprisonment. The response by these institutions to this query was, in broad outline, that Estonia's foreign policy priorities and the Europe Agreement have both been approved by Parliament, which in turn had been elected in free elections, and that accession is

[95] Tatham, 'Constitutional Judiciary', pp. 919–20.

[96] Küpper, 'Integration mit Hindernissen', pp. 334–5.

[97] P. Vehar, 'Constitutional Problems in the Period of Pre-Accession in the Republic of Slovenia' in Kellermann, De Zwaan and Czuczai, *EU Enlargement*, n. 14.

[98] e.g., in the Estonian Europe Agreement, reference to the application of Community rules is made in Articles 63(5), 65 and in Joint Declaration 1 to Article 36(1).

not a legal obligation. In 2001, the Christian People's Party filed an official application to the Estonian Defence Police to investigate the government's alleged activity against Estonia's national sovereignty and independence by its efforts to join the European Union.[99] The Defence Police rejected the claim, partly on the grounds of the immunity of top state officials.

In fact, the validity of the concerns about legitimacy has been acknowledged by the Estonian Constitutional Expert Commission in its Report on the constitutional consequences of EU accession,[100] to which we will come in more detail in chapter 5. The Expert Commission suggested an option of introducing a two-step constitutional amendment. The first wave of amendments would have introduced norms:

> which would create the legal preconditions for the accession of the Estonian Republic to the Union. These would ensure that Estonia's accession application, negotiations, which concern the conclusion of an accession treaty that would constrain sovereign powers of the state, and ultimately the whole process of harmonisation of legislation, reorganisation of institutions etc., which take place on the basis of the state budget resources . . . , would be in conformity with the Constitution. The norms introduced in the first step would form a general basis for the accession to the European Union and for a possibility to delegate to this effect certain state powers.[101]

However, the Expert Commission preferred a one-step amendment shortly before the actual accession, in order to avoid holding two referendums within a short period of time. Somewhat strikingly, the Expert Commission pointed out that the citizens have under article 54 of the constitution the right to defend the independence of Estonia by initiating resistance; however, that article envisages this right only for situations where the 'change of the constitutional order' takes place 'by force'.

Finally, the Legal Department of the Estonian Parliament has condemned the fact that legal acts had to refer to the concrete EC Directives

[99] 'Kristlik rahvapartei kaebas Eesti liitumise euroliiduga Kaposse' [Christian People's Party brought a complaint on Estonia's EU entry to the Defence Police], *Eesti Päevaleht Online*, 18 August 2001, www.epl.ee

[100] *Võimalik liitumine Euroopa Liiduga ja selle õiguslik tähendus Eesti riigiõiguse seisukohalt* [Potential Accession to the European Union and its Consequences for Estonian Constitutional Law], Report of the Constitutional Amendment Expert Commission of Estonia (1998), in Estonian at www.just.ee/juridica2.html

[101] *Ibid.*, p. 19 (author's translation).

and their publication details, for the reason that this implies a reference to the legislation of foreign states.[102]

The Latvian European Integration Bureau has also very briefly touched upon the issue of legitimacy in its Report on the constitutional implications of EU accession. According to it, the requirement of approximation 'raises a number of difficult legal issues: the constitutional authority to approximate EC law prior to full membership; the practical limits on approximation which can be completed without full membership and a methodology to determine this; and [the] government's authority to harmonise EC law on its own initiative'.[103]

The issue of sovereignty has also been raised earlier with regard to the EFTA states in the EEA. According to Ilkka Saraviita, 'it is widely thought in the EFTA States that the EEA will restrict the sovereignty of particular EFTA States considerably in all of the three areas of state powers – but in a covert, subtle way'.[104] This is mainly for the following reasons: the *acquis* was adopted by a single parliamentary decision, compared with decades of development within the Member States; in interpreting the EEA, the EFTA states are bound by the ECJ rulings made prior to their signature; and an EFTA member is not represented in the EU decision-making institutions. Because of the last point, Saraviita finds that the sovereignty of an EFTA state in the EEA may be even more restricted than the sovereignty of the members of the EC. While the constitutions of the Scandinavian countries do not mention sovereignty, the issue of sovereignty was particularly relevant in Finland, where the act for incorporating the EEA was regarded as conflicting with the constitution due to its restrictive influence on the legislative power of the Parliament and the President.[105]

Considering the above, the issue of sovereignty in the context of pre-accession adaptations certainly appears to be of relevance in the CEE countries, where the constitutions protect sovereignty in stricter terms and, as will be seen in chapter 6, legal theory has hitherto taken a traditional

[102] Reported in J. Laffranque, 'Influence of European Community Law on Estonian Law and, in Particular, Law-Making' (1999) 4 *Juridica International, Law Review of Tartu University* 90.

[103] *Constitutional and Administrative Facilitation of Effective Law Approximation and European Union Membership*, Report composed under the auspices of the European Integration Bureau and PHARE Technical Assistance to the Approximation of the Latvian Legislation to that of the European Communities (Riga, 1999), p. 2.

[104] I. Saraviita, 'European Economic Integration in the Framework of the EEA Treaty and its Impact on the Sovereignty of the EFTA Countries' (1993) 35 *Acta Juridica Hungarica* 247, see also at pp. 244–5 and 248.

[105] *Ibid.*, p. 242.

approach towards the concept of sovereignty. During the last decade, the legislative activity and policy-making in CEE Parliaments has been largely predetermined by a foreign organisation. Meanwhile, only Poland has prepared its constitution for EU accession at an early stage of integration. Purely from the perspective of constitutional legitimacy, it would have perhaps been more correct to carry out the integration-related constitutional amendments and corresponding referendums in the earlier years of integration, although the political realities of course need to be taken into account. With the amendment of constitutions and holding of referendums shortly before accession, CEE populations were effectively left with a choice of providing an *ex post facto* approval to the adaptations that had already been irreversibly carried out.

In practical terms, the sovereignty of CEE countries in the pre-accession phase could perhaps have been better protected by a collective approach to negotiations. Although CEE countries are in many respects different, they shared several fundamentally similar interests, such as more favourable transition periods in costly areas. Instead, the process of negotiations has been underlined by individual competition in respect of the speed of closing the negotiation chapters. For instance, Estonia consistently distanced itself from its two Baltic counterparts in this process, and Bulgaria has stressed that it is not in tandem with Romania. There has been more cooperation amongst the Vishegrad countries, albeit occasionally some of them declared their objection to having to wait for the others.

Issues of democratic deficit in the pre-accession adaptations

Another aspect of legitimacy regarding the pre-accession adaptations concerns the issue of democratic participation and accountability in the process of harmonisation and accession negotiations. The relationships between the CEE candidate countries and the EU fell, as foreign relations, under the competence of the governments, leading to a large shift of powers to the executive branch. In the Europe Agreement spheres, the political decision-making and supervisory powers belonged to the Association Councils, composed of the foreign ministers of the EU and CEE countries.

Democratic involvement took place through the following mechanisms. The harmonisation of laws was carried out by usual parliamentary procedures, although the margin of manoeuvre was relatively limited due to the laws having been previously controlled for compatibility with EU law. The crux of democratic involvement lay in the European Affairs

Commissions of the Parliaments, which usually included representatives from all political parties represented in the Parliament. Amongst main activities, these Commissions harmonised national legislation with EU law, cooperated with and issued recommendations to the governments, examined the economic and social aspects of integration and kept in contact with Parliaments of the Member States and with the European Parliament. The European Affairs Commissions usually formed the candidate country's part in the Association Parliamentary Committees, which, in turn, formed the bodies of democratic control in the Europe Agreement areas. The democratic control also took place through the Parliaments' plenary sessions devoted to deliberating on the EU issues.[106]

However, Parliament members themselves as well as scholarly studies have pointed out a number of weaknesses in the democratic control over the pre-accession adaptations. To start with, EU issues were in most candidate countries discussed just in two or three plenary sessions during the first decade of integration (until 2000). For instance, in Poland, only two parliamentary debates took place on European integration, in 1999 and 2000.[107] In Estonia, EU integration was deliberated in three plenary sessions: in a session on the ratification of the Europe Agreement in 1995, and in sessions devoted to the process of EU integration in 1998 and 2000. In Hungary, a substantial debate took place only in one of the five plenary sessions dealing with EU issues held during 1991–1997.[108] However, since 2000, the plenary sessions in CEE countries became more frequent due to the final phase of the accession negotiations and deliberation of constitutional amendments for EU entry.

Secondly, the substance of the parliamentary debates remained rather general until the last couple of years before accession, and little specific information was provided about potential economic and social implications of harmonisation and accession negotiations. Attila Agh, who has researched the participation of CEE Parliaments in the pre-accession process, has concluded that '[t]he EU committees have not been able to use their institutional potentials, including their control capacity over the negotiations of the national executives with the EU authorities. The [CEE] national parliaments are only in the initial phase of meeting the

[106] See on parliamentary involvement in individual countries, Mansfeldová and Klíma, *Role of the Central European Parliaments.*

[107] 'Organisational Structure of Accession Negotiations in Poland' in *Accession Negotiations: Poland on the Road to the European Union* (Chancellery of the Prime Minister of the Republic of Poland, Warsaw, October 2000), p. 26.

[108] Györi, 'Parliaments and the European Union', p. 83.

challenge of the European integration process.'[109] For example, it has been reported that in Slovenia, the Euro-capacity of the Parliament was insufficient due to the lack of foreign relations specialists working in the Parliament compared with the government, and due to the deputies' lack of motivation to deal with the complicated European issues. European matters were viewed in Parliament as international in the classic way, that is as something 'foreign'.[110] In Estonia, transcripts of the Parliament's European sessions showed discussions of a rather general nature. For instance, the Parliament and its European Affairs Commission were provided no information on the economic effects of the abolition of tax-free shopping in ships, which had attracted Finnish mass tourism to the country and therefore generated a large part of Estonia's tourism and retail revenue.[111] In Hungary, it has been reported that 'no genuine debate with regard to the accession to the EU has been pursued in the National Assembly at plenary sessions. Integration . . . remained the business of few in the Parliament and the majority of MPs place this subject quite close to the bottom of their "check list".'[112] A study by Heather Grabbe and Kirsty Hughes concluded that there was strikingly little debate over EU conditionality within the CEE Parliaments, media and within governments, and this is one of the reasons why the CEE countries did not make effective use of bargaining in the accession negotiations.[113] Grabbe has also pointed out that '[b]ecause of the lack of debate about accession requirements, CEE policy-makers . . . [were] often constrained more by EU conditions than by their domestic policies'.[114]

Thirdly, harmonisation took place at a rather fast pace, which often left insufficient time for normal deliberation between the coalition and opposition, as well as with interest groups and society. In Estonia, the underlying message of parliamentary presentations by ministers was the need to speed up harmonisation and negotiations. Only towards the final phase of the negotiations in 2001 did Prime Minister Mart Laar declare that Estonia's previous goal to close as many chapters as possible within

[109] A. Agh, 'Role of ECE Parliaments in the Pre-Accession Strategy' in Mansfeldová and Klíma, *Role of the Central European Parliaments*, p. 116.

[110] D. Zajc, 'The Responsibilities of a Central European Parliament in the Process of European Integration: the Case of the Parliament of Slovenia and its Commission for European Affairs' in Mansfeldová and Klíma, *Role of the Central European Parliaments*, p. 98.

[111] L. Tõnisson, intervention in the Parliament's session of 18 January 2001, www.riigikogu.ee

[112] Györi, 'Parliaments and the European Union', p. 84.

[113] Grabbe, 'A Partnership for Accession', p. 34, with reference to Grabbe and Hughes, *Eastward Enlargement*.

[114] Grabbe, 'A Partnership for Accession', pp. 24, 36.

the shortest possible time would be replaced by seeking the best possible position for the country.[115] In some countries where deliberations took longer, the EU reproached the slowness of harmonisation in its annual Reports. For instance, in Slovenia, the Progress Report of 1999 noted that the Slovenian government needed to speed up parliamentary processes.[116] In Slovakia, the constitutional amendment of 2001 facilitated harmonisation by authorising the government to issue decrees for executing obligations under the Europe Agreement (Article 120(2)). In the Czech Republic, there have been a number of efforts to speed up the harmonisation process via a constitutional amendment, as a response to the criticism of slowness by the European Commission's Progress Reports. The harmonisation process has been particularly hasty in the countries that were invited to join the negotiations in the second round at the Helsinki summit, as these countries had an even shorter period at their disposal.

Fourthly, in some countries, the government's positions submitted to Brussels were confidential. In Poland, the issue of land sales to foreigners caused the initiation of a vote of confidence in 2001 by the opposition parties against Minister Wlodzimierz Cimoszewicz, who had noted that it had been a mistake not to present all Polish positions in Warsaw before going to Brussels, adding that, in future, all such positions would be presented to Parliament beforehand in a written form.[117] In Estonia, some members of the Parliament condemned the fact that although Parliament and its Commission of European Affairs were allowed access to the positions, they were not allowed to make these publicly available.

Finally, in some countries there were no clear procedures for consulting Parliament and interest groups. This, coupled with the speed and lack of information, led to a situation where important questions were in fact resolved by a small number of officials. For instance, in Estonia, there was neither public debate nor parliamentary deliberation on the issue of land sales to foreigners; the chapter was closed quickly without a transition period being sought. As another example, no transition period was requested with regard to the expected fourfold rise in the price of sugar in the aftermath of accession, which could potentially trigger bankruptcies and social problems. The pertinent working group,

[115] 'Estonia Changes Tactics in EU Membership Talks', *RFE/RL Newsline*, vol. 5, no. 220, Part II, 20 November 2001.

[116] 'Constitution Watch: Slovenia' (1999) 8(3) *East European Constitutional Review* 45.

[117] 'Constitution Watch: Poland' (2002) 11 *East European Constitutional Review* no. 1/2.

composed of officials and some foreign experts, did not involve representatives of Estonian industries despite their requests to participate. Further, the parliamentary committees on EU integration issues themselves were not always included in the decision-making: a former member of the European Affairs Commission of the Estonian Parliament pointed out that during her two-and-half-year membership of this Commission, the Commission was normally informed *a posteriori* about the negotiation positions, and its vote had been asked for on just one occasion.[118]

Another issue to consider in respect of legitimacy is that until shortly before accession, the populations of CEE countries were largely uninformed about EU-related issues in general. A study by Heather Grabbe and Kirsty Hughes shows that the public debate about European integration took place mainly at the elite level, and concentrated on the historical, security and geopolitical aspects, while the people were largely uninformed about the implications of joining the EU, such as its economic and social aspects or impact on their daily lives.[119] In Poland, the public began to discuss the EU in a more detailed way rather than generalities only as of 1998–1999.[120] A study concerning the opinions of Czech local politicians revealed their lack of knowledge about the EU, and complaints about deficiency and the abstract level of information, because of which they had not been able to form opinions on more specific issues.[121] In a number of countries, the adaptations also suffered from a weak empirical legitimacy, as public support for European integration was rather low (see chapter 7).

Similar problems of democratic control have also been encountered in the countries that joined earlier. For instance, the Constitutional Committee of the Swedish Parliament criticised the secrecy surrounding the work of the Integration Office during the harmonisation under the EEA: industrial representatives were excluded from the working group on

[118] The above comments concerning the Estonian Parliament have been made by parliamentary deputies L. Tõnisson, J. Marrandi, S. Oviir and V. Rosenberg in the Parliament's sessions of 19 January 2000, 18 January 2001 and 25 October 2001; transcripts are available in Estonian at www.riigikogu.ee

[119] Grabbe and Hughes, *Eastward Enlargement*, pp. 70, 71, and H. Grabbe and K. Hughes, 'Central and East European Views on EU Enlargement: Political Debates and Public Opinion' in K. Henderson (ed.), *Back to Europe* (UCL Press, London, 1999), pp. 185, 186, 189.

[120] G. Blazyca and M. Kolkiewicz, 'Poland and the EU: Internal Disputes, Domestic Politics and Accession' (1999) 15 *Journal of Communist Studies and Transition Politics* 137.

[121] C. Perron, *Views of Czech Local Politicians on European Integration* (European University Institute, Robert Schuman Centre Working Paper No. 2000/39, Florence, 2000), pp. 4–5.

institutional questions; reference groups for the working groups within the Integration Office were not regularly called to meet; the working groups on trade policy, consumer issues and competition policy never reported on questions of public concern, regardless of the obvious importance of such questions for the economy.[122] Distribution of powers regarding the EEA was also considered problematic in Finland, where the EEA-related amendments were introduced to the constitution in 1993, in order to secure Parliament's participation in the decision-making structures of the EEA, which otherwise would have fallen under the President's competence as part of foreign policy.[123]

While pre-accession adaptations have usually been approached in terms of technicalities concerning the process of approximation and negotiations, this chapter has attempted to point out some broader issues pertaining to legitimacy, in view of the strict protection of sovereignty in the CEE constitutions (except for Poland where a new constitution was adopted in 1997). Throughout the 1990s, the CEE countries were engaged in a gigantic venture of harmonising their legislation to EU law, which, besides the 80,000 pages of *acquis*, also covered some core functions of statehood. For instance, the harmonisation included foreign policy and internal security, some areas beyond EU domestic competences, such as social system reform and nuclear safety, as well as those which were not binding on all Member States, such as Schengen and EMU. Meanwhile, unlike the EEA-countries, these countries effectively did not participate in the creation of this law, even as regards legislation that was in the drafting phase. Thus, it could paradoxically be said that more sovereignty was given away in the pre-accession period, and that the candidate countries regained some of it upon accession, as they were included into the decision-making process.

[122] Evans, *Integration of the European Community*, p. 308; Evans, 'Voluntary Harmonization', pp. 218–19.

[123] M. Scheinin and T. Ojanen, 'Finland' in J. Rideau (ed.), *États Membres de l'Union Européenne: Adaptations, mutations, résistances* (LGDJ, Paris, 1997), p. 188 *et seq.*

5

Revision of CEE constitutions for EU membership

Wider package of EU amendments

Slovakia

Having explored the constitutional background in CEE countries, the experiences in the 'old' Member States and the constitutional aspects of pre-accession adaptations, we will now turn to the central issue – the adaptation of constitutions of Central and Eastern European countries for membership of the European Union. We will start our inquiry into the chain of constitutional amendments across the region with the countries where the package of EU amendments was most comprehensive: Slovakia, the Czech Republic and Slovenia.

The process started in Slovakia, where the constitution is one of the easiest to amend amongst the countries in question: it requires the approval of a three-fifths majority[1] of all deputies (article 84(4)). Amongst earlier amendments, the division of powers was modified in 1998, and direct presidential elections were introduced in 1999, at the same time curbing the President's prerogatives.[2] These were followed in 2001 by a comprehensive revision of the constitution, which, *inter alia*, introduced reforms in respect of public administration, local government and the judicial system, created the institution of the ombudsman, clarified the separation of powers and prepared the country for membership of the EU and NATO. This package of altogether eighty-five amendments, produced by the Parliament's Commission for Constitutional Amendment which had been established in 1999 from amongst the deputies of the ruling coalition, was adopted by Parliament on 23 February 2001. Preceded by a heated debate of almost three weeks, the package was adopted by 90 pro-votes out of the

[1] Until 1995 a three-fourths majority.

[2] See in more detail D. Malova and E. Lastic, 'The Gradual Amending of the Slovak Constitution: Combating the Ambiguous Rules in 1992–2001' (2001) 2 *Central European Political Science Review* 103.

148 members present (57 against, 1 abstention). It was rejected *en masse* by the opposition, Vladimir Meciar's Movement for the Democratic Slovakia and the Slovak National Party.[3] The EU provisions were mainly placed into article 7; their text is available in Table A3 in the Appendix.

Central to the amendments is new paragraph 2 of article 7, which provides that the 'Slovak Republic may, by an international treaty ratified and promulgated as stipulated by law, or on the basis of such treaty, transfer the execution of a part of its rights to the European Communities and European Union'. Alongside the new provisions on membership of NATO (see chapter 8), a constitutional basis is thus created for a transfer of powers. As mentioned earlier, this was not considered possible under the existing clause on 'state alliances' in article 7, which according to most commentators was aimed at a potential closer relationship with the Czech Republic.[4] The entry into the European Union is subject to a special majority: the accession treaty has to be ratified by at least a three-fifths majority of all deputies (article 84(4)). In comparison, the ratification of the treaties establishing membership of other international organisations under article 7(4) takes place by a simple majority of Parliament.

Another key change is the move from a dualist to a monist approach towards international law. Previously, article 11 granted direct applicability and precedence only to ratified and promulgated human rights treaties in the event of a conflict with domestic acts. Other treaties were applied 'by reference' through a national law; they ranked the same as statutes and were subject to the *lex posterior* rule.[5] The amendments deal separately with supremacy of EU law and with that of international treaties. The former is addressed in the second sentence of article 7(2): '[l]egally binding acts of the European Communities and European Union shall take precedence over the laws of the Slovak Republic'. Supremacy of international agreements is established in the new paragraph 5 of article 7, which accords precedence to the ratified and promulgated human rights treaties, to treaties the execution of which does not require the adoption of further acts and to treaties which directly impose rights or obligations on natural

[3] 'Constitution Watch: Slovakia' (2001) 10 *East European Constitutional Review*, no. 1; Malova and Lastic, 'Gradual Amending', pp. 102, 123.

[4] M. Hoskova, 'Legal Aspects of the Integration of the Czech Republic and Slovakia into European Security and Economic Structures' (1994) 37 *German Yearbook of International Law* 91, and E. Stein, 'International Law in Internal Law: Towards Internationalization of Central-Eastern European Constitutions?' (1994) 88 *American Journal of International Law* 443.

[5] Hoskova, 'Legal Aspects', p. 84.

or legal persons. According to new article 1(2), Slovakia 'recognises and honours general rules of international law, international treaties by which it is bound and its other international obligations'. In addition, article 87(4) provides that the rules on publication of EU law will be specified by law. The position of EU law and international law is further strengthened by provisions on the role of the courts. Article 144 provides that judges are bound, along with the constitution and constitutional laws, by EU law and directly applicable treaties, and the courts have to initiate constitutional review proceedings should they be of the opinion that an act is at odds with the constitution, EU law or with a directly applicable treaty. On the initiative of the President or the government, the Constitutional Court may decide on the constitutionality of the treaties that require the consent of Parliament, prior to their submission to parliamentary debate (new article 125a). Where a conflict is found with the constitution or with a constitutional law, the ratification may proceed only after the respective amendments.

Four other amendments are of direct relevance to EU membership. Article 30(1) grants to foreigners who have permanent residence the right to vote and stand in elections of self-governing bodies of municipalities and of superior territorial units; this right was previously restricted to national citizens under article 69(3). Article 120(2) facilitates the implementation of EU obligations, authorising the government to issue decrees in order to execute obligations under the Europe Agreement and the EU Treaties. Article 13(1) permits the imposition of duties on citizens by government decrees pursuant to this article (article 120(2)), as well as by international treaties under article 7(4). A number of amendments concern the position of the judiciary, forming a response to the European Commission's pertinent request presented in the Regular Report of 2000,[6] with a view to meeting the Copenhagen Criteria.

Besides these remarkably comprehensive amendments, the constitution underwent another amendment in respect of the EU in May 2004. The amendment provides that a person cannot be simultaneously a member of the European Parliament and of the Slovak Parliament, and it enables the Constitutional Court to decide whether the elections to the European Parliament are legitimate.[7] Another draft amendment has been

[6] European Commission, *Regular Report on Slovakia* (2000), www.politika.host.sk/Prispevky/dokument_slovensko_EU2_politicalcriteria.htm

[7] Amendment to the Constitution Passed in Parliament, 14 May 2004, www.slovensko.com/news/1255.

on the agenda since December 2003, concerning the participation of the Slovak Parliament in the government's activities in the EU decision-making process. The resolution of this issue has been postponed due to disagreement as to whether the parliamentary positions should take the form of recommendations or be of a binding character.[8]

Before commenting on Slovakia's set of EU amendments, we will briefly outline the developments in the Czech Republic and Slovenia.

Czech Republic

Shortly after Slovakia, the Czech Republic passed on 18 October 2001 a fairly similar package of amendments preparatory to EU membership, the main difference being that it was addressed more broadly to 'international organisations'. The Czech comprehensive set of amendments is noteworthy given the notoriously eurosceptic public opinion in the country, as well as a more demanding constitutional amendment procedure – the amending of the constitution requires the approval of both houses of Parliament.[9] Indeed, the process of constitutional revision was markedly more troubled than in Slovakia, and the amendments were the result of a lengthy constitutional amendment odyssey: Parliament had deliberated thirteen amendment proposals since 1996, intended to make the Czech constitutional system compatible with EU membership. The focal part of these proposals was the quest to facilitate and speed up the harmonisation process by endowing the government with the power to adopt decisions that would have the legal force of a law, in order to meet the European Commission's demands presented in the Regular Reports.[10] Only seven proposals survived the first reading in Parliament, and even those were later rejected, not least because of opposition by Vaclav Klaus (current President and former leader of the Civic Democratic Party), who has been notorious for his euroscepticism and for outcries about the European Union undermining sovereignty. Previously, the Czech Constitution had been amended on

[8] 'Slovak Coalition Split over Constitutional Amendment Linked to EU Accession', *RFE/RL Newsline*, vol. 7, no. 238, Part II, 19 December 2003.

[9] A three-fifths majority of all deputies, coupled with a three-fifths majority of the senators present, with the quorum of at least one-third of all senators.

[10] 'Constitution Watch: Czech Republic' (1999) 8 *East European Constitutional Review*, no. 3, p. 11; I. Slosarcik, 'The Reform of the Constitutional Systems of Czechoslovakia and the Czech Republic in 1990–2000' (2001) 7 *European Public Law* 543; see also V. Balas, 'Legal and Quasi-legal Thresholds of the Accession of the Czech Republic to the EC' in A. Kellermann, J. De Zwaan and J. Czuczai (eds.), *EU Enlargement: The Constitutional Impact at EU and National Level* (Asser Press, The Hague, 2001), p. 273.

two occasions: with regard to the reform of self-governing territories in 1997, and peace-keeping missions in 2000.[11] Unsuccessful constitutional amendment proposals have included the abolition of Parliament's second chamber, the introduction of direct presidential elections, reform of the judiciary and replacement of the proportional electoral system with a majoritarian one.[12]

The amendments pertaining to EU membership are dispersed throughout the constitution; their full text is available in Table A4 in the Appendix. As with Slovakia, an express constitutional basis is created for participation in international organisations: the new article 10a provides that '[s]ome powers of the Czech Republic may be transferred to an international organisation or institution' by an international agreement. The ratification of treaties on joining such organisations requires the approval of a three-fifths majority of all deputies, and a three-fifths majority of all senators present, unless a constitutional law subjects it to a referendum (articles 10a(2), 39(4)). In contrast, membership of other international organisations not involving a transfer of powers is subject to ordinary parliamentary ratification by both parliamentary chambers (article 49).

Another common trait of the amendments with those in Slovakia is the move from dualism to monism, that is, direct applicability and precedence were previously accorded solely to human rights treaties, provided that these were ratified and promulgated (then article 10). Other treaties were applied 'by reference' through a national law, and their rank equalled that of statutes, being subject to the *lex posterior* rule.[13] The amendments considerably strengthen the position of international law: the reworded article 10 provides that promulgated, ratified and binding international agreements 'constitute part of legislation', and are applied in the event of a conflict with domestic statutes. In addition, article 1(2) declares that the Republic observes obligations arising from international law. The method of promulgating international agreements, according to article 52, is to be regulated by law. These provisions are reinforced by amendments concerning the role of the judiciary: judges are bound by those international agreements that constitute a part of legislation, and

[11] See for the latter chapter 8.

[12] See on these in more detail P. Kopecky, 'The Czech Republic: From the Burden of the Old Federal Constitution to the Constitutional Horse Trading among Political Parties' in J. Zielonka and A. Pravda (eds.), *Democratic Consolidation in Eastern Europe*, vol. I, *Institutional Engineering* (Oxford University Press, 2001), pp. 342–4.

[13] See Slosarcik, 'Reform of the Constitutional Systems', p. 539; Balas, 'Legal and Quasi-legal Thresholds', p. 267; Hoskova, 'Legal Aspects', p. 84.

they are entitled to assess the conformity of legal acts with such international agreements (article 95). Where a conflict is found, the matter is referred to the Constitutional Court. Furthermore, ratification of international agreements under articles 10a and 49 (respectively on accession to international organisations which involve a transfer of powers, and to those which do not) may be subject to a preliminary constitutional review by the Constitutional Court (articles 89(3) and 87(2)). In case the agreement is found to infringe the constitution, ratification can proceed only after the elimination of the conflict.

The remaining set of EU-related amendments deals with the participation of Parliament in EU affairs. Article 10b establishes that the 'Government informs the Parliament regularly and in advance of issues related to obligations issuing from the Czech Republic's membership of an international organisation or institution stipulated in Section 10a' (paragraph 1), and that the parliamentary chambers 'make statements on the decisions of such an international organisation or institution that are being prepared as provided by their rules of procedure' (paragraph 2). The Act on the principles of conduct of the chambers may entrust this competence to a joint body of the two chambers (paragraph 3).

Finally, it is also interesting to note that an amendment is in process with regard to the protection of the Czech language 'as an inseparable component of state and national identity', in an apparent quest to counterbalance the opening up of the constitutional system to international governance by an added safeguard to national identity.[14] As will be seen later, a similar 'protection clause' has been introduced in Latvia, and is under consideration elsewhere.

Slovenia

The last country in the group featuring a relatively extensive package of amendments is Slovenia. Before the EU amendments, the constitution had been amended twice: in 1997 with regard to the ownership rights of foreigners, and in 2000 with regard to the modification of the electoral system.[15] The former is of interest to our study, as it has led to another amendment in 2003 as part of the EU amendments. In order to be able

[14] Initiated by the Communist party, this amendment passed the first parliamentary reading on 31 March 2004: 'Will the Communist Party Save the Czech Language?', *RFE/RL Newsline*, vol. 8, no. 61, Part II, 1 April 2004.

[15] See in more detail M. Cerar, 'Slovenia: From Elite Consensus to Democratic Consolidation' in Zielonka and Pravda, *Democratic Consolidation*, pp. 392–3.

to ratify the Europe Agreement, Slovenia had to revise article 68 of the constitution, which provided that foreigners may not acquire land except by inheritance in circumstances where reciprocity of such rights is recognised.[16] The Constitutional Court had found[17] that there was a conflict between this article and the so-called 'Spanish Compromise' (Annex XIII) of the Europe Agreement, which allowed foreigners to own property in Slovenia. The 'Spanish Compromise' formed a response to Italy's strong pressure on the EU to enable the pre-1945 inhabitants of Slovenia, who had been under pressure to choose Italian citizenship and to leave their homes on the basis of the peace agreement between Italy and Yugoslavia, to buy back their former estates. On 14 July 1997, the Parliament amended article 68, providing that foreigners may acquire ownership rights to real estate under the condition of reciprocity. However, on the threshold of EU membership, the amendment of this article came up again. At the initiative of Rome and Brussels, the Swedish Foreign Minister stated that before becoming an EU member, Slovenia needed to abolish the principle of reciprocity in article 68.

The preparations for EU amendments started in 2001, when a government-established Expert Group published a set of draft amendments in the *Official Gazette*.[18] In October 2001, deliberations started in the Parliament's Constitutional Commission. The final amendments were adopted by a parliamentary procedure on 7 March 2003.[19] The EU amendments formed part of a wider package of amendments, which included reforms of the government and local self-government. Given that the constitution was closed with regard to the transfer of sovereign rights due to

[16] See 'Constitution Watch: Slovenia' (1997) 6 *East European Constitutional Review*, no. 2/3; P. Vehar, 'Constitutional Problems in the Period of Pre-Accession in the Republic of Slovenia' in Kellermann, De Zwaan and Czuczai, *EU Enlargement*, pp. 371–3; D. Zajc, 'The Responsibilities of a Central European Parliaments in the Process of European Integration: the Case of the Parliament of Slovenia and its Commission for European Affairs' in Z. Mansfeldová and M. Klíma (eds.), *The Role of the Central European Parliaments in the Process of European Integration: Proceedings of International Conference, Prague, 12–14.09.1997* (Academy of Sciences, Prague, 1998), pp. 95–7.

[17] Decision No. RM-1/97, 5 June 1997, *Uradni list RS*, No. 40/97, on Europe Agreement, in English www.us-rs.si/en/

[18] Predlog za začetek postopka za spremembe ustave Republike Slovenije [Proposal to initiate the Procedure of Changes to the Constitution of the Republic of Slovenia], in *Poročevalec – Državnega zbora Republike Slovenije*, 6 August 2001, p. 4.

[19] The Slovene Constitution can be amended by a two-thirds majority vote of all deputies (article 169). Where requested by at least thirty deputies, the amendment is additionally submitted to a referendum (article 179), the validity of which requires a minimum turnout of 50 per cent.

the principle that all powers derive from the nation and are executed by national institutions,[20] the new article 3a(1) lies at the centre of gravity of the EU provisions. It provides that:

> Slovenia may transfer the exercise of part of its sovereign rights to international organisations which are based on respect for human rights and fundamental freedoms, democracy and the principles of the rule of law.

According to the same paragraph, the ratification of the treaty on joining such an organisation requires a two-thirds majority of all deputies, and a referendum may be called beforehand. The above clauses also apply to the entrance into 'a defence alliance with states', aimed at NATO membership. A higher majority is thus required for the EU and NATO accession treaties, in comparison with the regime that continues to govern, under article 86, the ratification of other treaties, for which a majority of votes cast by the deputies that are present is sufficient.

The position of EU law is regulated in para. 3 of the same article. According to it, '[l]egal acts and decisions adopted within international organisations to which Slovenia has transferred the exercise of part of its sovereign rights shall be applied in Slovenia in accordance with the legal regulation of these organisations'. Thus, the law of the organisations mentioned in article 3a(1) has a privileged position, given that Slovenia has also earlier been a monist country where, under article 8, laws and regulations are to comply with the generally accepted principles of international law and binding international agreements, and ratified and published international treaties are applied directly. The Constitutional Court has confirmed that international agreements 'rank above statutory provisions in the hierarchy of legal acts' and ratified treaties 'are integrated in the internal legal system', therefore being able to create rights and obligations for natural and legal persons in the country, provided that they are of self-executing nature.[21] Unlike the Czech and Slovak Constitutions, the Slovene Constitution already contains the mechanism for the constitutional review of treaties: in the process of ratifying a treaty, an opinion on the conformity of the treaty with the constitution can be requested by the President, the government or one-third of the Parliament's members. Parliament is bound by the outcome of such an opinion (article 160(2)).

[20] Vehar, 'Constitutional Problems', p. 370, with reference to B. Šinkovec, 'Prblizhevanju clanstvu v Evropski uniji in ustava' (1999) *Pravna praksa*, no. 6, pp. I–VI.

[21] Decision No. RM-1/97, 5 June 1997, *Uradni list RS*, No. 40/97, on Europe Agreement, paras 12, 18 and 20, at www.us-rs.si/en/. See also Vehar, 'Constitutional Problems', pp. 373–4.

The three remaining amendments are as follows. The first, contained in article 3a(4), concerns the participation of the Slovene Parliament in EU affairs. It obliges the government to inform Parliament of the acts that are in the process of adoption in international organisations to which sovereign rights have been transferred, and of the government's activities in this respect. Parliament may adopt positions, which the government 'shall take into consideration in its activities'; a more detailed relationship is to be regulated by law. Secondly, article 47 removes the conflict regarding the Schengen system and the European Arrest Warrant,[22] by opening the possibility of extraditing Slovenian citizens where so required by a treaty under which Slovenia 'has transferred the exercise of part of its sovereign rights to an international organisation'. Finally, the above-discussed condition of reciprocity is removed from article 68. The full text of the draft amendments is available in Table A5 in the Appendix.

Some common observations

The remarkably wide package of EU provisions in these three constitutions in general appears to cover the amendments that were deemed necessary in scholarly studies,[23] and on occasions even reach beyond that. None of these constitutions previously contained provisions on delegating powers to external bodies, and they have now been 'opened up' in this respect. However, the 'international organisation' approach taken in the Czech and Slovenian amendments appears to be a setback, as a direct reference to the EU would have better recognised the far-reaching impact of the EU on national governance. In addition, the chosen formulation is rather clumsy from the point of view of legal technique, in that a distinction has to be drawn between international organisations which do involve 'transfer of powers' and those which do not, whether speaking about ratification of treaties, application of law or participation of national Parliaments. This distinction is also unnecessarily obscure for citizens.

[22] Council Framework Decision 2002/584/JHA, 13 June 2002 on the European Arrest Warrant and the surrender procedures between Member States (OJ 2002, L190).

[23] See e.g. Hoskova, 'Legal Aspects', p. 88 *et seq.*; V. Kunova, 'Constitutional Aspects of the Accession of the Slovak Republic to European Union' in Kellermann, De Zwaan and Czuczai, *EU Enlargement*, p. 327 *et seq.*; Balas, 'Legal and Quasi-legal Thresholds', p. 267 *et seq.*; Vehar, 'Constitutional Problems', p. 369 *et seq.*; V. Tyc, 'Czech Republic' in A. Ott and K. Inglis (eds.), *Handbook on European Enlargement* (T. M. C. Asser Press, The Hague, 2002), p. 237; J. Zemanek, 'The Amendments of the Czech Constitution for the Accession to the European Union' in Kellermann, De Zwaan and Czuczai, *EU Enlargement*, pp. 423–34.

According to Czech commentators, the formula of 'international organisation' reflects the aim of equally encompassing membership of other organisations, such as NATO and the International Criminal Court.[24] Besides this, it is possible that lower public support for the EU both in the Czech Republic and Slovenia partly accounts for the 'international organisation' approach, in view of the efforts in many accession countries to downplay the significance of the EU upon national sovereignty ahead of the then imminent accession referendums. While in Slovakia, the amendments benefited from consistently firm public support for the EU – 65–69 per cent in the period of 2000–2002[25] – the support rates were moderate in Slovenia, varying according to different polls between 42–56 per cent, and even lower in the Czech Republic, ranging between 38–51 per cent. High levels of euroscepticism in the latter were not least fuelled by Vaclav Klaus' (current President and former opposition leader) consistent rhetoric of the EU as a superstate.[26] As will be seen in chapter 6, the 'international organisation' approach also appears to represent the prevailing theoretical views regarding the EU across Central and Eastern Europe, and it has been present in the drafting phase or final amendments in most countries. Indeed, also in Slovakia, an earlier draft amendment, presented by a group of Parliament members on 14 June 2000, was addressed more broadly to 'international organisations' and international commitments.[27] We will discuss in more detail these and some other factors which may have conditioned the 'international organisation' approach, towards the end of this chapter.

Amongst some specific issues that may, despite the relatively extensive set of amendments, cause questions about the compatibility with EU law, the following could be mentioned. As seen, the Slovak Constitution has been amended once more with regard to membership of the European Parliament, and the issue of the role of the national Parliament

[24] Slosarcik, 'Reform of the Constitutional Systems', p. 544.

[25] Here and later in the text, a range of support levels will be given, based on Eurobarometer surveys and national polls during 2000–2002. The national polls tend to show lower support rates. Eurobarometer surveys are available at http://europa.eu.int/comm/enlargement/opinion/, and national polls in *RFE/RL Newsline* (www.rferl.org). Support rates for the EU and reasons for euroscepticism will be discussed in more detail in chapter 7.

[26] See P. Bugge, *Czech Perceptions of the Perspective of EU Membership: Havel vs Klaus* (European University Institute, Robert Schuman Centre, Working Paper No. 2000/10, Florence, 2000) and C. Perron, *Views of Czech Local Politicians on European Integration* (European University Institute, Robert Schuman Centre Working Paper No. 2000/39, Florence, 2000).

[27] Reported in Kunova, 'Constitutional Aspects', p. 335.

has been on the agenda of constitutional revision. Another issue that appears to be unresolved concerns article 23(4) which, providing that a citizen 'must not be forced to leave his homeland and he must not be deported or extradited', is at odds with the Schengen system and European Arrest Warrant. As seen, a similar provision was amended in Slovenia. In the Czech Republic, it has been commented that there is a conflict in this respect with the Charter of Fundamental Rights and Freedoms, which forms a part of the constitutional order of the Czech Republic,[28] as article 14(4) of this Charter prohibits forcing a citizen to leave his or her country. Although an amendment Bill has been drafted, it has not yet been adopted at the time of writing.

As regards the rights of EU citizens, only the Slovak Constitution is amended in respect of the electoral rights of resident EU citizens in local elections. This leaves open the question of EU citizens' right to participate in the European Parliament elections, given that article 30(1) presently contains a general rule that electoral rights belong to national citizens, and article 29(2) restricts the right to belong to political parties to citizens. This, as well as the electoral rights of EU citizens in the two other countries, is apparently accommodated by way of interpretation. For instance, the Czech Constitution (article 100(1)) defines the units of territorial self-administration as 'territorial communities of citizens', which leaves room for interpretation. The Slovene Constitution permits determining by a statute the voting rights of foreigners, containing thereby an exception to the general rule that the right of active and passive suffrage belongs to citizens (articles 43 and 44). Another question, which may also arise in respect of the other CEE constitutions, is that the entitlement to social security and state assistance is restricted to citizens (e.g. Slovenia, article 50(1); Slovakia, articles 35(3) and 39(1)), which may affect the effective exercise of EU citizens' rights to free movement. In Slovakia, the restriction of the entitlement to work in public service to citizens (article 30(4) of the constitution) needs to be interpreted in a way which takes into account the fact that the scope of public service that may be restricted to citizens has been interpreted rather narrowly by the European Court of Justice. Finally, as regards the potential need to adjust monetary provisions in view of the transition to a common currency at a later stage after accession, it appears that unlike many other CEE countries, the monetary

[28] I. Slosarcik and S. Klouckova, 'Czech Republic' in *Criminal Law in the European Union: A Giant Leap or A Small Step? FIDE 2004 National Reports*, www.fide2004.org/reports/mc/mc04b.pdf, p. 46.

provisions in these three constitutions are worded broadly enough so as to leave a sufficient margin of interpretation, and expressly allow making changes by laws rather than requiring the amending of the constitutions. For instance, in Slovakia, article 56 provides that the Republic 'establishes a bank of issue'. The Czech Constitution provides that the Czech National Bank 'is the central bank of the State' and '[i]ts activities are primarily oriented towards currency stability' (article 98(1) of the constitution). As will be discussed later in respect of Poland and Estonia, the obligation to safeguard 'currency stability' in the Czech Constitution may need revision so as to replace this obligation with the safeguarding of price stability. However, as noted, this may also be effected by means of a law rather than requiring a constitutional amendment.

Medium package of EU amendments

Poland

Although Slovakia was the first country to pass the EU amendments, it was in fact the Polish Constitution of 1997 which was the first to be, in broad outline, ready for EU entry. The new constitution replaced the constitutional documents that had partly kept in force a modified form of the 1952 Communist Constitution. The new constitution's provisions on international organisations and on the application of international law in Poland were, according to the *travaux préparatoires* in the Constitutional Commission, mainly prepared with a view to joining the European Union.[29] The basis for accession can be found in paragraph 1 of article 90, which provides that Poland may, by an international agreement, 'delegate to an international organization or international institution the competence of organs of State authority in relation to certain matters'. The ratification of an international agreement on joining such international organisation

[29] See S. Meintapoulos, 'Le droit constitutionnel polonais face à l'adhésion à l'Union Européenne' (1999) 45 *Osteuropa Recht* 18; S. Biernat, 'Constitutional Aspects of Poland's Future Membership in the European Union' (1998) 36 *Archiv des Völkerrechts* 398; S. Biernat, 'The Openness of the Constitution of the Republic of Poland towards European Integration' in G. Amato, G. Braibant and E. Venizelos (eds.), *The Constitutional Revision in Today's Europe* (Esperia Publications, London, 2002), pp. 439–51; J. Barcz, 'Membership of Poland in the European Union in the Light of the Constitution of 2 April 1997' (1997–98) 23 *Polish Yearbook of International Law* 21; K. Wojtowicz, 'Proposed Changes in the Polish Constitution of 1997 ahead of Poland's Accession to the European Union' (2001) 25 *Polish Yearbook of International Law* 27; A. Lazowski, 'International Agreements in the Legal Orders of the Candidate Countries: Poland' in Ott and Inglis, *Handbook on European Enlargement*, pp. 305–7.

requires a two-thirds majority both in the Sejm (lower house of Parliament) and in the Senate, in the presence of at least half of the deputies and senators (article 90(2)). It may also be submitted to a referendum (article 90(3)).

The *travaux préparatoires* of this article demonstrate the sensitivity of the question of delegating sovereignty, which was a central issue in the debates in the parliamentary commission.[30] In order not to affect the feelings of a part of the population, reference to the notion of limitation of sovereignty had to be quickly abandoned by the constitutional drafters. Furthermore, the provision on the transfer of competences, which had been moved several times back and forth between the first chapter on general principles, and the third chapter on sources of law, was finally placed into the latter. This formed a concession to those who saw in the former option a threat to national sovereignty. Another dispute concerned the issue of whether the legal basis of accession should be regulated immediately or after accession: the latter solution was advocated by those who believed that accession was a matter of the distant future, and by those who were opposed outright to the very idea of EU accession, regarding it as a threat to sovereignty and national interests. However, the option of immediate regulation prevailed in order to underline the country's political will to join the EU. The loss of sovereignty under articles 90 and 91 also became one of the two key issues in the referendum on the adoption of the constitution, alongside the dispute on whether the Preamble to the constitution should make a reference to God, as demanded by a highly popular Catholic radio station, Radio Maria.[31] The coalition of different parties, united around the Solidarity Labour Union, accused the drafters of intending to deprive Poland of its sovereignty. They succeeded in mobilising a large part of society to reject the presented draft: it was adopted on 25 May 1997 by a narrow margin of 52.7 per cent against 46 per cent, with a turnout of just 43 per cent. The Polish experience demonstrates the sensitivity of the issue of sovereignty in the amendment debates, which equally appeared to be present elsewhere in the region,

[30] See Meintapoulos, 'Le droit constitutionnel', pp. 22–4; A. Wasilkowski, 'International Law and International Relations in the New Polish Constitution of 2 April 1997' (1997–98) 23 *Polish Yearbook of International Law* 15; Biernat, 'Constitutional Aspects', p. 400.

[31] See E. Letowska, 'A Constitution of Possibilities' (1997) 6 *East European Constitutional Review*, no. 2/3; J. Justynski, 'The Impact of the European Integration Process on the Creation of the Broad Lines of the Constitution of the Republic of Poland and on the Political Practices of the Country' in Kellermann, De Zwaan and Czuczai, *EU Enlargement*, p. 283, with reference to W. Skrzydlo, *Konstytucja Rzeczypospolitej Polskej, Komentarz* (Krakow, 1998), p. 10.

although relatively little literature is yet available in the other countries due to their later start of the amendment process.

Besides the transfer of powers, the new constitution extensively regulates the relationship between national and international law.[32] According to article 91, a ratified and promulgated international agreement 'shall constitute part of the domestic legal order and shall be applied directly, unless its application depends on the enactment of a statute' (para. 1), and it takes 'precedence over statutes if such an agreement cannot be reconciled with the provisions of such statutes' (paragraph 2). The third paragraph of article 91 prepares Poland for the application of EU secondary law, granting direct applicability and precedence to laws established by the above-mentioned international organisations, where so provided by the agreement establishing such organisation.[33] The position of international law is further specified in various other provisions. Article 9 provides that Poland shall respect international law binding upon it. This declaratory provision is meant to encompass all international law, and may form a basis for the courts and other state bodies for applying norms not addressed elsewhere in the constitution, such as customary law, non-ratified treaties and law-making resolutions of international organisations. Article 87 provides that ratified international agreements form part of the sources of universally binding law in Poland. Differently from direct applicability, supremacy is granted only to those treaties that have been ratified by a statute of Parliament (articles 89 and 91); the status of the treaties ratified by the President (article 133(1)) has not been directly addressed. Article 88(3) provides that treaties ratified with the prior consent granted by a statute are promulgated in accordance with the procedure required for statutes. Prior to ratification of a treaty, the President can seize the Constitutional Tribunal to review the constitutionality of the law on ratifying the international agreement (articles 133(1.2) and 188(1)). Before the adoption of the 1997 Constitution, the status of international law was not regulated in the constitutional acts, but a monist approach was taken by the Constitutional Tribunal.[34]

In the current form, however, the 1997 Constitution appears to leave a number of conflicts with EU law unresolved, which has led to debates

[32] See articles by W. Czaplinski, 'The Relationship between International Law and Polish Municipal Law in the Light of the 1997 Constitution and Jurisprudence' (1999) *Droit Polonais Contemporain* 19 at pp. 19–26; Wasilkowski, 'International Law', pp. 7–19; Lazowski, 'International Agreements', pp. 299–305.

[33] Full text of the EU-related provisions is available in Table A6 in the Appendix.

[34] See for overview of the case law Czaplinski, 'Relationship between International Law and Polish Municipal Law', p. 21.

about revising the constitution again before or after EU accession.[35] The following issues have been pointed out in particular. To start with, article 62(1) restricts the right to vote in local elections to Polish citizens. Further, article 67(1) and (2) restrict the right to social security to Polish citizens, which may be at odds with the rights of EU citizens exercising the right to free movement. Article 227(1), which bestows on the National Bank of Poland the exclusive right to issue the Polish currency, to formulate monetary policy and to safeguard the value of the Polish currency, may need revision in respect of all these responsibilities in view of future membership of Monetary Union. Besides these issues, obligations arising from the Schengen *acquis* and the European Arrest Warrant have been found to be in conflict with articles 52(4) and 55, which prohibit the extradition of Polish citizens from the country.[36] One could also point out that in interpreting article 60, which restricts the entitlement to work in public service to citizens, account should be taken of the ECJ's restrictive interpretation of the scope of public service that may be restricted to national citizens.

Since two of the issues concerned – local elections and accession to the common currency – are expected to take place some years after accession (local elections in 2005), the governing view preferred to amend the constitution after accession, and overcome potential conflicts in the meantime by interpretation. However, there have been voices doubting the constitutionality of the Accession Treaty. For instance, in March 2003, the Peasant Party and the Law and Justice Movement called on President Alexander Kwasniewski to present Poland's Accession Treaty for screening by the Constitutional Tribunal. The reason given was that the priority of the constitution over international law is one of the basic conditions for preserving Poland's independence in the EU, and leaving the issue unresolved could result in questions over the legal status of the constitution after the country's entry into the EU.[37]

The amendment of the constitution at the time of accession negotiations and ratification of the Accession Treaty, however, would have entailed a number of political problems,[38] not least by presenting a risk of

[35] See Wojtowicz, 'Proposed Changes', pp. 40–4, and Biernat, 'Openness of the Constitution', p. 445.

[36] A. Grzelak, 'Poland' in *Criminal Law in the European Union: A Giant Leap or A Small Step? FIDE 2004 National Reports*, www.fide2004.org/reports/mc/mc17b.pdf, at 262. According to Grzelak, the majority of scholars prefer the resolution of this conflict by interpretation.

[37] 'As Some Doubt Constitutionality of Accession Treaty', *RFE/RL Newsline*, vol. 7, no. 50, Part II, 17 March 2003.

[38] See also Biernat, 'Openness of the Constitution', p. 448.

strengthening the nationalist anti-EU movements such as Self-Defence, which enjoyed the support of nearly 30 per cent of the population in the first months of 2004. Furthermore, since the new constitution has not yet undergone any amendments, there was a risk of the parliamentary opposition adding other issues on the agenda. Indeed, in September 2003, opposition party Liberal Civic Platform, the second force in the Parliament, adopted a resolution on a major constitutional revision, which would include a reduction in the size of the two parliamentary chambers, and introduction of a first-past-the-post electoral system.[39] In fact, proposals to amend the constitution had been put on the agenda by the opposition parties immediately after the 1997 referendum, due to some unresolved institutional issues as well as because of the weak public support for the constitution demonstrated by the referendum outcome.[40] The procedure for amending the new constitution does not make this an easy task: it requires the approval of two parliamentary chambers, and may involve a referendum.[41]

Hungary

In Hungary, the second half of the 1990s was marked by preparations for adopting a new constitution as envisaged in the Preamble to the 1949 Constitution, which, albeit comprehensively amended, had been formally retained in force. A parliamentary committee was established to this effect in 1995, and a draft of a new constitution was widely published and discussed in 1996.[42] The text of the current constitution was retained where there was no overwhelming majority in the Committee to change it. Article 3 of the draft constitution offered two formulations on

[39] *RFE/RL Newsline*, vol. 7, no. 170, Part II, 8 September 2003.

[40] 'Constitution Watch: Poland' (1997) 6 *East European Constitutional Review*, no. 2/3.

[41] See on this point also Biernat, 'Openness of the Constitution', p. 446. According to article 235 of the constitution, the amendments have to be first adopted by the Sejm (lower house of Parliament), by at least a two-thirds majority in the presence of at least half of all deputies. The amendments then have to be approved in the same wording by the Senate, by an absolute majority of votes in the presence of at least half of all senators. A confirmatory referendum may be held on the amendment of the provisions of Chapter I (fundamental provisions of the state), Chapter II (human rights) or Chapter XII (constitutional amendment procedure).

[42] For an English version of the draft constitution see 'Constitution of the Republic of Hungary (Draft)' (1997) 38 *Acta Juridica Hungarica, Hungarian Journal of Legal Studies* 5. See also A. Racz, 'Major Phases of Constitutional Development' in A. Harmathy (ed.), *Introduction to Hungarian Law* (Kluwer Law International, The Hague, 1998), p. 10 and K. Hiller, 'Neue Verfassung für Ungarn?' (1998) *Recht in Ost und West*, No. 2, pp. 75–6.

international cooperation, both authorising to 'transfer legislative, executive or judicial powers defined by the Constitution' to 'international organisations or institutions'.

However, in 1997, the draft constitution was dropped from the agenda, and amendments were introduced instead to the 1949 Constitution in respect of referendums, status of ministers and reform of the court system.[43] In 2000, another amendment was introduced concerning the obligations under NATO (see chapter 8). The governing opinion deemed it necessary to amend the constitution once again with regard to EU accession. The government opened a public debate on constitutional revision in its White Paper on the legal aspects of Hungary's accession to the European Union.[44] The White Paper recommended the introduction of a single Europe article, since it was found to be impracticable to list the elements of sovereignty to be exercised by the Community in respect of each and every field of the exercise of state powers (i.e. courts, National Bank, etc.). The parliamentary debates started in September 2002, when the leaders of Hungary's four parliamentary groups signed a declaration to approve the amendments before a referendum on EU accession, and pledged not to link domestic political conflicts to European integration.[45] In designing the amendments, two main options were on the table: a wider package of EU amendments 'to the necessary extent', and a minimum solution where the details concerning EU membership would not be addressed.[46] In early December 2002, four parliamentary parties had agreed in principle to introduce amendments on transferring sovereignty to the EU in respect of a number of supranational issues.[47] However, the final amendments, adopted unanimously on 17 December 2002, dropped many issues from the agenda, and provided a more modest solution in order

[43] See Hiller, 'Neue Verfassung', p. 64. The constitution had also been amended in 1995, when the majority required for constitutional amendment was increased from a three-fourths to a four-fifths majority.

[44] Reported in O. Varhely, 'International Agreements in the Legal Orders of the Candidate Countries: Hungary' in Ott and Inglis, *Handbook on European Enlargement*, p. 265.

[45] 'Hungarian Parties Sign EU Declaration', *RFE/RL Newsline*, vol. 6, no. 178, Part II, 20 September 2002.

[46] Presentation of J. Czuczai, at the conference 'EU Enlargement and European Constitutional Process', College of Europe, Natolin, Warsaw, 31 January–1 February 2003; see also J. Czuczai, 'National Preferences in Light of the Constitutional Adaptation Process to the EU Accession Acquis: The Hungarian Experiences in a Comparative Dimension of Central and Eastern Europe' in *Europe 2002* (Budapest, March 2004), vol. V/I, p. 35.

[47] 'Hungary's EU Referendum Date Approved by Parliament', *RFE/RL Newsline*, vol. 6, no. 225, Part II, 3 December 2002.

to join the EU. The constitutional amendment procedure is relatively flexible: the passing of an amendment requires a four-fifths majority of all deputies.

The choice for a minimal solution appears to reflect the sudden change in the political climate: after the 2002 elections, FIDESZ, one of the leading parties, had to resign from the government into opposition, where it took a markedly more eurosceptic stance towards the accession process. Boycotting the amendments and staying away from consultations, the party insisted on formulating the amendments so that Hungary's independence would not be surrendered and so that EU legislation would not take precedence over the Hungarian Constitution.[48] The difficulty of reaching a compromise led the Prime Minister Peter Medgyessy to announce the possibility that should the opposition not vote for the amendments, the government would appeal directly to the people on the issue.[49] In parallel, the formerly high public support for EU accession plummeted in January 2003 ahead of the accession referendum: only 45 per cent believed the country's EU accession to be advantageous, compared with 62 per cent six months earlier.[50] The rise in anti-EU sentiment was ascribed to FIDESZ's repeated stressing of the disadvantages of accession, as well as to the weak handling of the accession negotiations by the government.

The main amendment was introduced in the new article 2A of the constitution. Paragraph 1 provides that:

> [t]he Republic of Hungary for the purpose of becoming a Member State in the EU through the conclusion of an international treaty . . . [to] the necessary degree in order to fulfil the obligations and to exercise the rights stemming from the founding Treaties establishing the EU and the European Communities – can exercise certain constitutional powers jointly with other Member States. This joint exercise can be conducted also separately through the institutions of the EU.[51]

[48] 'Hungarian Parties Argue over Constitutional Amendment Vital for EU Accession', *RFE/RL Newsline*, vol. 6, no. 194, Part II, 15 October 2002; 'Doubts Persist over Fate of Hungarian Constitutional Reforms', *RFE/RL Newsline*, vol. 6, no. 209, Part II, 5 November 2002; 'Former Hungarian Premier Warns of Lost Sovereignty to EU', *RFE/RL Newsline*, vol. 6, no. 216, Part II, 18 November 2002.

[49] 'Doubts Persist over Fate of Hungarian Constitutional Reforms', *RFE/RL Newsline*, vol. 6, no. 209, Part II, 5 November 2002; 'Hungarian Delay on "Big-Bang" EU Enlargement', *RFE/RL Newsline*, vol. 6, no. 187, Part II, 3 October 2002.

[50] 'Support in Hungary for EU Accession Drops', *RFE/RL Newsline*, vol. 7, no. 14, Part II, 23 January 2003.

[51] Translation by Czuczai, 'National Preferences', pp. 53–4.

Pertinent international agreements may be adopted by a two-thirds majority of the Parliament's members (para. 2). The previous regime of ordinary parliamentary ratification (under article 19(3f)) remains applicable for other treaties. Other amendments include the following. Article 6(4) refers to 'establishing European unity for the accomplishment of the freedom, welfare and safety of European peoples'. The Hungarian and EU citizens will be entitled to vote in the European Parliament elections, and EU citizens in local elections (article 70). Hungary is to be represented in the EU institutions by the Government; detailed rules on parliamentary control are to be established by a law (articles 35 and 35A). Article 32D(1) redesigns the National Bank's role, with a special law to be adopted. Article 79 provides for a referendum on EU accession.

However, commentators have regretted that these amendments intentionally left the resolution of some potential conflicts to the Constitutional Court. This concerns in particular the question of supremacy of EU law, given that the Hungarian legal order is clearly a dualist one, where the norms of international law have not had precedence.[52] Hungary is the only country amongst the CEE candidate countries that clearly adheres to dualism.[53] Article 7(1) of the constitution provides that the legal system of Hungary accepts the generally recognised principles of international law, and that the country's domestic law shall be harmonised with the obligations assumed under international law. This means, according to the case law of the Constitutional Court, that only generally recognised norms of international law are incorporated and take precedence within the Hungarian legal system, whereas other forms of international law, including treaties, share the legal status of their promulgating legislation. In accordance with the strict dualist setting, the Hungarian Constitutional Court has repeatedly established that the internal legislation implementing the international agreement is applied instead of the international agreement itself.

On the other hand, the amendments resolved many issues the adjustment of which was deemed necessary, for instance, by the Congress of the Hungarian Lawyers' Association in May 2000.[54] Some potential conflicts

[52] Czuczai, 'National Preferences', p. 53.

[53] A. Harmathy, 'Constitutional Questions of the Preparation of Hungary to Accession to the European Union' in Kellermann, De Zwaan and Czuczai, *EU Enlargement*, p. 324; see generally also I. Pogany, 'Constitutional Reform in Central and Eastern Europe: Hungary's Transition to Democracy' (1993) 42 *International and Comparative Law Quarterly* 353.

[54] Harmathy, 'Constitutional Questions', p. 326, with reference to 'Az Ötödik Magyar Jogászgyûés ajánlásai', *Magyar Jog*, 2000, p. 321.

remain though, such as article 70/E(1) which guarantees only to the Hungarian citizens the right to social security, which may unduly restrict the rights of EU citizens exercising free movement. In addition, the restriction of the entitlement to work in public service to citizens under article 70(4) may need a liberal interpretation.

In fact, after the success in the accession referendum, Parliament re-introduced, in September 2003, some of the EU-related issues on the agenda of constitutional revision. These included the introduction of the Constitutional Court's review of international treaties, the review of compatibility of domestic laws with international commitments and facilitation of the deployment of military forces for peace-keeping and humanitarian missions under the aegis of the EU, NATO and United Nations.[55] Another Bill has been submitted to Parliament with the aim of introducing amendments on questions such as the relationship between the government and the Parliament in EU affairs, reform of electoral rules, and the implications of joining EMU.[56] Besides the amendments related to the EU, the government is also considering constitutional amendments on the reduction of the size of the Parliament and on the introduction of direct presidential elections.[57] In summer 2003, talks have also emerged in Parliament about preparing a new constitution, considering that the present constitution has been amended too many times, and that the year 2004 marks fifty-five years of the present constitution.[58]

Altogether, as indicated in the title of this section, the package of amendments in Poland and Hungary could be characterised as a medium one, compared to the first group. This is because Poland left a number of conflicts unresolved, but its Constitution contains a provision on the direct application and supremacy of the law of international organisations; the wording is aimed to cover both primary and secondary EU law. Hungary resolved many conflicts and the amendments are addressed directly to the EU rather than to international organisations, but the important question of supremacy of EU law remained unresolved in the context of Hungary's strongly dualist setting. In addition, the principle of sovereignty in these

[55] *RFE/RL Newsline*, vol. 7, no. 143, Part II, 30 July 2003; *RFE/RL Newsline*, vol. 7, no. 182, Part II, 24 September 2003.

[56] Reported in Czuczai, 'National Preferences', p. 54.

[57] 'Hungarian Premier to Call Plebiscites on Constitutional-Amendment Proposals?', *RFE/RL Newsline*, vol. 8, no. 39, Part II, 1 January 2004.

[58] 'Hungarian President Rejects Talk of New Constitution', *RFE/RL Newsline*, vol. 7, no. 160, Part II, 22 March 2003; 'Hungarian Government Proposes Constitutional Amendment', *RFE/RL Newsline*, vol. 7, no. 143, Part II, 30 July 2003.

constitutions is not protected as strictly as in the Baltic constitutions, which will be discussed next.

Minimal EU amendments

The process of amendment has been most difficult and controversial in the Baltic countries, Estonia, Latvia and Lithuania, where the rigid constitutional amendment procedures include a referendum for amending articles on sovereignty and independence.[59] This requirement proved too challenging to comply with in the process of EU accession, against a background where public support for EU membership was consistently the lowest amongst the candidate countries and the question of delegation of sovereignty was particularly sensitive due to the recent regaining of independence. We will explore below the developments in each of the three countries.

[59] The amendment procedures in the three Baltic countries are as follows. In Estonia, Chapter XV of the constitution provides three modes of amendment. First, although a referendum may be used for all amendments, its use is obligatory where the amendments concern Chapters I 'General Provisions', including sovereignty and independence, and Chapter XV 'Amendment of the Constitution'. Secondly, ordinary provisions may be amended by two successive memberships of the Parliament. In this case, the amendment Bill must be supported by a majority of all deputies and, in an unmodified form, by the succeeding Parliament in the first reading, with a three-fifths majority. The third option, which according to the *travaux préparatoires* of the constitution is meant for technical issues of minor importance, is the procedure of urgency. In this case, a resolution to consider an amendment Bill requires a four-fifths majority of the Parliament; the Amendment Act has to be passed by a two-thirds majority of all deputies. A rejected amendment may not be re-initiated within a year. In Latvia, a constitutional amendment Bill has to be passed in three readings by a majority of at least two-thirds of the members present, with the participation of at least two-thirds of all deputies (article 76). The Bill must be submitted to a referendum where the amendments concern articles 1 and 2 on sovereignty, other fundamental provisions in articles 3, 4 or 6, or the constitutional amendment procedure established in article 77. The validity of such a referendum requires a minimum turnout of 50 per cent. A referendum must also be held if one-tenth of the voters submit a fully elaborated draft of a constitutional amendment to the President, and the Parliament does not adopt it without modifying its content (article 78). In Lithuania, the amendment procedure is regulated in articles 147–9 of the constitution. Amendments to article 1 (independence and democracy), Chapter 1 (fundamental provisions of state) and Chapter 14 (constitutional amendment procedure) require a referendum (article 148). Furthermore, the amendment of article 1 requires the approval of a three-fourths(!) majority of all citizens who have the right to vote, while the amendment of the other above-mentioned chapters requires the minimum turnout of 50 per cent. Amendments to the other chapters of the Constitution require a two-thirds majority of all deputies in two votes. A rejected amendment may not be resubmitted within one year.

Estonia

Due to its rigid amendment procedure, the Estonian Constitution had been previously amended only on one occasion: the term of office of local councils was extended in 2003, shortly before the EU amendments.[60] In 1996, a comprehensive analysis of the constitution was undertaken by the Constitutional Expert Commission, which was established by the government from leading lawyers and scholars, with a view to ascertaining issues where a revision may be necessary. The results, published in 1998, included a Report, *Potential Accession to the European Union and its Consequences for Estonian Constitutional Law*,[61] in which the Expert Commission concluded that the constitution did not permit entry into the EU. The primary obstacle, according to the Report, lay in article 1, which declares the eternity and inalienability of Estonia's sovereignty and independence, and article 123(1), which prohibits the conclusion of treaties that are in conflict with the constitution. The Expert Commission therefore offered amendment proposals, to be approved at a referendum, as required in article 162 of the constitution. Central to the proposed amendments was new draft paragraph 1, to be added to article 1, which would have provided that 'Estonia may, on the basis of a referendum, participate in the European Union, which is an association of states created by its Member States on the basis of the Treaties'. Draft article 123^1 would have specified the conditions for the delegation of powers: reciprocity, equality and respect for 'the basic principles and functions of Estonian statehood, manifested in the Preamble to the Constitution'. In addition, the Expert Commission pointed out the need for a provision which would establish Parliament's relations with the government in EU affairs. It also recommended the elimination of two manifest conflicts with EU law: the Bank of Estonia's exclusive right to issue Estonia's currency (article 111), in view of the future adoption of a common currency, and the restriction of membership of political parties to Estonian citizens (article 48), in view of the effective exercise of EU citizens' right to stand in elections for local councils and the European Parliament. The Expert Commission

[60] See on previous amendment debates P. Roosma, 'Amending or Adjusting? Comments on Estonia' in E. Smith (ed.), *The Constitution as an Instrument of Change* (SNS Förlag, Stockholm, 2003), p. 105 *et seq.*

[61] *Võimalik liitumine Euroopa Liiduga ja selle õiguslik tähendus Eesti riigiõiguse seisukohalt* [Potential Accession to the European Union and its Consequences for Estonian Constitutional Law], Report of the Constitutional Amendment Expert Commission of Estonia (1998) in Estonian at www.just.ee/juridica2.html

also offered an optional clause on the direct applicability of EU law, since article 123 grants direct applicability and supremacy only to the treaties ratified by Parliament, and hence would not cover EU secondary legislation. Until early 2002, the amendment discussions proceeded mainly from the Expert Commission's Report. Although the opinions concerning the issues and the extent of the constitutional amendments varied, most foreign experts,[62] domestic lawyers[63] and the Legal Chancellor[64] deemed it necessary to amend the constitution in order to join the EU, and a relatively wide agreement could be discerned in respect of a similar range of issues. The main dispute revolved around the issue of whether the amendments should include article 1, and thus involve a constitutional amendment referendum, or should rather be placed into Chapter IX on foreign relations or in a new special EU Chapter.

However, in the wake of rising euroscepticism, which peaked in May 2001 when the polling agencies recorded that 59 per cent of the voters were against joining the EU, the amendment of the constitution became a political rather than a legal issue, and the question of amending article 1 was increasingly exploited by the eurosceptic movements. In this context, the then Prime Minister Mart Laar expressed uncertainty as to whether the constitution needed to be amended at all,[65] and it was not clear until March 2001 whether a referendum would be held – for instance, the then President Lennart Meri recommended holding a referendum some years after EU membership on whether the Estonians wished to withdraw from the Union.[66]

[62] e.g. L. Lopez Guerra, M. Niemivuo, J. Gardner, G. Carcassone and H. Beemelmans, whose opinions are available in the collection *Põhiseaduse Juriidilise Ekspertiisi Komisjoni Tegevuse Aruande Lisa 'Välisekspertiisid'* [Appendix 'Foreign Expert Opinions' to the Report on the Activity of the Constitutional Expert Commission] (Justiitsministeerium, Tallinn, 1998).

[63] Different views are discussed in more detail in A. Albi, 'Estonia's Constitution and the EU: How and to What Extent to Amend It?' (2002) *Juridica International, Law Review of Tartu University* 39. See also J. Laffranque, 'Constitution of the Republic of Estonia in the Light of Accession to the European Union' (2001) *Juridica International, Law Review of Tartu University* 207, and R. Maruste, 'Eesti enne euro-otsustust' [Estonia before the EU Decision], *Postimees*, 16 December 2001.

[64] The Legal Chancellor's opinion on amending the constitution, submitted to the European Affairs Committee, is available in annotated form in the Parliament's press announcement of 12 October 2001, www.riigikogu.ee

[65] Speech by M. Laar at the Parliament's session of 18 January 2001, transcript available in Estonian at www.riigikogu.ee

[66] H. Roonemaa, 'Meri: rahvas võiks aastate pärast hääletada euroliidust välja astumist' [Meri: the People Could Vote on Secession from the EU after a Few Years], *Eesti Päevaleht*, 5 May 2001.

Against this backdrop, the Ministry of Justice, insisting on the time constraints and the difficulty of finding a consensus in Parliament, started in 2002 to promote the idea of not amending the constitution, but 'supplementing' it with the so-called 'Third Constitutional Act', which would exist beside the constitution and the Implementing Act of the Constitution. After a speedy and relatively closed deliberation within an ad hoc commission, composed of representatives of the party factions, civil servants and academia, the Act on Supplementing the Constitution of Estonia was indeed initiated in Parliament in May 2002. Article 1 of this laconic Act provides that 'Estonia may belong to the European Union, proceeding from the founding principles of the Constitution of the Republic of Estonia'. Article 2 continues that '[i]n case Estonia belongs to the European Union, the Constitution of the Republic of Estonia will be applied, taking into consideration the rights and obligations deriving from the Accession Treaty'. The third article subjects the amendment of this Act to a referendum. The reference to the safeguarding of the basic values of the constitution in article 1 of the Act is known as a so-called 'crisis clause', and it was inserted on the request of the Legal Chancellor. The Act passed all three readings by 18 December 2002. It was opposed only by the People's Union Party, who advocated a clause on the people's right to decide upon the ratification of future treaties which may bring about fundamental changes to the character of the EU polity.[67] The Act was approved in a referendum on 14 September 2003, where two referendums – on accession and on the 'supplementing' of the constitution – were fused into one, following an amendment to the Referendum Act. According to the accompanying media coverage, the initiators of the Act were convinced that Estonia did not harm its sovereignty by adopting the Act.[68] Besides reducing the sensitivity of the issue of sovereignty ahead of the accession referendum, the Third Act also provided a means to avoid the EU amendments being hijacked by another topical and controversial amendment – the introduction of direct presidential elections, which had been initiated in Parliament in October 2002.

[67] 'Rahvaliit põhiseaduse täiendamise vastu' [The People's Union is against the Supplementing of the Constitution], *ETA News*, reported in *Delfi news portal*, 28 May 2002; J. Reiljan, 'Rahvas põhiseaduse kaitsjana' [People as the Guardian of the Constitution], *Postimees*, 15 July 2002.

[68] Ü. Mattheus, 'Põhiseaduse muutjad Eesti suveräänsuse kahjustamist ei karda' [The Amenders of the Constitution are Not Afraid of Harming Estonia's Sovereignty], *Raadio Vaba Euroopa Online*, 16 May 2002, www.vabaeuroopa.org

The Third Constitutional Act should inevitably be seen in the context of geopolitical and economic pressures for joining the EU. Because of its tragic history, Estonia simply could not have afforded the risk of remaining outside the EU, in a geopolitical 'grey zone' next to Russia. However, some questions have been raised about the correctness of such a solution. The procedural and substantive shortcomings of the Act attracted criticism by prominent lawyers such as Allar Jõks (Legal Chancellor),[69] Rait Maruste (Judge of the European Court of Human Rights and the former President of the National Court),[70] and by some lawyers in a joint public statement.[71] The critique has revolved around the following issues. First, the Third Constitutional Act does not fit well into the Estonian legal order, unlike in some countries where constitutional laws possess a status equal to the constitution and are amended in accordance with constitutional amendment procedure (e.g. Austria, Sweden, the Czech Republic). The Estonian Constitution does not provide for such kind of constitutional acts, and the legal position of the Implementing Act of the Constitution is not equal to the constitution because it regulates an initial transitional period and has predominantly expired. Secondly, the three rigid amendment procedures do not include the possibility of adopting an act which would exist independently beside the constitution. Thirdly, as mentioned in chapter 3, the constitutions of Central and Eastern Europe are regarded as legal rather than political documents. In this respect, the Third Act risks obscuring and devaluing Estonia's clear, directly applicable and up-to-date constitution, since it will be interpreted in the light of one general principle deriving from the Third Act, a document standing outside the current constitutional system. Fourthly, the content of the Third Act fails to reflect how membership of the EU impacts upon the exercise of state powers, nor does it eliminate some manifest conflicts

[69] Õiguskantsleri arvamus Justiitsministeeriumis välja töötatud eelnõu 'Põhiseaduse rakendamine Euroopa Liidu liikmeks oleku tingimustes' kohta [The Legal Chancellor's Opinion on the Draft Law of the Ministry of Justice 'Implementation of the Constitution in the Conditions of European Union Membership'], 16 April 2002, unpublished document; A. Jõks, 'Põhiseadus muutuste künnisel' [Constitution at the Doorstep of Changes], *Postimees*, 17 April 2002.

[70] R. Maruste, 'Põhiseadust tuleks siiski muuta' [The Constitution Should Still be Amended], *Postimees*, 30 January 2002.

[71] A. Albi, M. Gallagher, I. Koolmeister, R. Maruste, L. Mälksoo and P. Roosma, 'Ühispöördumine seoses nn Põhiseaduse Kolmanda akti riigiõiguslike probleemidega' [Joint Statement concerning the Constitutional Problems of the Third Constitutional Act] (2002) 5 *Juridica* 352.

between the constitution and EU law. Indeed, Justice Maruste has characterised this Act as 'nihilism towards the constitutional state'.[72] Not surprisingly, the problems were also highlighted by the eurosceptic movement. Its leader, Kalle Kulbok, sent official communications to the main state institutions, declaring that the Third Act entitles the Estonian people to initiate resistance against the change of the constitutional order under article 54 of the constitution.

The Constitutional Chamber of the National Court also encountered some constitutional challenges in these respects. After the referendum, altogether nine cases were brought to the National Court, challenging the mode of constitutional revision and the fusion of the two types of referendums; we deal with the latter issue in more detail in chapter 7. One of the challenges was brought jointly by the Estonian Voters' Union and Helle Vilu, who claimed that it was impossible to retain eternal and inalienable independence, while transferring part of it to the European Union. In addition, these claimants argued that under articles 102, 161, 162 and 163, the constitution may only be 'amended' and not 'supplemented' by an independent act. Another major case was brought by the afore-mentioned Mr Kulbok, who asked the court to review the compatibility of the Accession Treaty with the constitution. Referring to the 1998 Opinion of the Constitutional Expert Commission, where it had been found that EU entry requires a prior amendment of article 1 by means of a referendum, Kulbok argued that the Accession Treaty should not have been concluded until after such an amendment. Kulbok also referred to an official communication by the then Legal Chancellor Eerik-Juhan Truuväli, who had upheld the same view as the Constitutional Expert Commission in this respect. All cases were rejected by the Constitutional Chamber on procedural grounds; the substance of the challenges was not addressed.[73] The court stated that constitutional review of treaties can only be initiated by courts and by the Legal Chancellor, not by individuals,[74] and that the deadline had expired long before the referendum for challenging the constitutionality of Parliament's decision

[72] Maruste, 'Põhiseadust tuleks siiski muuta'.

[73] e.g. *Kulbok*, Decision No. 3–4–1–12–03, 29 September 2003 and *Vilu and Estonian Voters Union*, Decision No. 3–4–1–11–03, 24 September 2003, both available in Estonian at www.nc.ee

[74] According to the Law on the Procedure of Constitutional Review 2002, the control of constitutionality of treaties may take place both before ratification and on a treaty in force, on the initiative of the Legal Chancellor.

on 'supplementing' the constitution and on fusing the two types of referendums.

Following these controversies, the debates on constitutional revision have been resumed after the successful holding of the accession referendum, and there are proposals to start work towards a new constitution, to be produced in a few years' time.[75] The Reform Party has adopted a resolution calling on Parliament to convene a Founding Assembly to this end.[76] The new constitution is expected to contain a wider set of EU provisions. These would include participation in EMU, collective defence in the framework of the EU and NATO, the government's role in Brussels and the appointment of judges to the EU courts. To add some other issues that may deserve an amendment but have attracted less attention, the following could be mentioned. First, the drafting of a wider provision on the position of EU citizens and their equal rights with those of Estonian citizens, to the extent provided by EU law, deserves consideration. This is because the right of EU citizens to stand and vote in the elections of local authorities and the European Parliament would be restricted by articles 57 (the voting right belongs to Estonian citizens), 156 (election of the local municipalities) and 48 (only Estonian citizens may belong to political parties). In addition, EU citizens' rights related to free movement may be obstructed by articles 28–32, 34, 36 and 44 of the constitution, which permit the restriction of certain rights to Estonian citizens, such as the right to state assistance in the case of old age, inability to work, loss of a provider, as well as the right to work in public service. Another issue that may need amendment is the extradition of citizens. Although the Estonian Constitution allows extradition of citizens under conditions prescribed by international treaties, it has been pointed out that article 36 of the constitution subjects extradition to the government's decision, whereas the European Arrest Warrant system requires a judicial decision.[77] Beyond EU issues, the new constitution is also expected to offer a more sustainable institutional organisation for a small country, to elaborate the chapter on

[75] e.g. R. Maruste, 'Eesti vajaks uut põhiseadust' [Estonia Needs a New Constitution], *Eesti Päevaleht*, 26 March 2004; U. Reinsalu (Chairman of the Constitutional Affairs Commission of the Parliament), 'Eesti põhiseadus 21. sajandil' [Estonian Constitution in the 21st Century], *Postimees*, 30 January 2004.

[76] 'Reformierakond käivitab töö uue põhiseaduse koostamiseks' [Reform Party Launches Work on the Creation of a New Constitution], *Postimees*, 24 January 2004.

[77] K. Raba, 'Estonia' in *Criminal Law in the European Union: A Giant Leap or A Small Step?*, *FIDE 2004 National Reports*, www.fide2004.org/reports/mc/mc06b.pdf, pp. 89–90.

fundamental rights and freedoms, and to deal with the two amendment Bills that have been on the Parliament's agenda of constitutional revision – on the introduction of direct presidential elections and on the creation of a constitutional court.

Latvia

Latvia encountered very similar challenges: in a context where euroscepticism was rife, the constitution was eventually amended by parliamentary procedure, notwithstanding the requirement of a referendum for amending articles 1 and 2 on sovereignty. The overall climate for EU amendments was well characterised in a 1999 Report on the impact of EU accession on the Latvian Constitution.[78] Taking into account the difficult history of Latvia, combined with the high symbolic importance of the 1922 Constitution as the expression of Latvia's independence and nationhood, and the feasibility of passing the amendments in the referendum, the Report suggested that 'it is unlikely that major constitutional changes in relation to EU membership would be acceptable to the Saeima or [the] people of Latvia'. The picture is not complete without mentioning that public support for EU accession has been the lowest amongst the candidate countries: in the period of 2000–2002, only 38–42 per cent of the population supported EU accession, with a solid figure of 31–43 per cent opposing it.

Official discussions about amending the constitution for EU accession started in August 2000, when a special Working Group, composed of representatives from leading state institutions, was set up by the Prime Minister's decree in order to draft the amendments. The draft amendments were presented in March 2001,[79] but due to the political sensitivity of EU accession, no further official moves were taken until the parliamentary elections of October 2002. The Working Group had also considered the possibility of not amending the constitution at all but rather re-interpreting it, since from the legal point of view, Latvia already lives

[78] *Constitutional and Administrative Facilitation of Effective Law Approximation and European Union Membership*, Report composed under the auspices of the European Integration Bureau and PHARE Technical Assistance to the Approximation of the Latvian Legislation to that of the European Communities (Riga, 1999).

[79] The amendments and their explanatory part are available in *The Theoretical Foundation of the Amendments to Satversme proposed by the Working Group* (Ministry of Justice, Riga, November 2001). See for an overview also D. Luthers-Thümmel, 'International Agreements in the Legal Orders of the Candidate Countries: Latvia' in Ott and Inglis, *Handbook on European Enlargement*, pp. 279–80.

under rules harmonised to EU law.[80] The constitution was eventually amended by parliamentary procedure on 8 May 2003, keeping largely the same format as that proposed by the Working Group.

The amendments are laconic. They were mostly placed into article 68, which had previously dealt with parliamentary ratification of international agreements. A new paragraph was added, which provides that '[u]pon entering into international agreements, Latvia, with the purpose of strengthening democracy, may delegate a part of its State institution competencies to international institutions'. The ratification of such international agreements requires the approval of a two-thirds majority of the members, in the presence of at least two-thirds of all members. The second new paragraph provides that membership of the European Union is subject to a referendum. A referendum may also be held on 'substantial changes in the terms regarding the membership of Latvia', where requested by at least half of all members of the Parliament. This provision is meant to include Latvia's potential secession from the EU and was included as a concession to the eurosceptics. Some European legal experts have expressed concern that such a provision could undermine the stability of the EU and brand Latvia as a politically problematic state.[81] In article 79, the minimum turnout is reduced for EU referendums, from 50 per cent (as required for constitutional amendment referendums under article 79) to half of the turnout rate of the previous parliamentary elections.[82] Since the turnout rate was 72 per cent in the 2002 parliamentary elections, the minimum turnout for the EU accession referendum thus constituted 36 per cent. This move was explained by the argument that the constitution does not provide for the possibility of holding an EU referendum, since accession to the EU would be nothing more than fulfilling obligations undertaken by an international treaty, and therefore would not affect the principles of sovereignty and independence in articles 1 and 2 of the constitution,[83] for the amendment of which a referendum with a minimum turnout of 50 per cent is required.

Overall, these minimal amendments appear to stand in stark contrast with the earlier amendment practice: Latvia's Constitution, which is the

[80] S. Habracevica in her presentation on the Working Group's draft amendments at the conference 'The Sovereignty of Latvia and Membership of the EU', organised by the Ministry of Justice on 23 November 2001 in the Riga Graduate School of Law.

[81] 'Constitution Watch: Latvia' (2001) 10 *East European Constitutional Review*, no. 1/2, p. 24.

[82] The full text of the amendments is available in Table A9 in the Appendix.

[83] *Theoretical Foundation of the Amendments to Satversme*, p. 6 *et seq.*

re-instituted 1922 Constitution, has been amended on several occasions. In 1994, the voting age was lowered; in 1996, the Constitutional Court was established; in 1997, a wider package of amendments, mainly dealing with technical issues concerning the Parliament and President, were introduced; in 1998, a new chapter on human rights was inserted.[84] Two subsequent amendments are interesting in relation to the EU, in that while EU accession usually leads to opening up the constitutions to the international level, these amendments represent a more protectionist direction. In 1998, a new provision was introduced declaring the Latvian language to be the state language (article 4), and in 2001, the position of the Latvian language was further reinforced by declaring it to be the official procedural language in Parliament and in local offices. This forms a symbolic response to the nationalistic wing, given that Parliament had shortly before dropped from the Election Law the requirement of fluency in the Latvian language for candidates to public offices, in order to bring the country a step closer to joining the EU and NATO.[85]

In fact, the above EU amendments, according to their drafters, were not meant to be the end of the story, but rather form a minimum procedural precondition for EU accession, which may be complemented by substantive amendments after the accession referendum.[86] Indeed, various studies have pointed out issues that may need amendment, whether by amending several articles in the existing chapters or introducing a new EU Chapter.[87] This solution would take into account the strong tradition of normative regulation in Latvia, as well as correspond to the present structure of the constitution and its historical development.[88] In addition to the issue of delegating sovereignty, the new chapter would regulate issues such as the coordination of the government's activities with Parliament

[84] See in more detail A. Usaĉka, 'The Impact of the European Integration Process on the Constitution of Latvia' in Kellermann, De Zwaan and Czuczai, *EU Enlargement*, pp. 337–9, and A. Sprudzs, 'Rebuilding Democracy in Latvia: Overcoming a Dual Legacy' in Zielonka and Pravda, *Democratic Consolidation*, pp. 159–60.

[85] V. Mite, 'Latvia Adjusts Language Laws, but the Issue Remains Divisive', *RFE/RL Newsline*, vol. 6, no. 93, Part II, 20 May 2002; 'Constitution Watch: Latvia' (2002) 11 *East European Constitutional Review* no. 1/2.

[86] E. Levits, presentation on the Working Group's draft amendments at the conference 'The Sovereignty of Latvia and Membership of the EU', organised by the Ministry of Justice on 23 November 2001 in the Riga Graduate School of Law.

[87] Reported in Usaĉka, 'Impact of European Integration', pp. 343–4. On the other hand, minimal amendments have been advocated e.g. by E. Levits, 'The Satversme and the European Union' (2000) *Latvijas Vestnesis*, no. 213/218, p. 2 (in Latvian), cited in Usaĉka, 'Impact of European Integration', p. 343.

[88] *Ibid.*, pp. 343–4.

in EU matters, the procedure for electing European Parliament members and the relationship between EU law and Latvia's legal system.[89] Indeed, an amendment concerning the last issue appears particularly necessary, as the Latvian Constitution does not regulate the application of treaties. New article 89, introduced in 1998, states in a general manner that the state shall recognise and protect human rights in accordance with binding international treaties. The precedence and direct applicability of treaties is regulated on a statutory level: article 13 of the Law on International Treaties 1994 provides that where a ratified treaty contains a provision divergent from Latvian laws, the former shall be applied. However, international treaties do not directly form part of the national legal system: they are applied through reference in legislative acts where the priority of treaties is declared, or by way of analogy. International law is kept in mind when drafting the laws, but a treaty becomes applicable only if there is no domestic legislation on a particular matter.[90] Under the Law on the Constitutional Court 1996, the Court reviews the constitutionality of international agreements signed or entered into by Latvia, on the initiative of individuals or the President, at least twenty members of the Parliament, the government, the Prosecutor General or certain other state institutions.

Amongst other conflicting provisions are article 101, which restricts the right to participate in local elections to citizens, and article 8, which contains a general rule that electoral rights belong to citizens. The combination of these may render practically ineffective the right of EU citizens to vote and stand in the elections of the European Parliament and local councils. Another conflicting provision is article 98 which prohibits the extradition of Latvian citizens, and thus goes against the Schengen system and European Arrest Warrant.[91] In addition, as with many other countries, the restriction of work in public service to citizens under article 101 should take into account the limited scope of public service in the interpretation of the European Court of Justice. As regards participation in Monetary Union, the margin of interpretation appears to be wider because Latvia's laconic constitution does not regulate monetary issues.

[89] *Ibid.*, pp. 343–4.

[90] Reported by I. Ziemele, 'Incorporation and Implementation of Human Rights in Latvia' in M. Scheinin (ed.), *International Human Rights Norms in the Nordic and Baltic Countries* (Kluwer Law International, Dordrecht, 1996), pp. 79, 84–6.

[91] A. Zikmane, 'Latvia' in *Criminal Law in the European Union: A Giant Leap or A Small Step? FIDE 2004 National Reports*, www.fide2004.org/reports/mc/mc12b.pdf, p. 184.

In 2004, another Working Group, established by the Ministry of Justice, proposed an additional set of amendments to Parliament in order to eliminate further constitutional conflicts with EU law. These proposals concern mainly article 98 on extradition, and article 101 on the voting rights of EU citizens in local elections. There have also been suggestions to replace the eighty-years-old document with a new modern constitution in view of EU accession.[92] Although the adoption of a new constitution had been envisaged already in the 1990 Declaration 'On the Renewal of the Independence of the Republic of Latvia', it has never been implemented. A new draft constitution has been presented by the Latvian Social Democratic Workers Party and its chairman Juris Bojars, a scholar of international law, but the idea has not found wider support.[93]

Lithuania

Although in Lithuania, the constitution already contains a provision on joining international organisations (article 136) and two provisions have been amended to eliminate conflicts with EU law, it will be addressed in this group because of similar controversies concerning the referendum requirement for amending Chapter I on sovereignty and independence to those encountered in the other Baltic counterparts. Furthermore, the amendment of article 1 is subject to a particularly high threshold majority, requiring a three-fourths approval of all the citizens who have the right to vote.[94]

The constitution has earlier been amended on one occasion, which was necessitated, as with Slovenia, by the ratification of the Europe Agreement. Adopted on 20 June 1996, the amendment reformulated article 47 so that foreigners could acquire non-agricultural land, necessary for the construction and operation of the buildings and facilities designated for the purpose of their direct activities. According to a special constitutional law accompanying it, this expression encompassed the nationals and enterprises of the EU, for the purpose of carrying out economic activities; such an approach had disappointed Lithuania's ethnic minorities, especially the Poles. The amendment of this provision had already

[92] Reported in Usaĉka, 'Impact of European Integration', p. 338.

[93] 'Constitution Watch: Latvia' (2001) 10 *East European Constitutional Review*, no. 1/2, p. 23.

[94] The amendment of the other chapters requires the minimum turnout rate of 50 per cent. See, for a more detailed account of the amendment procedure, above n. 59.

been proposed in 1993, in order to take advantage of the then easier amendment procedure.[95] The debates continued for another three years but the amendment was not adopted until 1996, when the issue of land sales became the primary obstacle to the ratification of the Europe Agreement.[96] In November 1996, a referendum was held on the issue of purchase of agricultural land by EU citizens, but it failed due to an insufficient turnout. As will be seen later, this provision necessitated another amendment ahead of accession, so as to make available equally the sale of agricultural land. As regards the amendment proposals not related to EU accession, these have included the enhancing of presidential powers, the reduction of the size of Parliament and the relationship between Parliament and the judges.

The work on preparing the Lithuanian Constitution for EU membership started in 1998, when the Chancellery of the Lithuanian Parliament established a special Working Group in order to elaborate pertinent draft amendments. The Report, submitted to the Chancellery of the Parliament in September 1998, concluded that accession would not be contrary to the constitution because the EU is an international organisation not impinging upon Lithuania's independence.[97] The Working Group nonetheless deemed some amendments advisable, in order to better prepare for accession, but rejected at the same time the need for holding a constitutional amendment referendum.[98] The sensitivity of the issue becomes evident if we consider that Lithuania had earlier held as many as seven referendums. The Rapporteur of the Working Group pointed out that achieving a majority with a 50 per cent turnout would be problematic given the low

[95] During the first year of the application of the constitution, one parliamentary reading, with the approval of a three-fifths majority, was sufficient for amending certain articles (under article 153).

[96] See N. Gelazis, 'Institutional Engineering in Lithuania: Stability through Compromise' in Zielonka and Pravda, *Democratic Consolidation*, pp. 165–85; J. Žilys, 'The New Constitution of the Republic of Lithuania in the Context of the European Law System' in T. Jundzis (ed.), *The Baltic States at Historical Crossroads: Problems in the Context of International Cooperation on the Doorstep of the 21st Century* (Academy of Sciences of Latvia, Riga, 1998), pp. 244–5; V. Vadapalas and I. Jarukaitis, 'International Agreements in the Legal Orders of the Candidate Countries: Lithuania' in Ott and Inglis, *Handbook on European Enlargement*, pp. 286–7.

[97] 'Republic of Lithuania Constitutional Law on the Amendment of Articles 136 and 138 of the Constitution of the Republic of Lithuania. Draft of the Working Group established under the Seimas Chancellery' in *Stojimas I Europos Sajunga Ir Konstitucija. Seminaro Medziaga 29–30.06.1999* (Eugrimas, Vilnius, 2000), p. 141.

[98] 'Republic of Lithuania Constitutional Law', p. 141 *et seq.*

support rates towards the EU.[99] Indeed, until 2000, public support for EU accession was just 47–50 per cent. However, since then it has consistently increased, being the highest amongst the Baltic countries – in 2002, 57 per cent supported accession and 17–25 per cent were opposed to it. Understandably, none of the Lithuanian commentators have mentioned the amendment of article 1, which requires the approval by a three-fourths majority of all citizens who have the right to vote.

The Working Group recommended amending articles 136 and 138, by introducing four provisions. The focal part was new paragraph 2, to be added to article 136, which would have established the basis for Lithuania's entry into international organisations involving 'delegation of the competence of State institutions'. It is noteworthy that one of the purposes for joining such organisations, according to the proposed provision, would have been 'assuring security and independence', which appeared to recognise at the constitutional level the EU as a security guarantee, an issue which has been one of the central reasons for European integration in the Baltic countries. The second draft sentence proposed to establish parliamentary control over the government in the process of adopting legal acts in such international organisations. The remainder of the draft amendments were aimed at dealing with the position of EU law, albeit being addressed more broadly to 'international organisations': draft article 138(3) would have provided that where it follows from the founding treaty of an international organisation, the law of such organisations forms 'a constituent part' of Lithuania's legal system and takes supremacy over national law. Following discussions with foreign experts, who drew attention to the advantages of addressing the amendments directly to the EU rather than to international organisations,[100] the European Law Department of the government presented in October 2000 new draft amendments,[101] in which the provisions were indeed addressed directly to the European Union. The new draft also contained provisions on EU citizens' right to purchase agricultural land and to participate in local elections.[102]

[99] V. Vadapalas, 'Lithuania: The Constitutional Impact of the Enlargement at National Level' in Kellermann, De Zwaan and Czuczai, *EU Enlargement*, p. 351.

[100] Comments on Lithuanian draft amendments by F. Frowein, P. C. Müller-Graff, I. Pernice and others are available in English in the collection *Stojimas I Europos Sajunga.*

[101] These are available in Vadapalas, 'Lithuania: Constitutional Impact', pp. 366–8.

[102] See also V. Vadapalas and I. Jarukaitis, 'International Agreements in the Legal Orders of the Candidate Countries: Lithuania' in Ott and Inglis, *Handbook on European Enlargement*, pp. 287–9.

Amongst the above proposals, only the last two issues ultimately led to the amendment of the constitution. First, the above-discussed article 47 underwent another revision so as to also permit the sale of agricultural land to EU citizens. Initially, the full liberalisation of this regime had been proposed, and the negotiation chapter on free movement of capital had been closed. However, the government change in mid-2001 led to a request to re-open the negotiation chapter, and a transition period of seven to ten years was sought. To strengthen the pressure, a referendum on a transition period was proposed by the Union of Farmers and New Democracy parties, and the farmers' organisations threatened to organise road blockades, should the amendment be adopted before settling this issue.[103] In November 2002, the Danish Presidency accepted the candidate countries' request for a transition period concerning land sales to EU citizens. Following this, the amendment was finally adopted on 23 January 2003 (116 for, 4 against, 4 abstentions),[104] but land sales will effectively become possible as of 2011, due to the seven-year transition period.

The second amendment reworded article 119, so as to grant to all permanent residents, including non-citizen residents, the right to vote and stand in local government elections. The amendment passed its first reading in January 2002, and the second, final reading on 20 June 2002 (105 for, 14 against, 4 abstentions). The second vote had been postponed on several occasions due to disagreement over whether the right to participate should be granted to all permanent residents, including the Russian minority, as supported by the left-wing coalition parties, or be restricted to Lithuanian and EU citizens. The amendment will enter into effect in 2006.[105] Contrary to the controversial situation in Latvia and Estonia, Lithuania does not have a sizable Russian minority; it amounts to less than 7 per cent of the total population.

Although the afore-mentioned documents have recommended amendments on the delegation of sovereign powers and on the effect of EU law upon national law, these issues were, until recently, missing in the Parliament's amendment debates. Parliament's Constitutional Affairs

[103] 'Constitution Watch: Lithuania' (2002) 11 *East European Constitutional Review*, no. 1/2; 'Two Referendums to be Proposed in Lithuania', *RFE/RL Newsline*, vol. 6, no. 103, Part II, 4 June 2002.

[104] 'Lithuania Approves Land Sales to Foreigners – Eventually', *RFE/RL Newsline*, vol. 7, no. 15, Part II, 24 January 2003.

[105] 'Lithuania Postpones Vote on Constitutional Amendment', *RFE/RL Newsline*, vol. 6, no. 86, Part II, 9 May 2002; 'Lithuania Amends Constitution on Local Elections', *RFE/RL Newsline*, vol. 6, no. 116, Part II, 21 June 2002; 'Constitution Watch: Lithuania' (2002) 11 *East European Constitutional Review*, no. 3.

Commission decided in summer 2001 that there was no need for an amendment concerning the delegation of powers, based on the opinions of prominent constitutional scholars. Consequently, the accession took place under the existing, general regime of parliamentary ratification of treaties concerning Lithuania's participation in international organisations (article 138(1.5)), coupled with an accession referendum (but not a constitutional amendment referendum; see chapter 7). Ratification of treaties may be preceded by the Constitutional Court's opinion on their conformity with the constitution (under existing articles 105 and 106), on the initiative of the Parliament and the President.

However, since the participation of the Parliament's members in the Convention on the Future of the Union led to a wider understanding about 'what is really going on in the EU' with regard to sovereignty, Parliament has made a decision to re-open the issue of delegating sovereignty. There have also been proposals for adopting a separate constitutional act on EU membership, rather than amending the constitution, a proposal that fits better with the Lithuanian constitutional system compared with the experience in Estonia.[106] In fact, as with many other countries, the amendment process is set to continue after the accession referendum was successfully held: a Bill on further amendments has been put on the Parliament's agenda in spring 2004. This can be welcomed, as experts have pointed out the need for further amendments, such as on Parliament's participation in EU affairs and the possibility of adopting a common currency (article 125 presently limits the right 'to issue bank notes' to the Bank of Lithuania).[107] Although Lithuania amended the provisions on local elections, questions may remain with regard to EU citizens' right to participate in the elections of the European Parliament, given that electoral rights and the right to belong to political parties (articles 34 and 35) are restricted to national citizens. As with many other countries, the restriction of social security rights to national citizens (article 52) may unduly restrict EU citizens' rights related to free movement, and citizens' entitlement to work in public service (article 33) needs to take account of the narrow interpretation of the scope of public service in the ECJ case law. The Lithuanian Constitution does not appear to conflict with the

[106] Lithuania has a tradition of constitutional laws because the constitution (article 150) declares two laws to form a constituent part of the constitution: Constitutional Law on the State of Lithuania 1991 and Constitutional Act on the Non-Alignment of the Republic of Lithuania with Post-Soviet Eastern Alliances 1992.

[107] See comments by F. Frowein, P.-C. Müller-Graff, I. Pernice and others in *Stojimas I Europos Sajunga*.

European Arrest Warrant because article 13(2), albeit generally prohibiting the extradition of citizens, does allow for the extradition of citizens where so provided by international treaties concluded by Lithuania.[108] As regards the position of EU law, a provision in this respect would be welcome even though Lithuania is a monist system, given that only ratified treaties (not including secondary law) are granted the position of a 'constituent part' of Lithuania's legal system (article 138(3)).

Developments in Romania and Bulgaria

Romania

Although Romania's and Bulgaria's accession has been postponed until 2007 at the earliest, these two countries are included in our study due to their similar constitutional background and their commencement of accession negotiations together with other CEE countries. In fact, in terms of constitutional provisions, Romania paradoxically appears to be the best-prepared country for EU membership, in the aftermath of the package of amendments which was adopted in October 2003. It should be noted that Croatia will not be covered in this study, as it joined the accession process considerably later.

Romania's case is particularly interesting as its constitutional amendment procedure is the most rigid amongst all the countries in question. All amendments require the holding of a referendum and, furthermore, it is prohibited to amend the provisions concerning the following issues: the national, independent, unitary and indivisible character of the Romanian state, the republican form of government, territorial integrity, independence of the judiciary and political pluralism and official language (article 148).[109] Not surprisingly, the new constitution had not been amended prior to 2003, when a wide-ranging constitutional reform was carried out all at once. The preparations for adjusting the constitution for EU membership started in December 2000, when the government established a Working Group of experts from amongst various ministries to

[108] V. Vadapalas, 'Lithuania' in *Criminal Law in the European Union: A Giant Leap or A Small Step? FIDE* 2004, www.fide2004.org/reports/mc/mc13b.pdf, p. 197.

[109] The amendment procedure is regulated in articles 147–8. A draft amendment has to be adopted by the Chamber of Deputies and the Senate by at least a two-thirds majority of all members in both chambers. If no agreement is reached, the draft may be adopted by a mediation procedure, where both chambers decide in a joint session by at least a three-fourths majority of all deputies and senators.

study the compatibility of the constitution with EU law.[110] In July 2002, an ad hoc Parliamentary Commission on constitutional amendments began its work.[111] The amendments were approved on 18 September 2003, in separate sessions of the Chamber of Deputies and the Senate, following agreement in the mediation commission. The mediation procedure was necessitated by the boycotting of the amendments throughout the process by the extremist Greater Romania Party, who objected to the rights given to ethnic minorities to use their language in courts and in public administration. In the Senate, the vote was supported by 100 senators (37 voted against), while in the Chamber of Deputies 265 members supported the amendments (62 voted against). The opponents came in both chambers mainly from the opposition's Greater Romania Party.[112] The amendments were then approved by the people in the referendum held on 18–19 October 2003. The EU amendments formed part of a rather extensive package of altogether seventy-nine amendments. Other reforms concerned issues such as amplification of human rights protection and development of mechanisms of judicial review. One long-standing dispute concerned the abolition of the proviso that Romania is a 'national state' from article 1, which has been consistently requested by the Hungarian minority movement, but this provision remained unmodified.

The core of the amendments lies in the five paragraphs of article 145.1, located in the new section V.1, which is entitled 'Euro-Atlantic Integration'. The first paragraph lays down the basis for the transfer of powers to the EU:

> Romania's accession to the constituent treaties of the European Union, with a view to transferring certain powers to Community institutions, as well as to exercising in common with the other Member States the abilities stipulated in such treaties, shall be carried out by means of a law adopted in the joint session of the Chamber of Deputies and the Senate, with a majority of two thirds of the number of deputies and senators.

As with most countries, there was previously no basis for a transfer of powers to international organisations. Only a general clause

[110] I. Grozavescu, 'International Agreements in the Legal Orders of the Candidate Countries: Romania' in Ott and Inglis, *Handbook on European Enlargement*, p. 320.

[111] 'Romanian Parliamentary Commission on Constitutional Amendments Begins Work', *RFE/RL Newsline*, vol. 6, no. 136, Part II, 23 July 2002.

[112] 'Romanian Parliament Gives Final Green Light to Constitutional Amendments', *RFE/RL Newsline*, vol. 7, no. 179, Part II, 19 September 2003.

existed according to which the President concludes international treaties negotiated by the government, and submits them to Parliament for ratification (article 91).

Supremacy of EU law is the next central issue of the amendments. Paragraph 2 of article 145.1 establishes that after accession, the provisions of the Treaties and of mandatory Community regulations 'shall take precedence over the opposite provisions of the national laws, in compliance with the provisions of the accession act'. This provision is also applied to the acts that revise the EU's constituent treaties (paragraph 3). These provisions are reinforced by paragraph 4, which obliges Parliament, the President, the government and the judicial authorities to guarantee the implementation of the obligations arising from the Accession Act and acts mentioned in paragraph 2. These provisions are significant, because Romania is considered to be a partially dualist country, where precedence has been given only to human rights treaties. Article 11 of the constitution provides that the state pledges to fulfil in good faith its obligations deriving from the treaties to which it is a party, and that ratified treaties are part of national law. Article 20 adds that the constitutional provisions concerning human rights are interpreted and enforced in conformity with the Universal Declaration of Human Rights and other treaties to which Romania is party, and that human rights treaties take precedence in case of inconsistencies with internal law. It is interesting to note that with the exception of the regime applied to EU law and human rights treaties, Romania remains a dualist country. In fact, a limit on the priority of international law has been added in the second paragraph of article 20, which now provides that 'where any inconsistencies exist between the covenants and treaties on fundamental human rights to which Romania is a party, and the national laws, the international regulations shall take precedence, *unless the Constitution or national laws comprise more favourable provisions*' (emphasis added). As regards the position of EU law, article 11(3), which introduces a preliminary review of the constitutionality of treaties, is also of relevance. If a treaty is found to be unconstitutional, it cannot be ratified; on the other hand, if it has been found constitutional, it 'cannot be the subject of an objection of unconstitutionality' (article 145(3)). Earlier, the Constitutional Court's review was only possible on the constitutionality of domestic laws which ratify international treaties, prior to their promulgation, on the initiative of the President, presidents of both chambers of Parliament, the government, the Supreme Court, at least fifty deputies or at least twenty-five senators (article 144).

Finally, the supremacy of the constitution is reaffirmed in article 1(5), which provides that 'the observance of the Constitution, its supremacy and the laws shall be mandatory'.[113]

Several amendments deal with the position of citizens in relation to EU issues. EU citizens are accorded the right to elect and be elected in local elections (article 16(4)). Romanian citizens, after the country's accession to the EU, explicitly have the right to elect and be elected to the European Parliament (article 35.1). Article 19(1) introduces the possibility of extraditing Romanian citizens, in accordance with international agreements. Article 41(2) introduces the possibility for foreigners to acquire land 'under the terms resulting from Romania's accession to the European Union and other international treaties Romania is party to, on a mutual basis, as well as a result of lawful inheritance'. This provision forms a response to the European Commission's demand presented in its Progress Reports to abolish the ban in this respect.[114] In the Europe Agreement, Romania had been granted a ten-year transitional period on land sales to EU citizens.

The remainder of the provisions pertaining to the EU are as follows.[115] Article 145.1(5) obliges the government to send to the Parliament's chambers draft mandatory acts before their submission to the EU institutions. Further, the possibility of adopting a common currency is opened in article 136(2), which previously provided that the national currency is the *leu*, with its subdivision, the *Ban*. Several provisions deal with membership of NATO, to which we come in chapter 8. Finally, a significant part of the amendments regulate various aspects concerning the judiciary, following the European Commission's request presented in the Regular Reports where the country's compliance with the Copenhagen Criteria was assessed.

Romania's amendments paradoxically appear to be the most comprehensive amongst the Central and Eastern European countries, and go far beyond the regulation of the EU in most constitutions of the 'old' Member States. They appear to meet, and even go beyond, what has been deemed necessary by scholarly studies.[116] This outcome was certainly facilitated

[113] In parallel, a similar provision was deleted from article 51.

[114] Opinion on Romania's Application for EU Membership, Brussels, July 1997, p. 81.

[115] The full text of the amendments is reproduced in Table A11 in the Appendix.

[116] See e.g. A. Ciobanu-Dordea, 'Constitutional Problems of Accession in Romania' in Kellermann, De Zwaan and Czuczai, *EU Enlargement*, pp. 312–14; V. Duculescu, 'La réforme constitutionnelle en Roumanie et les exigencies de l'intégration européene' (2004) *Revue Internationale de Droit Comparé* 193.

by the high level of support for EU membership in the country, and the absence of urgency which became decisive in many countries elsewhere.

However, the amendment process was not entirely uncontroversial. At the outset of the constitutional amendment discussions, sensitivities surrounded the prohibition to amend the 'national' and 'independent' character of the state, contained in article 148 of the constitution. To overcome this delicate situation in view of the expected entry to the EU, proposals existed in favour of a parliamentary ratification of the Treaties, without amendment of the constitution.[117] A question of constitutionality of the EU amendments *vis-à-vis* the prohibition of amendment in article 148 was also referred to the Constitutional Court by the Greater Romania Party which asserted that the amendments 'diminish the unitary national character of the state and its official language'. The Court rejected the claim on procedural grounds.[118]

Bulgaria

In Bulgaria, the amendment of the constitution involves a mechanism that is unique in Central and Eastern Europe: in order to amend the fundamental provisions, the Grand National Assembly (GNA), consisting of 400 members, has to be specially elected under the procedure of parliamentary elections. This challenging method is envisaged for cases where the amendments concern the adoption of a new constitution, changes related to Bulgaria's territory and ratification of any international instruments envisaging such issues, changes in the form of state or the form of government, direct applicability of the constitution or application of ratified international treaties, irrevocability of fundamental rights or amendments concerning the constitutional amendment procedure.[119] Not surprisingly, the constitution has not previously been amended. Unsuccessful amendment proposals have included the question of endowing the President with a power to issue legislation, the strengthening of the

[117] Reported in N. Rosner, *The Constitutional Limits to the Application of European Union Law* (LLM Thesis No. 1998/7, Central European University, Law Department, Budapest, 1998), pp. 141–2 and 145–6.

[118] Constitutional Court Decision No. 356, September 2003, reported in 'Romanian Nationalists Appeal to Constitutional Court over Amendments', *RFE/RL Newsline*, vol. 7, no. 181, Part II, 23 September 2003.

[119] According to Chapter 9 of the constitution, a two-thirds majority of all GNA members is required to amend the constitution, in three ballots on three different days. Ordinary constitutional provisions are amended by Parliament. The passing of the amendment requires a three-fourths majority of all deputies, in three ballots on three different days.

President's position as a political arbiter, introduction of the ombudsman and endowing citizens with a right of direct recourse to the Constitutional Court.[120]

The issue of amending the constitution for EU accession appeared on the agenda only recently; until 2001 there had been no amendments in this respect in the legislative agenda of the Parliament.[121] In 2002, proposals for constitutional reform were put forward by some leading politicians,[122] and a temporary ad hoc parliamentary commission to this effect was set up in April 2003.[123] However, it was decided to draft the amendments only in respect of the position of the judiciary, an issue to which the European Commission had drawn attention in the Progress Reports under the Copenhagen Criteria, and to leave the EU amendments to a later stage. Indeed, on 24 September 2003, Parliament unanimously passed a series of amendments pertaining to the mandates and immunity of magistrates and judges.[124] As regards the EU amendments, President Georgi Parvanov has said that it would be prudent to postpone these until the adoption of the European Constitution.[125] The main debate pertaining to the EU amendments has revolved around the issue of whether the convening of the Grand National Assembly is necessary. The Constitutional Court ruled in 2003 that only the Grand National Assembly could change the structure of the judiciary or the powers of the President, the Council of Ministers, the Parliament and the Constitutional Court.[126] On 21 April 2004, the Constitutional Court was asked whether amendments pertaining to EU membership require the involvement of the Grand National Assembly (GNA). In its decision of 5 July 2004, which is not yet available

[120] See in more detail E. Tanchev, 'National Constitutions and EU Law: Adapting the 1991 Bulgarian Constitution in the Accession to the European Union' (2000) 6 *European Public Law* 229, and V. Ganev, 'Bulgaria: The (Ir)Relevance of Post-Communist Constitutionalism' in Zielonka and Pravda, *Democratic Consolidation*, pp. 190–1.

[121] E. Tanchev, 'Constitutional Amendments due to Bulgarian Full EU Membership' in Kellermann, De Zwaan and Czuczai, *EU Enlargement*, p. 303.

[122] 'Bulgarian European Affairs Minister Says Constitution Must be Amended by the End of 2003', *RFE/RL Newsline*, vol. 6, no. 116, Part II, 21 June 2002; 'Bulgarian Parliamentary Speaker Demands Constitutional Changes', *RFE/RL Newsline*, vol. 6, no. 51, Part II, 18 March 2002.

[123] 'Bulgarian Parliament Sets up Commission to Draft Constitutional Amendments', *RFE/RL Newsline*, vol. 7, no. 78, Part II, 24 April 2003.

[124] 'Bulgarian Parliament Unanimously Adopts Constitutional Changes', *RFE/RL Newsline*, vol. 7, no. 183, Part II, 25 September 2003.

[125] 'Bulgarian Parliament Unanimously Adopts Constitutional Changes', *RFE/RL Newsline*, vol. 7, no. 183, Part II, 25 September 2003.

[126] Decision of 10 April 2003.

in English at the time of writing, the Court found that the involvement of the GNA is not required. Constitutional lawyers have proposed that it is more practical to interpret EU accession in a way that would not require the exclusively difficult mode of constitutional revision by the GNA.[127] On the other hand, in the light of the above-mentioned 2003 decision on the need to involve the GNA for the amendments concerning the judiciary, it is somewhat surprising that the EU amendments were not found to be of such importance as to justify the convening of the GNA. As with many other CEE countries, this judgment may indicate the difficulty of reconciling the accession process with the rigid constitutional requirements.

Constitutional provisions the amendment of which have been under debate include the following. To start with, the European Commission has requested the lifting of the ban on foreigners buying land (article 22).[128] Scholarly studies have additionally considered it necessary to introduce a clause on the transfer of powers to the European Union.[129] Currently, Parliament ratifies international instruments that concern Bulgaria's participation in international organisations (article 85(1) paragraph 2), but there is no clause enabling the delegation of powers. Further, although Bulgaria is a monist country, supremacy and direct effect of EU secondary law would not be sufficiently guaranteed by article 5(4), which applies only to ratified and promulgated treaties.[130] In addition, the supremacy of EU law over the Bulgarian Constitution would be in conflict with article 85(3) (which provides that the constitution shall be amended before concluding

[127] Tanchev, 'Constitutional Amendments', pp. 308–9.

[128] *Agenda 2000: For a Stronger and Wider Union, Bulletin of the European Communities*, Supplement 5/97; Tanchev, 'Constitutional Amendments', p. 307.

[129] Tanchev, 'Constitutional Amendments', pp. 303–7; E. Evtimov, 'Die Bulgarische Verfassung und das Europarecht: Spannungsfelder und Lösungsansätze' (2001) 47 *Osteuropa Recht* 403.

[130] Tanchev, 'National Constitutions', pp. 233–4, 241. The Constitutional Court has confirmed that article 5(4) provides for the immediate and direct inclusion of the provisions of international agreements as an integral part of the internal law of Bulgaria. Direct effect is subject to the condition that the treaty must be ratified, published in the state gazette and entered into force, otherwise Bulgaria remains bound by the treaty under international law but the treaty has no direct effect. Non-ratified treaties need transformation by legislative means. This is established in the Constitutional Court's Decision No. 7, 2 July 1992, published in *Durzhaven Vestnik* 56/92, where the Prosecutor General requested interpretation of articles 85(3) and 149(1.4) of the constitution, as reported in E. Konstantinov, 'The Implementation of International Treaty Obligations in the National Legal Order: the Answer of the Bulgarian Constitution' (1995) 2 *Journal of Constitutional Law in Eastern and Central Europe* 66 at pp. 69–70. See also Evtimov, 'Die Bulgarische Verfassung', p. 396.

treaties that so require), and article 149(4) (the Constitutional Court rules on the compatibility of a treaty with the constitution prior to ratification).[131] Further, articles 65(1) and 93(2) restrict electoral rights to Bulgarian citizens. As with many other constitutions, it should be pointed out that articles 51(1), 52 and 58(1), restricting certain social rights to citizens, may affect EU citizens' rights pertaining to the effective exercise of free movement, and article 25(4) which prohibits the extradition of citizens may need an amendment with a view to the Schengen system and the European Arrest Warrant.

Some overarching trends in the EU amendments

The previous sections show a large degree of diversity in adjusting the constitutions of Central and Eastern Europe for EU accession, but some overarching trends nonetheless emerge. In the initial phases, the experience of the 'old' Member States was reflected upon, and issues were raised which had triggered amendments in their constitutions: delegation or transfer of powers to the EU, participation of national Parliaments, voting rights of EU citizens in elections of local councils and the European Parliament and a common currency. On occasions going even further than the experience in the 'old' Member States, there were proposals to clearly posit the direct effect and supremacy of EC law. Some issues were specific to the constitutions of the accession countries, such as the removal of the ban on extradition of nationals, and on the sale of land to foreigners. Another novelty of this round of accession is that under the Copenhagen Criteria, the European Commission's Regular Reports have called for amending the provisions concerning the position of the judiciary (Slovakia, Romania, Bulgaria) and the speed of harmonisation (the Czech Republic).

However, in the final phases of passing the amendments, the political practicalities became decisive, and in the majority of countries the amendments remained relatively minimal, albeit in different respects (with the exception of Slovakia and Romania). To start with, the extent of EU-related provisions remained minimal in comparison with the amendments that were deemed necessary in Estonia, Latvia, Lithuania and Poland; several manifest conflicts remained unresolved in these countries. In fact, the

[131] On the initiative of one-fifth of all deputies, the President, the Council of Ministers, the Supreme Cassation Court, the Supreme Administrative Court or the Chief Prosecutor (article 150).

amendment exercise could be characterised as the 'end of stage one', as these countries, as well as Hungary and Slovakia, are set to introduce further amendments or even consider preparation of new constitutions, after the accession referendums were successfully won.

The second aspect of minimalism is that rather than explicitly addressing the EU, a number of countries accommodated the accession under general provisions on international organisations (the Czech Republic, Poland, Lithuania, Slovenia and partly Latvia). It should be pointed out, however, that while at the initial stages the 'international organisation' approach was taken almost universally, some countries later opted for direct provisions on the EU.

The third aspect, procedural minimalism, is specific to the Baltic countries, where the requirement of a referendum for amendments affecting sovereignty was rather liberally interpreted. The search for constitutional solutions for accommodating EU membership often balanced here on the border of constitutional correctness and political feasibility: there were high-profile views in the three Baltic countries that their constitutions did not necessarily need to be amended for EU accession and, indeed, the Estonian Constitution was not amended but 'supplemented' by an independent constitutional act. None of the Baltic countries held a constitutional amendment referendum, creating instead new types of referendums, with the procedural requirements being facilitated. The amendments in all three countries remained minimal, and have attracted criticism for sidestepping the amendment procedures, as well as not eliminating conflicts with EU law.

The fourth aspect of minimalism is common to a large number of countries: many have not mentioned the delegation of powers at all, not to mention the word 'sovereignty', and the amendments were inserted into chapters other than the first chapters on sovereignty and independence. For example, in Poland, the location of the amendments – First or Third Chapter – became one of the key issues in the drafting debates; the latter option prevailed as a concession to those who saw the EU as a threat to sovereignty. A reference to the limitation of sovereignty had to be dropped in an early phase of drafting, so as not to inflame public sentiment; the amendment speaks instead about the transfer of part of the competences. In Hungary, the FIDESZ party demanded that the draft constitutional amendments be formulated in a way that would not entail the surrender of Hungary's national sovereignty. In the Baltic countries, the avoidance of the issue of sovereignty enabled them to hold 'ordinary' types of referendums, which have procedural and psychological advantages in comparison with the constitutional amendment referendums. Drafting debates in the other countries equally revealed the effort to downplay the impact on sovereignty.

Perhaps the following factors can be discerned, which played some overarching role in conditioning this 'minimal' approach. First, the amendments were influenced by the parallel preparations for accession referendums: we will see in chapter 7 that many governments were concerned whether the referendums would be successful, against the background of eurosceptic public opinion and previous experience with invalid referendums due to insufficient turnouts. In this context, an extensive set of EU amendments in the national constitutions could have posed the risk of becoming a dangerous tool in the hands of eurosceptic parties. Therefore, more extensive amendments were mainly possible in those countries where the accession process enjoyed firm public support, such as Slovakia and Romania, which were able to adopt the most extensive package of amendments, and the overall process was also smoother. At the same time, the solutions remained minimal in the Baltic countries where popular support for EU accession has been under or on the border of 50 per cent. In Hungary, a wider package of amendments had been planned at the time when people were supportive of accession, but some important issues such as supremacy were eventually left out, as the support rates plummeted towards the end of 2002. The support rates and reasons for euroscepticism will be addressed along with the accession referendums in chapter 7, which will show that many countries considered the option of not holding a referendum at all, and had to engage in various procedural 'manoeuvres' to secure positive results.

Secondly, there appears to be a tendency that the amendments were adopted earlier in the countries where constitutions can be amended by a relatively flexible parliamentary procedure – the Czech Republic, Slovakia and Hungary.[132] In addition, in all these countries, plus Slovenia, the amendments pertaining to the EU are more extensive. Meanwhile, the revision took place at a late stage ahead of accession, and remained minimal in the Baltic countries, where the amendment of sovereignty provisions requires a referendum. The overall pattern of previous constitutional amendments in CEE countries (see Table A2 in the Appendix) equally appears to indicate that countries with a relatively simple parliamentary amendment procedure (Slovakia, Hungary and the Czech

[132] A comparative overview about the constitutional amendment procedures in the CEE countries is available in Table A1 in the Appendix.

Republic) have introduced several amendments, whereas those with the most rigid amendment procedures, the constitutions of Estonia, Romania and Bulgaria, had not been amended before 2003.

It is noteworthy that also among the 'old' Member States, those countries where the constitutions mention the EU in a minimal manner or not at all, tend to share fairly rigid constitutional amendment procedures, as discussed in chapter 2. In fact, this seems to be broadly in line with a theory proposed by Donald Lutz, who has in a cross-national analysis demonstrated that the degree of rigidity of a constitution affects its amendment rate.[133] Eivind Smith has also commented that it is typical in the case of those constitutions that are very hard to amend (e.g. the constitutions of the USA and Denmark) to engage instead in 'a creative interpretation'.[134] The experience of Romania, however, diverges from the above pattern: due to high public support for EU integration and the absence of time pressure, Romania's amendment package is remarkably extensive notwithstanding the exceptionally rigid amendment procedure.

Thirdly, the 'international organisation' approach appears to reflect to a certain degree the constitutional theory which prevailed in the region until the end of the 1990s: the EU has been regarded as an international organisation to which some powers are delegated, applying the traditional concept of sovereignty. Chapter 6 will explore the theoretical debates in more detail.

Altogether, the constitutional amendment debates showed a great deal of political tension and delicate manoeuvring in an effort to find a balance between, on the one hand, geopolitical and economic imperatives to join the EU and, on the other hand, the constitutional safeguards to sovereignty that were designed in response to the painful experiences of the past. The minimalism of the solutions is, of course, justified in view of the political costs of amending the constitutions, especially considering factors such as difficult amendment procedures, high minimum turnout requirements for referendums, public sentiment concerning the delegation of sovereignty merely a decade after having regained it and, in a number of countries, eurosceptic public opinion. One equally has to pay tribute to the role of implicit amendments and interpretation. However, the plans to resume the amendment process in many countries after

[133] D. Lutz, 'Towards a Theory of Constitutional Amendment' (1994) 88 *American Political Science Review* 355.

[134] E. Smith, 'The Constitution between Politics and Law' in Smith, *The Constitution*, p. 34.

accession should be welcomed, for the reasons to be explored in the next section.

Assessment in the light of the rationale of a constitution

Although the comparative landscape lends support to minimal solutions, recourse to comparison, as has been pointed out by Joachim Hesse, should be subject to a critical examination of the Western models themselves before transposing them to the East. Hesse has put forward stimulating questions in a wider context of adopting Western constitutional models in Central and Eastern Europe,[135] which remain equally acute with regard to the EU amendments. According to him:

> For the West the need to consider carefully how best to advise and assist the process of constitutional reconstruction in the East imposes an obligation to examine closely the West's own institutions. How are they functioning? Do they meet contemporary demands? On what values do they rest and how effectively do they sustain them? This kind of critical approach to democratic constitutionalism in the West must surely be an integral part of any consideration of the models which it may be practicable and desirable to recommend to the East.

Indeed, the process of ever deeper integration has raised the fundamental question about the role of national constitutions in the European construction. Constitutions are compared to social contracts by which the *pouvoir constituant* agrees upon the legitimate exercise of power in a state. The rationale of constitutions – their purpose, essence and justification – is to determine the distribution and exercise of power competences. They are to establish the mutual relations and balance between the legislative, executive and judicial branches of governance, and to regulate the procedures under which state institutions fulfil their functions. The mechanisms of exercising power, established in the constitutions, are usually given an elevated status by being subjected to a stricter amendment procedure, in comparison with procedures for adopting or amending ordinary legislation. In all three branches of governance, EU membership involves delegation of far-reaching parts of sovereign powers to EU institutions. In fact, more than half of the Member States' legislation now derives, to a varying degree, from EU institutions, including in some core areas of

[135] J. Hesse, 'Introduction: Constitutional Policy and Change in Europe: the Nature and Extent of the Challenges' in J. Hesse and N. Johnson (eds.), *Constitutional Policy and Change in Europe* (Nuffield European Studies, Oxford University Press, 1995), p. 4.

sovereign statehood such as foreign, monetary and defence policy and internal security. Meanwhile, this substantial shift of exercising powers has not been reflected in a number of the Member States' constitutions, which in 2004 still contain minimal or even no references to EU membership. Therefore, such constitutions have rightly been characterised as suffering from a 'European deficit',[136] in that they remain obsolete to the actual distribution of powers.

In the case of the constitutions of Central and Eastern Europe, the regulation of the exercise of powers has additional distinct dimensions, which were discussed in chapter 3. First, as a reaction to their common history of being dominated by external powers, these constitutions underscore sovereign and autonomous exercise of powers. The second special dimension is that compared with some Western European constitutions, the new post-Communist constitutions establish with detail and precision the mechanisms and procedures for exercising power and the interrelationship between the governing institutions. In line with this, changes in the internal mechanisms of exercising powers have been preceded by revision of the constitutions, examples of which have been given in earlier sections of this chapter. There is no reason to undermine this tradition by changes caused by external factors, especially given the 'souverainist' character of the CEE constitutions. Minimal amendments, regrettably, may involve a devaluation of the clear, up-to-date and directly applicable constitutions of Central and Eastern Europe.

An adequate reflection of the impact of European integration in the constitutions would also be desirable from the point of view of the Constitutional Courts, so as not to leave them with an *a posteriori* task of stretching the elusive constitutional norms on international organisations in order to justify the constitutionality of successive shifts of powers to the EU level. From the point of view of legitimacy, this exercise should rather be undertaken by the Parliaments. Further, in case of manifest constitutional conflicts with EC law, the room for interpretation by the Constitutional Courts is more limited and may give rise to unnecessary confrontations between the national Constitutional Courts and the European Court of Justice, which may challenge the uniform application and effectiveness of EU law. This is particularly so for the reason that CEE constitutions expressly spell out the principle of supremacy of the

[136] B. De Witte, 'Constitutional Aspects of European Union Membership in the Original Six Member States: Model Solutions for the Applicant Countries?' in Kellermann, De Zwaan and Czuczai, *EU Enlargement*, p. 73.

constitution, which equally applies to international treaties, as has been reaffirmed by Constitutional Courts across the region (supremacy and the role of Constitutional Courts in European integration will be discussed in more detail in chapter 9).

In fact, some CEE Constitutional Courts have expressly stated that, based on the principles of legitimacy and the rule of law, the constitutions may only be amended by the prescribed procedure and not in a disguised way by parliamentary ratification of foreign treaties or by referendums. The Hungarian Constitutional Court's warning against a hidden modification of the constitution by ratifying treaties in its Europe Agreement decision was pointed out in chapter 4. A similar warning was echoed in the Slovene Constitutional Court's Europe Agreement decision.[137] The constitutional amendment procedure, which according to the Slovene Constitutional Court is a particularly demanding legal procedure and subject to the need for legitimacy, has to be followed because:

> According to article 1 of the Constitution, Slovenia is a democratic republic and a state governed by the rule of law (article 2 of the Constitution) . . . Paragraph 2 of article 160 of the Constitution places the public interest, for the State not to commit itself under international law to fulfil obligations which are not in conformity with its Constitution, at the level of a constitutional value. The respect for such public interest, which can also be described as international reputation or credibility of the State . . . cannot be, as is claimed by the petitioner, exclusively an object of political responsibility of the holders of power with regard to the electorate, for the respect for it should also be deemed to be a question of conformity with the Constitution.[138]

According to the Court, constitutional conflicts should be avoided during the negotiations, e.g. by means of making a reservation or adding an annex to the agreement or its protocols, or adding reservations after signing the agreement. If, however, the Constitutional Court finds a provision of a treaty to be incompatible with the constitution, the ratification may only take place if the state has added reservations, renegotiated the treaty or carried out a prior constitutional amendment.

Besides treaties, constitutions may equally not be amended by means of a referendum, where not so provided by the amendment procedure. In Slovakia, the Constitutional Court has underlined the importance of

[137] Decision No. RM-1/97, 5 June 1997, *Uradni list RS*, No. 40/97, on Europe Agreement, in English at www.us-rs.si/en/, paras 35–8.

[138] *Ibid.*, paras 35 and 38.

respecting the parliamentary amendment procedure that has been envisaged by the constitution, stating that no other institution, even the people directly by referendum, can amend it.[139] A referendum, according to the Court, would only demonstrate to Parliament the people's will to have the constitution amended. The Hungarian Constitutional Court has also stressed that amendment of the constitution may only take place by the constitutional amendment procedure and not in a disguised way by Parliament or a referendum: '[t]he exercise of rights arising from popular sovereignty, by referendum as well as by the National Assembly, may only proceed in accordance with the provisions of the Constitution'.[140]

In the Czech Republic, the Constitutional Court has emphasised the importance of respecting the prohibition, contained in article 9, on amending the principles of a democratic and law-observing state, which according to Czech legal theory include the principle of popular sovereignty.[141] According to the Czech Constitutional Court:

> in the framework of this Constitution, the constitutive principles of a democratic society are placed beyond the legislative power and are thus *ultra vires* of the Parliament. A constitutional state stands or falls by these principles. To do away with any of these principles, by whatever means carried out, whether by a majority or an entirely unanimous decision of Parliament, could not be otherwise interpreted than as the elimination of this constitutional state as such.[142]

Finally, it is worth pointing out that the European Constitution[143] is certainly 'taken seriously' – each of its articles has undergone a careful political and academic scrutiny. Meanwhile, taking the national constitutions seriously in relation to European integration sometimes appears to entail the risk of being associated with euroscepticism. This rather unjustified association should instead give way to a search for solutions to build a genuine 'European constitutional order',[144] where national constitutions form equal and credible building-blocks, alongside the European constitutional treaty, in legitimising European governance.

139 Decision No. 26/97, II, ÚS 31/97, summary in English at www.concourt.sk/A/a_index.htm

140 Resolution No. 2/1993 (I.22), (1996) 3 *East European Case Reporter of Constitutional Law* 26.

141 K. Vodicka, 'Unaufhebbare Grundprinzipien der tschechischen Verfassungsordnung' (1996) 42 *Osteuropa Recht* 225.

142 Pl. US 19/93 *on Lawlessness of the Communist Regime* (1997) 4 *East European Case Reporter of Constitutional Law* 159.

143 See chapter 10.

144 See discussion in chapters 9 and 10.

In view of the above observations, it would be appropriate to consider what an ideal set of EU amendments should include. First, the constitutions should provide for the delegation of powers for their common exercise in the European Union, besides the existing, broader provisions addressed to international organisations.[145] The 'international organisation' approach provides only an illusory mechanism for exercising powers in view of the EU's far-reaching effects on sovereignty, and it relies on the nation-state-centred values which are becoming obsolete in the globalising and interdependent world of the twenty-first century. Besides this, the distinction between international organisations which involve 'transfer of powers' and those which do not is unnecessarily confusing to citizens, and clumsy from the point of view of legal technique. For instance, do the former include only the EU, or also NATO, the Council of Europe and other organisations, and hence apply to the application of their law and to the participation of national Parliaments? At the same time, there is equally a need for clear provisions regarding participation in traditional international organisations.

As regards the formulation of whether sovereignty is transferred, delegated, pooled or shared, chapter 2 has shown that these terms appear to be used relatively interchangeably in the constitutions of the 'old' Member States. In fact, the European Court of Justice itself has also used in its decisions several expressions: 'a limitation of sovereignty', 'a transfer of powers', 'limited their sovereign rights', 'transfer . . . of the rights and obligations', 'permanent limitation of . . . sovereignty rights', 'powers have been conferred on . . . .'[146] The vocabulary has also been diverse in the decisions of the Constitutional Courts of the 'old' Member States, both within their successive decisions and within the individual decisions themselves. Overall, the verb 'delegate' appears to carry the undertone of paying a symbolic tribute to the national constitutional concerns about the ultimate basis of the exercise of powers. On the other hand, it has rightly been observed that the expression 'transfer' rather than 'delegate' would be preferable

[145] The introduction of a standard clause on EU membership has also been advocated by the MATRA project of the T. M. C. Asser Institute, calling for the EU's encouragement in this respect (see Annex VII, to Kellermann, De Zwaan and Czuczai, *EU Enlargement*, p. 591 *et seq*). However, it is important to emphasise that constitutions, due to their status as fundamental national documents, cannot be subject to approximation. On the other hand, academic institutions themselves are well positioned to increase the general public's awareness about the advantages of EU amendments.

[146] Case 26/62, *Van Gend en Loos* [1963] ECR 1; Case 6/64, *Costa* v. *ENEL* [1964] ECR 585; Euratom Ruling 1/78 [1978] ECR 2151 at 2178.

for the reason that the meaning of 'delegation' in constitutional law is limited to the transfer of powers to a lower institution or organisation. The transfer of state powers to the European institutions is, according to Community law, permanent and it is not possible to draw these powers back, as is suggested by the term 'delegation'.[147]

Secondly, the dual exercise of popular sovereignty deserves recognition in the constitutions, as democratic legitimacy derives both from the national and European level. The recognition of the exercise of democracy on the European level should involve both the intergovernmental aspect (control of national Parliaments over their governments' activity in the Council), and the direct European aspect (direct democratic representation of the peoples of Europe via the European Parliament). Although this proposal does not find support in the comparative perspective, it could be argued that the Member States' constitutions suffer from a 'European Parliament deficit', given that the principle of popular sovereignty forms an underlying principle of the constitutions. This is with the exception of Austria and Portugal, where the European Parliament elections are mentioned in the constitutions.

This is closely related to the third issue: several constitutions need to recognise various rights belonging to EU citizens, as these bring a further European dimension to the concepts of popular sovereignty and nation-state. This involves primarily EU citizens' right to vote and stand in the elections of local councils and the European Parliament. But it also includes EU citizens' rights concerning free movement, the effective exercise of which could be restricted in several constitutions by the limitation of certain rights to national citizens. For instance, under several constitutions, only citizens are entitled to social welfare and work in the public service.

Fourthly, the privileged position of EC law justifies it being reflected in the constitutions. Since EU law is directly applicable and takes supremacy over national law, it goes much further than the position granted to the ratified and published traditional international treaties. Although the issue of ultimate supremacy remains contested, express recognition of direct applicability and supremacy of EU law with regard to ordinary national law would better meet the requirements of transparency and legitimacy.

[147] These points have been made in 'Project Proposal: The Constitutional Impact of Accession at the National Level of the Candidate Countries' in Kellermann, De Zwaan and Czuczai, *EU Enlargement*, pp. 590–2.

Finally, manifest conflicts with EU law should be eliminated from individual constitutions, such as the national banks' exclusive rights to issue national currency to pave the way for the adoption of the Euro, and the prohibition on extraditing nationals, in view of the Schengen *acquis* and the European Arrest Warrant. The constitutions could also contain references to 'European affairs' in areas where the European Constitution has an impact.[148]

It is clear that such extensive amendments may involve complications with regard to the procedural tensions attendant upon constitutional revision, and popular sentiment among citizens and politicians in both the 'old' and 'new' Member States. Yet a number of countries have indeed introduced a similar set of constitutional provisions with regard to European integration – Germany, Portugal, Austria and France. Amongst the Central and Eastern European countries, the Slovakian Constitution and, paradoxically, the Constitution of Romania, still a candidate country, live up to these standards. In fact, these two constitutions could be recommended as a model for the constitutional reforms in current and future accession countries and, indeed, also in several 'old' Member States. It is noteworthy that those countries where the constitutions mention the EU in a minimal manner, or not at all, tend to share fairly rigid constitutional amendment procedures, as seen above. In these countries, the motives for rigid amendment procedures might perhaps deserve reconsideration in the light of the changing social context. Rigid amendment procedures were designed with the purpose of avoiding authoritarian tendencies or usurpation of power. As such developments are no longer acute, the need for securing the stability of constitutions may be outweighed by the need to keep the constitutions meaningful with regard to the exercise of powers in the context of European integration. In addition, clear constitutional provisions on European integration have the advantage of increasing citizens' awareness about European issues, and thus reducing the much-lamented democratic gap between the EU and its citizens.

Last but not least, the adaptation of constitutions in respect of EU membership is likely to be conducive to a more favourable interplay between the national and European legal orders, due to their imprint on national legal education. Constitutional law and EU law have often been taught as

[148] See P. Steinberg, 'A Tentative Survey of the Innovations of the Constitution for Europe that Might Impact Upon National Constitutions' in J. Ziller (ed.), *L'européanisation des droits constitutionnels à la lumière de la Constitution pour l'Europe* (L'Harmattan, Paris, 2003), pp. 139–56.

separate subjects, and many national constitutional law textbooks mention the EU in a marginal manner.[149] Therefore, students often leave universities with a traditional understanding of sovereignty and nation-state-centred views on democratic legitimacy, which result in a large gap between the perceptions of successive generations of national lawyers and EU lawyers, who in many ways seem to live in different legal universes.[150] This also keeps the potential for major constitutional conflicts ripe. However, the debate sparked by the German *Maastricht* decision[151] has significantly contributed towards an increasing convergence in the discourse between national constitutional law and EU law. This process has certainly been reinforced by the move towards a European Constitution.

Altogether, the above developments indicate that the concept of 'constitution' appears to be 'in transition'. Laying down the foundations of sovereign governance in a nation-state, constitutions have traditionally been associated with states. The increasingly intensifying challenges to this by various external organisations and bodies have caused the 'opening up' of the constitutions to accommodate international and European governance. The ongoing process of adopting a European Constitution is triggering another major change of paradigm, in that the notion of 'constitution' is being decoupled from statehood and used in the context of a transnational polity such as the EU. We will come to the debates concerning these developments in the last chapter.

[149] S. De la Sierra and F. Domínguez-García, 'The Treatment of European Law in the Study of Constitutional Law: Has an Effective Europeanisation of Constitutional Law Already Taken Place?' in Ziller, *L'européanisation des droits constitutionnels*, pp. 53–68.

[150] See on the role of legal training M. Aziz, 'Sovereignty Lost, Sovereignty Regained? Some Reflections on the *Bundesverfassungsgericht*'s Bananas Judgment' (2002) 9 *Columbia Journal of European Law* 134.

[151] See for discussion of this decision chapter 10.

6

Theoretical views of sovereignty and democratic legitimacy in CEE

Delegating sovereignty, preserving independence?

In the 'old' Member States, the concept of sovereignty has considerably transformed in the course of the European integration process. For instance, in France, debates about the transfer of sovereignty and shared sovereignty are replacing the traditional concept of national sovereignty, which used to be defined through clear elements, including its indivisibility, inalienability and manifestation through parliamentary sovereignty.[1] In Germany, it has been commented that 'the age of absolute sovereignty is regarded as an age which is rather akin to "paradise lost"'.[2] As will be discussed in more detail in chapter 10, scholarly studies are increasingly calling for a revision of the concept of sovereignty, or even casting doubt on the concept's explanatory value, due to factors such as the dispersion of ultimate authority between numerous regulatory and judicial entities on international, supranational and national levels.

In the meantime, the countries of Central and Eastern Europe, where sovereignty was only recently restored, have hitherto predominantly operated in a traditional language of sovereignty, independence, ethnically defined nation-state and national self-determination. In some cases, verbatim definitions of the pre-Soviet period have been used by authoritative constitutional amendment commissions to assess EU membership. Although CEE countries declared, soon after regime change, that EU accession forms their major foreign policy goal, their legal discourse has until recently focused on the re-established sovereignty and on the effects

[1] J. Ziller, 'Sovereignty in France: Getting Rid of the Mal de Bodin' in N. Walker (ed.), *Sovereignty in Transition* (Hart, Oxford, 2003), pp. 261–77, especially at p. 264, with reference concerning the criteria to J. Gicquel, *Droit constitutionnel et institutions politiques* (15th edn, Montchrestien, Paris, 1997), pp. 198–200.

[2] M. Aziz, 'Sovereignty Über Alles: (Re)Configuring the German Legal Order' in Walker, *Sovereignty in Transition*, p. 281.

of public international law upon sovereign legal systems, as the application of international law was not addressed by the constitutions and scholarly research during the Communist period. The awareness of the constitutional impact of the European Union has been weak in CEE literature;[3] it started to register mainly towards the very end of the 1990s and especially since the participation of CEE representatives in the Convention on the Future of Europe. Until 1998–1999, literature about the EU's effects upon national constitutions or sovereignty was scarce in the CEE countries, except for Poland where EU accession formed one of the key issues in the debate on adopting the new constitution in 1997. For instance, as regards the Czech Republic, Mahulena Hoskova has expressed surprise that the 1992 Czech Constitution was silent with regard to EU membership even though adopted at the time when accession was one of the Republic's most important goals. According to her, '[i]t is, however, more surprising that the question of whether and to what extent Czech accession to the European Union requires prior amendments of the Constitution is virtually absent in the Czech legal discourse'. By 1994, 'there was very little awareness of [the constitutional problems of EU accession] . . . among most of the officials charged with preparing the Czech legal system for such membership'.[4] According to her, this holds equally true for Slovakia. With regard to Slovenia, Primos Vehar has reported that the transfer of the exercise of legislative, executive and judicial powers to the institutions of the EU as a supranational organisation was 'scarcely understood or credible to many traditionally oriented lawyers and politicians who insist on the position that the Constitution is hierarchically the highest legal act and that all state authorities . . . have to ensure this hierarchy and respect it'.[5] Although constitutional awareness about the EU gained ground as accession drew closer, Central and Eastern European scholars tended to devote minimal space to analysing the nature of the EU polity, and to view the Union therefore merely as an international organisation

[3] Reported with regard to Hungary by A. Harmathy, 'Constitutional Questions of the Preparation of Hungary to Accession to the European Union' in A. Kellermann, J. De Zwaan and J. Czuczai (eds.), *EU Enlargement: The Constitutional Impact at EU and National Level* (Asser Press, The Hague, 2001), p. 123; with regard to the Czech Republic and Slovakia by M. Hoskova, 'Legal Aspects of the Integration of the Czech Republic and Slovakia into European Security and Economic Structures' (1994) 37 *German Yearbook of International Law* 91, see also p. 87, and with regard to Slovenia by P. Vehar, 'Constitutional Problems in the Period of Pre-Accession in the Republic of Slovenia' in Kellermann, De Zwaan and Czuczai, *EU Enlargement*, p. 370. The same holds true for Estonia, Latvia and Lithuania.

[4] Hoskova, 'Legal Aspects', p. 87.

[5] Vehar, 'Constitutional Problems', p. 370.

or a confederation of states,[6] finding that it would not significantly affect national sovereignty.

This background is one of the reasons why the EU was addressed as an international organisation in the constitutional amendments of several accession countries, an approach that had initially been taken almost universally. For instance, Polish legal theory did not distinguish until recently between international organisations and supranational organisations.[7] The 'international organisation' approach was taken in the new 1997 Constitution, as well as in all four draft constitutions submitted before 1993[8] and in most of the earlier drafts of the 1997 Constitution.[9] Some authors, however, have criticised the application of the notion of 'international organisation' to the EU.[10] In Lithuania, the Working Group proposed in 1998 a clause on delegating competences to bodies of international organisations. The Working Group explained that the EU forms an international organisation and, constitutionally, participation in the EU does not differ from participation in the United Nations or the Council of Europe.[11] However, following the opinion of a number of foreign experts on the disadvantages of such an approach,[12] a revised version of the draft amendments, submitted in 2000, proposed provisions on the transfer of competences directly to the European Union.[13] Nonetheless, the accession eventually took place under the existing provisions

[6] However, amongst those who have emphasised the EU's supranational character see E. Tanchev, 'National Constitutions and EU Law: Adapting the 1991 Bulgarian Constitution in the Accession to the European Union' (2000) 6 *European Public Law* 233 at pp. 236, 241; Hoskova, 'Legal Aspects', pp. 86–7; Vehar, 'Constitutional Problems', p. 370 *et seq.*; S. Biernat, 'Constitutional Aspects of Poland's Future Membership in the European Union' (1998) 36 *Archiv des Völkerrechts* 400; J. Barcz, 'Membership of Poland in the European Union in the Light of the Constitution of 2 April 1997' (1997–98) 23 *Polish Yearbook of International Law* 22.

[7] Comment by C. Mik on his paper 'Sovereignty and European Union: Polish Perspective', presented in the workshop 'Sovereignty in Transition', EUI, Florence, 21–22 September 2001.

[8] These are presented in A. Wasilkowski, 'The Future Polish Constitution in the Perspective of Poland's Membership of the European Union' (1993) *Droit Polonais Contemporain* 14.

[9] Biernat, 'Constitutional Aspects', pp. 400–1 and 407.

[10] *Ibid.*, pp. 400–1; Barcz, 'Membership of Poland', p. 22.

[11] 'Republic of Lithuania Constitutional Law on the Amendment of Articles 136 and 138 of the Constitution of the Republic of Lithuania, Draft of the Working Group established under the Seimas Chancellery' in *Stojimas I Europos Sajunga Ir Konstitucija. Seminaro Medziaga 29–30.06.1999* (Eugrimas, Vilnius, 2000), p. 142.

[12] See comments by F. Frowein, P.-C. Müller-Graff, I. Pernice and others in *Stojimas I Europos Sajunga.*

[13] V. Vadapalas, 'Lithuania: The Constitutional Impact of the Enlargement at National Level' in Kellermann, De Zwaan and Czuczai, *EU Enlargement*, p. 354.

on international organisations. The Czech constitutional amendments of 2001 permit the transfer of some powers to 'an international organisation or institution', an approach that also figured in earlier draft amendment proposals.[14] Slovene amendments are equally addressed to 'international organisations'; an earlier draft of 2001 had offered the formulation 'international organisations of supranational nature'.[15]

In those countries where the final amendments were addressed to the EU (Hungary, Slovakia, Estonia and Romania), the 'international organisation' approach was present in the preparatory phases of drafting. In Hungary, the international organisation approach was taken, as seen above, in the new draft constitution of 1997,[16] and the only alternative draft until 1999 had also been addressed to 'international intergovernmental organisations'.[17] In Slovakia, the initial draft constitutional amendments, submitted by a group of parliamentary deputies in June 2000, proposed an amendment on the transfer of sovereign rights to international organisations.[18] Although the initial draft amendments in Estonia, composed by the Constitutional Expert Commission in 1998, were addressed directly to the European Union, the EU was defined as an association or confederation of states.[19] The 'Third Constitutional Act' that was finally adopted provides a laconic authorisation for joining the EU, and was widely presented as not harming sovereignty.

[14] e.g. those proposed by J. Malenovsky, 'Résumé: Projet commenté des articles de la Constitution de la République tchèque régissant ses rapports au droit international' (1999) 5 *Pravnik* 403. On the other hand, J. Zemanek's amendment proposals have been directly addressed to the European Union (J. Zemanek, 'The Amendments of the Czech Constitution for the Accession to the European Union' in Kellermann, De Zwaan and Czuczai, *EU Enlargement*, pp. 432–3).

[15] 'Predlog za začetek postopka za spremembe ustave Republike Slovenije' [Proposal to Initiate the Procedure of Changes to the Constitution of the Republic of Slovenia], in *Poročevalec – Državnega zbora Republike Slovenije*, 6 August 2001, p. 4.

[16] 'Constitution of the Republic of Hungary (Draft)' (1997) 38 *Acta Juridica Hungarica, Hungarian Journal of Legal Studies* 5.

[17] Offered by J. Nemeth, 'Az Europai Integracio es a Magyar Alkotmany' in A. Bragyova (ed.), *Nemzetközi Jog az Uj Alkotmanyban – Tanulmanyok* (Közgazdasagi es Jogi Könyvkiado, Budapest, 1997), pp. 110–12, cited in G. Lissauer, *The Potential Impact of European Union Membership on Hungary's Constitution* (LLM Thesis, University of Kent at Canterbury, 1999), p. 55.

[18] Reported in V. Kunova, 'Constitutional Aspects of the Accession of the Slovak Republic to European Union' in Kellermann, De Zwaan and Czuczai, *EU Enlargement*, p. 335.

[19] *Võimalik liitumine Euroopa Liiduga ja selle õiguslik tähendus Eesti riigiõiguse seisukohalt* [Potential Accession to the European Union and its Consequences for Estonian Constitutional Law], Report of the Constitutional Amendment Expert Commission of Estonia (1998), in Estonian at www.just.ee/juridica2.html

In Latvia, an earlier draft amendment of 1999 recommended a provision authorising the conclusion of treaties on the entrance into international organisations.[20] The final amendments addressed the provision on the delegation of powers to international organisations, but also included a direct requirement of referendum for entry into the EU.

The 'international organisation' approach also appears to correspond to the way the concept of sovereignty is, in theoretical terms, reconciled with membership of the EU. With some variations, an underpinning idea can be discerned across the region according to which independence (external sovereignty) has to be retained, while some state powers (internal sovereignty) may be delegated to the EU. This explains the importance of the approach which regards the EU as an international organisation or a confederation – membership of these clearly preserves independence, compared with ambiguities associated with membership of a supranational or a federal entity. This is most straightforwardly posited in the Estonian constitutional theory, where the Expert Commission adopted the definition of sovereignty given by Anton-Tõeleid Kliimann, a constitutional scholar of the period of the First Estonian Republic (1918–1940).[21] According to Kliimann, 'independence' (*iseseisvus*) means the prohibition for a state to become a part of another state. 'Sovereignty' (*sõltumatus*), on the other hand, means that the law-giving authorities must not be subordinated to a foreign power so that the latter could prescribe to the Estonian legislative bodies how to organise life in the state, or control the exercise of these rules. According to these definitions, the Expert Commission found that Estonia may delegate part of sovereignty, i.e. legislative, executive and judicial powers, to a confederation of states. In the meantime, independence must be preserved: Estonia may not participate in a federal Union, which would emerge should the EU adopt a constitution or establish a bicameral European Parliament.

The same idea is present in Lithuanian constitutional theory. The Working Group stated on many occasions that '[a]ccession to the European Union does not mean loss of independence or its limitation; it means delegation of a part of . . . State competence to the EU bodies'. Independence

[20] *Constitutional and Administrative Facilitation of Effective Law Approximation and European Union Membership*, Report composed under the auspices of the European Integration Bureau and PHARE Technical Assistance to the Approximation of the Latvian Legislation to that of the European Communities (Riga, 1999).

[21] A.-T. Kliimann, 'Development of Estonia's Independence' (in Estonian) (1935) 2 *Õigus* 49, cited in *Võimalik liitumine*, pp. 3–5.

(external sovereignty) is retained as '[i]t has been universally recognised and is beyond doubt that Member States of the European Union are fully-fledged members of international relations and organisations'.[22]

The Latvian Working Group has stated that EU accession implies a delegation of state competences (internal sovereignty), but it does not harm Latvia's independence.[23] In doing so, however, it remarkably applied to the notion of independence a novel concept of 'open statehood', which will be discussed in more detail in chapter 10. Latvia is thus the first among the Baltic countries to recognise officially the need to revise the sovereignty concept of the First Republic period, and to adapt it to the needs of the twenty-first century. However, before adapting this new interpretation, the sovereignty concept used in the Latvian legal theory has mainly been based, as with the other Baltic countries, on the definitions of sovereignty and independence provided by the constitutional scholars of the First Republic, especially that of Karl Dishlers, a distinguished legal scholar of the period.

In Hungary, there is a widespread view in constitutional theory that sovereignty is indivisible and non-transferable. By joining the EU, Hungary will remain a sovereign and independent state, but the exercise of certain constitutional powers can be restricted.[24]

In Poland, the theories of sovereignty are more diverse, but a conceptually similar approach may be distinguished in some writings, although a somewhat different vocabulary has been deployed. Internal sovereignty is referred to by using the expression 'power competences', which may be delegated, whereas 'sovereignty' takes the meaning of external sovereignty, which must be preserved. Cesary Mik reports that according to Polish constitutional theory, the omission of the term 'sovereignty' from article 90 of the 1997 Constitution was significant in order to convey the idea that EU accession 'neither deprives nor restricts Poland in its sovereignty'; it is merely allowed 'to confer the competence of its organs to an international

[22] 'Republic of Lithuania Constitutional Law', p. 141, and Vadapalas, 'Lithuania: The Constitutional Impact', p. 353.

[23] *The Theoretical Foundation of the Amendments to Satversme proposed by the Working Group* (Ministry of Justice, Riga, November 2001), p. 6 *et seq.*

[24] Reported by J. Czuczai, 'National Preferences in Light of the Constitutional Adaptation Process to the EU Accession Acquis: The Hungarian Experiences in a Comparative Dimension of Central and Eastern Europe' in *Europe 2002* (Budapest, March 2004), vol. V/1, pp. 54–5. See also J. Czuczai, 'The Constitutional Challenges of Accession in Central and East European Countries: A Comparative Study on Hungary, Poland and Czech Republic' in Kellermann, De Zwaan and Czuczai, *EU Enlargement*, p. 420, n. 19.

organisation'.[25] A similar position is echoed by Wladyslaw Czaplinski, who, commenting on EU integration under the Polish Constitution, says that a state can either be sovereign or not, since the notion of limited sovereignty does not exist in international law, whereas competences may be transferred, except for transferring all of them.[26] Some other commentators share the view that joining the EU does not mean the loss of sovereignty, but associate the EU's impact on sovereignty with different aspects. For instance, Jan Barcz is of the view that the exclusive character of the powers of state authorities is relinquished in areas determined by the Treaties; the transfer of powers is not absolute and may be revoked.[27] According to Stanislaw Biernat, the literature on the constitutional solutions emphasises that article 90 allows only for the transfer of the execution of the powers of state authority to an international organisation, and not for the transfer of powers *per se*; such a concept means that Poland remains sovereign, and is merely giving up exclusivity in exercising the rights of a sovereign.[28] On the other hand, Janusz Justynski has taken a more novel view: by losing legislative power, 'Poland gains a broad power in the field of co-establishing law for the whole European Union'.[29]

In the Czech Republic, the amendment proposal was formulated so that it 'retains the present characteristic of the Czech Republic as a "sovereign, unitary, democratic law-abiding state"' under article 1 of the constitution, but 'modifies the existing constitutional concept of the state by the introduction of a new clause on the respect of the Czech Republic for the rules and obligations imposed by international law'.[30]

The tendency that the EU is found not to significantly affect sovereignty also appears from the fact that many CEE reporters in a relatively recent conference on the constitutional adaptations in Central and Eastern Europe did not mention the issue of sovereignty at all when discussing

[25] C. Mik, 'State Sovereignty and European Integration: Public International Law, EU Law and Constitutional Law in the Polish Context' in Walker, *Sovereignty in Transition*, p. 398.

[26] W. Czaplinski, 'L'Intégration européenne dans la constitution polonaise de 1997' (2000) *Revue du Marché Commun et de l'Union Européenne* 171.

[27] Barcz, 'Membership of Poland in the European Union', pp. 25–7.

[28] Biernat, 'Constitutional Aspects', p. 407.

[29] J. Justynski, 'The Impact of the European Integration Process on the Creation of the Broad Lines of the Constitution of the Republic of Poland and on the Political Practices of the Country' in Kellermann, De Zwaan and Czuczai, *EU Enlargement*, p. 283.

[30] I. Slosarcik, 'The Reform of the Constitutional Systems of Czechoslovakia and the Czech Republic in 1990–2000' (2001) 7 *European Public Law* 544.

the constitutional impact of EU accession.[31] There is also a tendency to focus on the conservatory elements of sovereign statehood, such as the right to secede from the Union, rather than exploring the EU's effects on sovereignty and new approaches to the concept. Altogether, as noted by Justice Miroslaw Wyrzykowski, 'European integration requires a relinquishing of the traditional notion of sovereignty, i.e. of the value most appreciated today in Eastern Europe as one of the greatest successes achieved due to the collapse of communism'.[32] In the words of Joachim Hesse:

> [w]hereas in the East there are many societies engaged in rediscovering themselves as nation-states and in giving constitutional shape to that new identity, . . . in the West it is more a question whether the nation-states will remain politically and constitutionally distinctive one from another, or commit themselves decisively to a merging of sovereignties and thus, in some degree, to a fusion of constitutional forms in a new political entity.[33]

The predominance of the traditional approach to sovereignty in Central and Eastern Europe has, in the author's view, the following reasons. First and foremost, the centrality of the paradigm of sovereign nation-state forms a corollary of the recently regained sovereignty, which has been a focal issue in CEE legal research. In addition, research on the international impact on constitutional theory was effectively suspended during the fifty years of Marxist-Leninist doctrine and due to the Iron Curtain.[34] Further, the EU's constitutional impact has mainly been assessed by experts of constitutional law and public international law, with EU studies being in an early phase. It is also interesting to note that some CEE countries have very small populations, which inevitably restricts the availability of specialist discussion, especially because CEE scholars have been actively involved in the legislative drafting during the process of rebuilding new independent

[31] See reports by V. Balas, A. Ciobanu-Dordea, P. Vehar, A. Harmathy and A. Nikodem in the collection of the conference proceedings edited by Kellermann, De Zwaan and Czuczai, *EU Enlargement*.

[32] M. Wyrzykowski, 'The Constitutions of the Eastern European Countries in the Structure of European Constitutionalism' in R. Bieber and P. Widmer (eds.), *L'Espace Constitutionnel Européen* (Schulthess Polygraphischer Verlag, Zürich, 1995), p. 161.

[33] J. Hesse, 'Introduction: Constitutional Policy and Change in Europe: the Nature and Extent of the Challenges' in J. Hesse and N. Johnson (eds.), *Constitutional Policy and Change in Europe* (Nuffield European Studies, Oxford University Press, 1995), p. 4.

[34] For an account of the theory of sovereignty during Communism see Aziz, 'Sovereignty Über Alles', pp. 301–3.

legal systems. Alongside these factors, the constitutional framework itself also appears to account for the theoretical discussions: it is sought to retain a meaningful substance to the distinction between sovereignty and independence and, by using the 'international organisation' approach, to build a psychologically neutral bridge for the move from the constitutional silence on international organisations to membership of a deeply integrated supranational organisation.

Popular sovereignty: from an ethno-cultural to a post-national concept?

There is a similar difference in discourse as concerns popular sovereignty and democratic legitimacy. In the Western side of Europe, there has been a mushrooming of literature decoupling democratic legitimacy from the nation-state, especially since the (in)famous German *Maastricht* decision.[35] The German Constitutional Court, in brief, took an essentialist, ethno-cultural approach to democratic legitimacy, finding that democratic representation is inherently bound to a culturally, linguistically and socially homogeneous community within the territorial boundaries of a nation-state. Against this backdrop, it posited that a minimum democratic legitimacy is sufficient on the supranational level, taking place predominantly via the national democratic mechanisms, such as the responsibility of governments in their EU activities *vis-à-vis* the national Parliaments, and the participation of national Parliaments by means of ratification of successive treaties. The European Parliament was attributed merely a complementary legitimising role. In the eyes of the German Constitutional Court, a shift of democracy to the EU level would weaken democracy due to the absence of a European people and a European political process.[36]

This controversial view fuelled a wider debate about democracy in the European Union, which resulted in a relatively widespread acknowledgement that there is enough content to a European demos to justify stronger democratic representation through the European Parliament, in parallel to democratic legitimacy deriving from the nation-state level. The recognition of a European demos drew particularly upon influential writings by

[35] *Brunner*, BVerfGE 89, 155 (1993), [1994] CMLR 57; see, for comment on this decision, chapter 10.

[36] See for a similar, so-called 'No Demos' view also U. K. Preuss, 'Problems of a Concept of European Citizenship' (1995) 1 *European Law Journal* 267; D. Grimm, 'Does Europe Need a Constitution?' (1995) 1 *European Law Journal* 282.

Joseph Weiler[37] and Jürgen Habermas.[38] Weiler suggests that the European demos is based on the common transcending cultural and political values expressed in the constituent documents, instead of the organic, ethno-cultural values. While national identity is more about emotional belongingness, European identity is a 'reflective, deliberative rational choice'. Habermas' theory of constitutional patriotism similarly proposes that it is the common universal principles of the constitution rather than shared cultural identity that bind a society together in the modern multicultural liberal democracies. This provides a legitimate base for twofold democratic representation, on the national and European level. Furthermore, the recognition of a European demos is inevitable because, as Weiler has pointed out, the national chains of democratisation of EU politics provide but illusory and formalistic democratic control, considering the 'volume, complexity and timing of the Community decisional process', as well as the wide use of qualified majority voting.[39] As Habermas says, it is our obligation to try to save democracy even if transcending the limits of the nation-state.[40] We will discuss the issue of the European demos in more detail in chapter 10, which deals with the implications of the European Constitution.

While Western Europe is thus redefining the national state in the context of European integration, in Central and Eastern Europe 'the nation is still strongly anchored with the nation-state'.[41] Central and Eastern European academic discourse, as well as the citizenship and language legislation, has hitherto been approaching the notion of people through the ethno-cultural concept of homogeneous sovereign nation-state; the nation is viewed as a community of fate sharing the same identity through a common language, history and culture.[42] The ethno-cultural approach

[37] J. H. H. Weiler, 'Does Europe Need a Constitution? Demos, Telos and the German Maastricht Decision' (1995) 1 *European Law Journal* 233 at p. 238; J. H. H. Weiler, *The Constitution of Europe: 'Do the New Clothes have an Emperor?' and Other Essays on the European Integration* (Cambridge University Press, 1999).

[38] J. Habermas, 'The European Nation State: Its Achievements and Its Limitations: On the Past and Future of Sovereignty and Citizenship' (1996) 9 *Ratio Juris* 125; J. Habermas, 'The European Nation-State and the Pressures of Globalization' (1999) 235 *New Left Review* 40.

[39] See Weiler, 'Does Europe Need a Constitution', pp. 233, 238.

[40] Habermas, 'The European Nation State', pp. 136–7.

[41] M. Lehti, *Sovereignty Redefined: Baltic Co-operation and the Limits of National Self-determination* (Working Paper of COPRI, Copenhagen, 1999), pp. 27–8; also Hesse, 'Introduction', p. 8.

[42] See in more detail U. Preuss, 'Patterns of Constitutional Evolution and Change in Eastern Europe' in Hesse and Johnson, *Constitutional Policy*, p. 110 *et seq.*; W. Sokolewicz, 'The

to popular sovereignty has also been expressly entrenched in several constitutions. Rather than establishing a more general principle of popular sovereignty, which could be interpreted as allowing for its exercise on the supranational level, many of them vest power explicitly in the concrete nations. For instance, the Latvian Constitution expressly states that 'sovereign power . . . is vested in the people of Latvia' (article 2). The Romanian Constitution declares that Romania is a 'national and unitary state' (article 1(1)), and national sovereignty resides with the 'Romanian people' (article 2). The Preamble to the Bulgarian Constitution speaks about expressing the will of the 'people of Bulgaria'. Although the same also holds true for the Polish and Slovene Constitutions, these specify that the nation is regarded in civic rather than in ethnic terms. The Polish Constitution, using the expression 'We, the Polish Nation' (Preamble) and stating that 'supreme power in the Republic of Poland shall be vested in the Nation' (article 4), makes it clear in the Preamble that the expression 'Polish Nation' means 'all citizens of the Republic'. Previously, however, popular sovereignty was understood in Polish constitutional theory in an ethno-cultural way: 'the people are the true "sovereign", endowed with a will of their own from which all legitimate political authority stems. A legitimate government must thus be grounded in a legislature that is really of the people in the strong sense of the *identity* of the rulers and the ruled.'[43] In Slovenia, the drafters of the constitution advocated the contemporary concept of sovereignty of the people, where the constitutive element of the state would not just be the 'Slovene nation', but the citizens of Slovenia (article 3(1)), irrespective of their national or ethnic origin.[44]

In Slovakia and Romania, the Hungarian minority parties have regularly called for amending the constitutions so as to replace the ethnic concept of nation with a civic one. In Slovakia, the Hungarian Coalition Party requested – although without success – that the 2001 amendments would include the replacement of the expression 'We, the Slovak nation'

Relevance of Western Models for Constitution-Building in Poland' in Hesse and Johnson, *Constitutional Policy*, p. 256; Wyrzykowski, 'Constitutions of the Eastern European Countries', p. 161; S. Bartole, *Riforme costituzionali nell'Europa centro-orientale* (Bologna, 1993), pp. 50–1.

43 Reported by A. Rapaczynski, 'Constitutional Politics in Poland: A Report on the Constitutional Committee of the Polish Parliament' in I. Dick and A. E. Howard (eds.), *Constitution Making in Eastern Europe* (Woodrow Wilson Centre Press, Washington, 1993), p. 113.

44 M. Cerar, 'Slovenia: From Elite Consensus to Democratic Consolidation' in J. Zielonka and A. Pravda (eds.), *Democratic Consolidation in Eastern Europe*, vol. I, *Institutional Engineering* (Oxford University Press, 2001), p. 391.

in the Preamble with 'We, the citizens of Slovakia'.[45] In Romania, the Hungarian Democratic Federation of Romania has, since the drafting of the constitution in the Constituent Assembly in 1991, insisted on replacing article 1, which declares Romania to be 'a national state', with one defining it as a 'civic state', but to no avail. Latvia and Estonia, where the ethnically constructed citizenship criteria have left a large percentage of the population without voting rights, have constantly been under pressure from the Council of Europe, OSCE, NATO and the EU to liberalise their citizenship laws and especially the language requirements. It is interesting that at the time of opening up for international governance, Latvia has amended the constitution to strengthen the position of the state language, and constitutional amendment proposals to this effect are under consideration in the Czech Republic, as seen in chapter 5. In Slovenia, national sentiments ran high in a 2004 referendum, where a government-sponsored Bill, which proposed to restore social security rights to the so-called 'erased persons', was rejected by an overwhelming majority of 95 per cent. The 'erased persons' means about 18,000 mainly former Yugoslav citizens who were removed from the Slovenian population registry in 1992, after failing to apply for citizenship or permanent residency.

Ethno-cultural views of democratic legitimacy also appear from the decisions of the Constitutional Courts. The Hungarian Constitutional Court affirmed in the 'Europe Agreement' decision that democratic legitimisation is based on people's sovereignty and that the norms applied in Hungary must be attributable to the people, as seen in chapter 4. In the Baltic states, the constitutional courts have underscored the indivisible bond between the national language, exercise of democracy and the nation-state, paying tribute thereby to the continuous sensitivity towards the delicate ethnic situation and previous forced domination of the Russian language in these countries. The Estonian Chamber of Constitutional Review has linked the effectiveness of democracy to the use of the national language in a decision concerning the amendments to the Language Act:

> Article 1 of the Constitution declares that Estonia is a democratic republic. Democracy fulfils its purpose when it works. One of the conditions for a working democracy is that the persons who exercise power have

[45] 'Constitution Watch: Slovakia' (2001) 10 *East European Constitutional Review*, no. 1, p. 38; D. Malova and E. Lastic, 'The Gradual Amending of the Slovak Constitution: Combating the Ambiguous Rules in 1992–2001' (2001) 2 *Central European Political Science Review* 103.

> comprehensive understanding of what is going on in Estonia and use a single sign system in doing business. Thus, the requirement that the Estonian language be used in representative democracy and doing state business is in conformity with general interests and justified in the historically developed circumstances . . . Pursuant to the preamble to the Constitution, one of the goals of the state is to guarantee the preservation of the Estonian nation and culture throughout the ages. The Estonian language is an essential component of the Estonian nation and culture, the preservation of the Estonian nation and culture without it is impossible.[46]

In Latvia and Lithuania, the Constitutional Courts have underlined the value of a state language in a nation-state in the decisions rejecting complaints about the adjustment of foreign names to the rules on spelling names in the national language. In Lithuania, the Constitutional Court has stated that:

> [t]he establishment of the status of the state language in the Constitution means that Lithuanian is a constitutional value. The state language preserves the identity of the nation, it integrates a civil nation, it ensures the expression of national sovereignty, the integrity and indivisibility of the state, and a smooth functioning of the state and local government establishments.[47]

The Constitutional Court of Latvia, in a decision concerning the adjustment of foreign names to the rules of the Latvian language, has made reference to the Lithuanian decision as regards the fact that 'the state language maintains the identity of the nation, unites it and ensures manifestation of the national sovereignty and indivisibility of the nation'.[48] The Latvian Constitutional Court added that:

> Taking into account the historical features and the fact that the numerical structure of the Latvians in the state territory has decreased during the 20th century and in the biggest cities, including Riga[,] Latvians are a minority . . . and that the Latvian language only recently has regained its status as the state language, the necessity of protecting the state language and strengthening its usage is closely connected with the state of Latvia democratic system . . . Taking into consideration that the Latvian language as the state language has been fixed in the Satversme (Constitution) and the fact that in the era of

[46] Decision No. 3-4-1-1-98, 5 February 1998, *On Language Law*, in English at www.nc.ee/english/

[47] Decision No. 14/98, 21 October 1999, in English at www.lrkt.lt/1999/n9a1021a.htm, para. 4.

[48] Decision No. 2001-04-0103, 21 December 2001, in English at www.riga.lv/minelres/NationalLegislation/Latvia/Latvia_ConstCourt2001_English.htm

> globalization Latvia is the only place in the world where the existence and development of the Latvian language[,] and together with it the existence of the main nation[,] may be guaranteed. Limitation of the usage sectors of the Latvian language as the state language in the state territory shall be regarded as the threat to the democratic system . . . Thus – the private life of the applicant is limited to protect the right of other inhabitants of Latvia to use the Latvian language freely in the entire territory and to protect the democratic state system.

In the EU context, CEE writings hitherto associated legitimisation with the intergovernmental and national democratic mechanisms, in line with the argument of the German *Maastricht* decision. Awareness about the legitimising role of the European Parliament has mainly emerged with the preparations for the elections to the European Parliament in June 2004. Earlier, legitimacy had predominantly been attributed to the participation of national Parliaments in EU affairs, the responsibility of the governments *vis-à-vis* the national Parliaments, and to the accession referendums. For instance, the Estonian Expert Commission, underlying the sovereign nation-state paradigm, explained that the principle of popular sovereignty would not allow any other (inter)governmental bodies authorised by a foreign nation, including the European Parliament, to possess higher power than the Parliament, since the former would then exercise higher power not only on the intergovernmental level but also in Estonia, which would be prohibited by the constitution. The Expert Commission has further explained that since the supreme state power is identical to the sovereign, the Estonian people as the source of sovereignty would not be legally bound by these rules. Under the right of national self-determination, as declared in the Preamble to the constitution, the *pouvoir constituant* belongs to the Estonian nation, which is the only source of supreme power and the only sufficient source of legitimacy. Furthermore, the Expert Commission has stated that the development of the European Parliament into a body comparable to the 'highest state authority body' would render the EU a federation, participation in which would be prohibited by the independence provisions of the constitution.[49]

The traditional intergovernmental approach to democracy, according to which the crux of legitimisation lies within the nation-state through the responsibility of the national governments *vis-à-vis* the national Parliaments, is also taken by the Lithuanian Working Group. The Working

[49] 'Võimalik liitumine', pp. 5, 8–9, 14–15.

Group has reiterated on many occasions that '[a]ccession to the European Union and delegation to its bodies of a portion of competence of the State bodies does not at all mean that this state loses . . . features of its democratic system'.[50] The President of the Working Group has earlier noted that '[d]emocracy philosophically and pragmatically cannot be realised without sovereignty'.[51] With regard to Poland, Wojciech Sokolewicz has pointed out:

> [a]s with other European states, Poland will face the unprecedented phenomenon recently termed constitutional pluralism, which stands in sharp contrast to what is popular in our part of the continent: the tendency to think mainly in terms of national sovereignty, self-definition, and often even the homogeneity of a national state.[52]

On the other hand, the 2001 draft amendments of the Latvian Working Group proceed from a modern interpretation that the democracy principle of article 1 is not harmed by EU accession, but democracy will be exercised directly by the election of the Latvian members of the European Parliament, and indirectly by the Latvian government's participation in the EU Council.[53]

Another change triggered by EU accession in the traditional ethnocultural approach towards the concept of demos is that it opens to EU citizens many rights that have traditionally been inextricably linked to citizens. These include the right to vote and stand in the elections of local authorities and the European Parliament. Further, the provisions which banned land sales to foreigners had to be abolished, and the prohibition on the extradition of citizens had to be removed in a number of constitutions. In addition, the effective exercise of the EU citizens' right of non-discrimination concerning free movement may necessitate revision or broad interpretation of constitutional provisions that entitle only citizens to work in public service, and to the rights of social security, including state assistance in the case of old age, unemployment, disability and medical aid.

The above discussion shows how in parallel to the amending of constitutions, constitutional theory in the region is equally undergoing a

[50] 'Republic of Lithuania Constitutional Law', p. 141.

[51] S. Staciokas, 'Democracy and Sovereignty (The Lithuanian Experience)' in *Philosophy and Democracy* (Vilnius, 1996), p. 99.

[52] Sokolewicz, 'Relevance of Western Models', p. 256, with reference to Preuss, 'Patterns of Constitutional Evolution'.

[53] *Theoretical Foundation of the Amendments to Satversme*, p. 6.

major change. In a very short period of time, the traditional nation-state-centred paradigm of sovereignty and democratic legitimacy is giving way to theories of supranational governance and post-national democracy. While the constitutional lawyers in the 'old' Member States have had time to adapt incrementally to and absorb new steps of integration, the accession of the CEE countries represents a major 'constitutional leap', in the sense that they are joining at a time when the Union is preparing a constitution which for many involves federal connotations. We will look at the responses in CEE countries to the EU's constitutional reform in chapter 10, where we will return to the question of sovereignty and democratic legitimacy by considering the implications of the European Constitution.

7

Referendums

Referendum experience: frequent and unsuccessful

In parallel to constitutional amendments, referendums[1] were held in the accession countries in order to legitimise EU membership. It was mentioned in chapter 5 that the sensitivities surrounding the accession referendums partly accounted for minimal EU amendments in CEE constitutions. This chapter will explore the process of accession referendums in more detail, starting with an inquiry into the general experience with referendums in the countries of Central and Eastern Europe.

At the outset, it should be pointed out that referendums are frequently held across Central and Eastern Europe, which perhaps gives grounds for characterising the region as one of direct democracy. The frequency of recourse to referendums could partly be ascribed to the totalitarian past and newly regained sovereignty, which has entailed a need to give higher legitimacy to decisions, as well as glorifying the notion of the people as the holders of sovereign power. To put it in numbers, there have been at least forty-three referendums since 1990 in the ten countries explored in this book.[2] Nine of these were held in relation to EU membership in 2003; the others have been held on issues of varying importance, from privatisation to NATO membership: the details are available in Table 7.2.[3] Referendums have been most numerous in Slovenia (altogether nine), Lithuania

[1] The term 'referendums' will be used instead of 'referenda', as recommended by the Oxford English Dictionary of 1989, and used in M. Gallagher and P. V. Uleri (eds.), *The Referendum Experience in Europe* (Macmillan, Basingstoke, 1996).

[2] According to some sources, the number of referendums has been higher, as separate questions presented in one referendum have often been counted as different referendums.

[3] See also for details of referendums in individual countries the website of Direct Democracy, http://c2d.unige.ch/, and A. Auer and M. Bützer (eds.), *Direct Democracy: The Eastern and Central European Experience* (Ashgate, Aldershot, 2001), as well as country reports in the *East European Constitutional Review* and *RFE/RL Newsline* (www.referl.org). Bulgaria and the Czech Republic have not held referendums over the last couple of decades (the latter until the EU referendum). Results of accession referendums are available in Table 7.4.

(altogether eight) and Slovakia (altogether six), since the countries' independence in 1991 and 1993 respectively. On the other hand, Bulgaria has held no referendums so far, and the Czech Republic has been reluctant to resort to referendums until the EU referendum of 2003; notoriously, no referendum was held on the dissolution of Czechoslovakia. In addition, there has been an abundance of referendum initiatives that have not been successful. For instance, recent referendum initiatives in Hungary include those on the indexing of pensions, amendments to the Labour Code, abolition of obligatory military service and free foreign language exams for high school students (spring 2001), on recounting votes cast at the preceding parliamentary elections (spring 2002), on reduction of the size of Parliament and introduction of direct presidential elections (February 2004), and on granting citizenship to ethnic Hungarians living in neighbouring countries (March 2004).

What is common to the referendums in a number of countries is that their validity is subject to rather high minimum turnout requirements: a minimum of 50 per cent participation is required in Slovakia, Lithuania, Bulgaria, Romania, for constitutional amendment referendums in Slovenia and Latvia and for ordinary referendums in Poland; details can be found in Table 7.1. Most extremely in Lithuania, three-fourths of all citizens who have voting rights must consent to amending article 1 of the constitution (on independence). Hungary, in fact, reduced the minimum turnout requirement of 50 per cent by a constitutional amendment in 1997, shortly before the NATO referendum; a valid referendum now requires a 25 per cent approval of the total electorate. Latvia did the same ahead of the EU referendum, to which we come in the next section.

These high turnout requirements render the securing of a successful referendum a challenging exercise. In fact, more than half of the referendums within recent years have failed to meet the quorum. Apart from the enthusiastic participation in the referendums of the early 1990s on independence and on the adoption of new constitutions, Table 7.2 shows that eleven out of twenty referendums from 1994 onwards (not including EU accession referendums) were invalid due to low turnout rates, and the turnout remained below 50 per cent in eighteen cases.

Another difficulty is that an unsuccessful referendum may block a treaty for several years. In the case of an invalid or a negative result, a new referendum on the issue may not be re-initiated within four years in Poland, three years in Slovakia, two years in the Czech Republic, one year in Slovenia and, in the case of a constitutional amendment referendum,

Table 7.1 *Minimum turnout requirements in CEE referendums*[a]

Country	Minimum turnout	Type of referendum	Prohibition on repeat of referendum
Lithuania	3/4 of all citizens who have voting rights	Referendum on amending article 1 on independence	1 year for constitutional amendment referendum
	50% turnout	Ordinary referendums and referendums on amending ordinary constitutional provisions	
Latvia	50% turnout	Constitutional amendment referendums	–
	Half of the turnout rate of the previous parliamentary elections	Ordinary referendums and, since 2003, for EU referendums	
Slovakia	50% turnout	All referendums	3 years
Bulgaria	50% turnout	All referendums	–
Slovenia	50% turnout	Constitutional amendment referendums	1 year
	–	Ordinary referendums	
Poland	50% turnout	Ordinary referendums, in order to be binding (otherwise consultative referendum)	4 years
	–	Constitutional amendment referendums	
Hungary	25% approval of all citizens who have voting rights	Since 1997 for all referendums as a result of an amendment adopted before NATO referendum	–
	50% turnout	Before 1997 for all referendums	
Estonia	–	All referendums	1 year for constitutional amendment referendum
Romania	50%	All referendums	–
Czech Republic	–	Currently referendum may be held only for EU accession	2 years

[a] This table is a modified version of a table published in A. Albi, 'Referendums in the CEE Candidate Countries: Impact on EU Treaty Amendment Procedure' in C. Hillion (ed.), *EU Enlargement: A Legal Approach* (Hart, Oxford, 2004), p. 66, and A. Albi, *Referendums in Eastern Europe: The Effects on Reforming the EU Treaties and on the Candidate Countries' Positions in the Convention* (European University Institute, Robert Schuman Centre Working Paper No. 2002/65, Florence, 2002), p. 10.

in Estonia and Lithuania (see Table 7.1). In Estonia, Parliament must also be dissolved.

The remaining aspects of referendum procedures were, until the changes introduced ahead of the EU referendums, the following. In Slovakia, referendums may be held on 'important issues of public interest' (article 93(2)) and on joining 'state alliances' (article 93(1));[4] the use of the latter was envisaged for potential decisions over a closer relationship with the Czech Republic. A referendum is to be called by the President, on the request of 350,000 citizens, or on the basis of a resolution of Parliament, which in turn can be initiated by the government or parliamentary deputies (articles 95(1) and 96). Questions concerning basic rights and freedoms, taxes, levies and the state budget may not be the subject of a referendum (article 93(3)).

In Hungary, referendums may be held on 'any question falling within the competence of Parliament' (article 28B(1)).[5] Referendums may be consultative or have the objective of taking a decision; the holding of a referendum may be obligatory or discretionary (article 28C(1)). A referendum must be carried out at the request of 200,000 voters (article 28C(2)), or alternatively, Parliament has a discretion of holding a referendum on the proposal of the President, the government, one-third of deputies or 100,000 voters (article 28C(4)). No referendums may be held, *inter alia*, on the obligations arising from the treaties in force, on the content of the laws containing these obligations (but may on the future acceptance of treaty obligations), or on the constitutional provisions on national referendums (article 28C(5)). The result is binding if the holding of the referendum is obligatory (article 28C(3)).

In Poland, there are three types of referendums. First, article 90(3) of the constitution provides for an optional referendum for ratifying the treaty on joining international organisations referred to in article 90(1). The issue of whether the ratification shall be carried out by Parliament or by a popular referendum has to be decided by an absolute majority vote, in the presence of at least half of the Sejm members (article 90(4)). Secondly, article 125(1) provides for the possibility of holding a referendum in respect of 'matters of particular importance to the State'. This referendum may be ordered by the Sejm or by the President, with the consent of the Senate, to be given by an absolute majority vote, in the presence of at least half of all senators (article 125(2)). Thirdly, article 235 provides

[4] See also Referendum Law 1992.

[5] See also Law on National Public Initiative and Referendums 1998.

Table 7.2 *Referendums in CEE (other than EU referendums)*[a]

Country	Year	Issue	Turnout	Remarks
Lithuania	1991	Independence	84%	
	May 1992	Constitutional amendment establishing a presidential system	58%	Failure, as 50% approval of the total electorate required
	June 1992	Withdrawal of Soviet troops	76%	
	October 1992	Constitution	74%	
	1994	Illegal privatisation; savings compensation for inflation victims; early parliamentary elections	37%	Invalid
	October 1996	Expenditure of state budget; compensation of the loss of assets prior to 1990; decrease in size of Parliament (by amending articles 55, 57 and 131 of the Constitution)	52%	
	November 1996	Purchase of agricultural land by EU citizens	40%	Invalid
Slovakia	1994	Transparency of privatisation	20%	Invalid
	1997	NATO membership; nuclear weaponry and military bases	9.5%	Invalid
	1998	Privatisation of main state companies	44%	Invalid
	2000	Early elections	20%	Invalid
	2004	Early elections	36%	Invalid
Poland	1996	Privatisation	33%	Invalid
	1997	New constitution	43%	No minimum
Hungary	1990	Procedure of presidential elections	14%	Invalid
	1997	NATO membership	49%	Threshold majority 25% of the total electorate

Latvia	1991	Independence	88%	
	1998	Amendments to Citizenship Act	67%	
	1999	Amendments to Pensions Act	25%	Invalid
Slovenia	1990	Independence	93%	
	1996	Amendments to the electoral law	38%	Declared successful by the Constitutional Court for reasons of three different referendum questions being submitted
	1998	Consultative referendum on reform of local government system	Only electors of affected border areas were asked to participate	
	1999	Referendum on funding the construction of power plant TET3	27%	No minimum
	2001	Amendments to Law on Infertility Treatment	33%	No minimum
	January 2003	On privatisation of Telephone Society and railroads	31%	No minimum
	September 2003	On Sunday sales	28%	No minimum
	2004	Rights of former Yugoslav citizens	31.5%	Non-binding
Estonia	1991	Independence	82%	
	1992	Constitution	67%	
Romania	1991	Constitution	66%	

[a] This table is an expanded version of a table published in A. Albi, 'Referendums in the CEE Candidate Countries: Impact on EU Treaty Amendment Procedure' in C. Hillion (ed.), *EU Enlargement: A Legal Approach* (Hart, Oxford, 2004), pp. 67–8 and A. Albi, *Referendums in Eastern Europe: The Effects on Reforming the EU Treaties and on the Candidate Countries' Positions in the Convention* (European University Institute, Robert Schuman Centre Working Paper No. 2002/65, Florence, 2002), p. 11.

for the possibility of holding a confirmatory constitutional amendment referendum in the case of amending the provisions of Chapters I, II or XII of the constitution. This type of referendum may be initiated by the institutions that are entitled to initiate constitutional amendment proceedings. The important difference is that the constitutional amendment referendum does not have a minimum turnout requirement, while the two former types of referendums require the turnout of at least 50 per cent (articles 90(3), 125(3)).[6]

In Slovenia, the Parliament may call a referendum on any issue which forms the subject of regulation by law (article 90(1)), and on amending the constitution (article 170). The former type of referendum may be called on its own initiative, and must be called where so required by at least one-third of the deputies, by the National Council (the upper chamber of Parliament, whose decision on calling a referendum requires, under article 99(2), a majority vote of all members), or by 40,000 voters (article 90(2)). The constitutional amendment referendum must be called where so required by at least thirty deputies (article 170(1)). The former type of referendum can be approved by a majority of votes (article 90(4)), whereas the latter requires a 50 per cent turnout (article 170(2)).[7]

In Romania, a referendum is obligatory for amending the constitution (article 147(3)), and optional for 'matters of national interest' (article 90).[8] Referendums are initiated by the President, after consulting Parliament (article 90).

In the Czech Republic, only local referendums were provided in the constitution (article 9); a law was adopted for the EU accession referendum, to which we come later.

In Bulgaria, referendums may be held on issues that fall under the Parliament's competence (article 84(p5)).[9] The pertinent decision has to be taken by Parliament, on the proposal of one-fourth of all deputies or the Council of Ministers. No referendums are allowed on amending the constitution.

In the Baltic countries, the legal provisions on referendums were considerably changed ahead of EU referendums; the previous regime that

[6] See for the referendum procedure also Statute on Referendum 1995; W. Czaplinski, 'L'Intégration européenne dans la constitution polonaise de 1997' (2000) *Revue du Marché Commun et de l'Union Européenne* 171; S. Biernat, 'Constitutional Aspects of Poland's Future Membership in the European Union' (1998) 36 *Archiv des Völkerrechts* 408.

[7] See also Law on Referendum and Popular Initiative 1994.

[8] See also Bill on the Organisation and Unfolding of a Referendum 2001.

[9] See also Law on the Forms of Direct Democracy 1996.

largely continues to apply to non-EU-related issues is as follows. In Latvia, referendums were provided under the constitution for four procedural cases: (a) constitutional amendment of the fundamental constitutional provisions, including sovereignty (article 77); (b) laws withheld by the President, if requested by one-tenth of the electorate (article 72); (c) a draft law or a fully-elaborated new constitution submitted by one-tenth of voters but not adopted by Parliament (article 78); and (d) the President's proposal to dissolve Parliament.[10] Article 73 prohibits referendums on ratification of international treaties, but it has been suggested that the requirement of sovereignty as a fundamental constitutional principle outweighs the prohibition of a referendum on the Accession Treaty.[11] A constitutional amendment referendum requires that at least half of all citizens who have voting rights have voted in favour, while referendums on draft laws need the approval by the majority of half of the number of voters who participated in the previous parliamentary elections (article 79).

In Lithuania, there were three types of referendums prior to changes related to EU accession: (a) obligatory referendums in the case of amending article 1 (independence and democracy), Chapter 1 (state of Lithuania) or Chapter 14 (constitutional amendment procedure) of the constitution (article 148(1)); (b) optional referendums on 'the most significant issues concerning the life of the State and the People' (article 9); and (c) optional referendums on adopting provisions of laws (article 69(4)).[12] The important procedural difference is that the amendment of article 1 by referendum requires approval by three-fourths of all the citizens who have voting rights, while other referendums require a 50 per cent turnout, and one-third of all of the country's voters have to vote in favour to adopt a decision. The right to initiate a referendum belongs to one-third of the deputies or 300,000 voters (article 9).

In Estonia, there were three types of referendums: (a) the constitutional amendment referendum, the holding of which is mandatory for amending the fundamental provisions including sovereignty (article 162); (b) the referendum on 'important national issues' (article 105); and (c) the referendum on draft laws (article 105).[13] The two latter referendums have several procedural advantages. For instance, while the constitutional

[10] See also Law on Public Referendums and Legislative Initiatives 1994.

[11] A. Buka and K. Jarinovska, 'Will Referendum on Accession to the EU Take Place in Latvia?' (in Latvian) (1999) *Likums und Tiesibas*, no. 1.

[12] See also Law on Amending and Supplementing the Law on the Referendum 1994.

[13] Referendum Law 2002.

amendment referendum may be initiated by one-fifth of deputies or the President and requires a two-thirds majority of the Parliament membership, the two other referendums may be initiated by a wider range of institutions, and a simple majority suffices in Parliament. The constitutional amendment referendum and the referendum on draft laws additionally require a longer period of readings in Parliament. Furthermore, an unsuccessful referendum on constitutional amendment may not be re-initiated within one year (article 168), and all types of unsuccessful referendums lead to a declaration of extraordinary elections of Parliament (article 105(2)). The result of a referendum is binding on all state institutions. Referendums on ratification of international treaties are prohibited under article 106 of the constitution. However, the Constitutional Expert Commission has deemed it possible to hold a referendum on the ratification law of the Accession Treaty, because the Accession Treaty, in comparison with ordinary treaties, forms an 'extremely important statal choice'.[14] The Expert Commission has recalled in this respect a draft constitutional provision discussed in the Constitutional Assembly, which required the holding of a referendum should Estonia join a political, economic or military union of states. This provision was not included in the constitution because the referendum requirement would have essentially duplicated article 1, which, establishing the eternity and inalienability of sovereignty and independence, was meant to subject Estonia's accession to treaties that restrict sovereignty to a prior constitutional amendment by referendum.[15]

Public opinion and euroscepticism

Although the accession referendums, as will be seen in the next section, were won by large majorities and thus appear to convey a great deal of enthusiasm towards membership of the European Union amongst the populations of Central and Eastern Europe, the preparations for these referendums, in fact, took place in a rather different environment. Regardless of EU accession being an undisputed priority amongst the political elites in the candidate countries, and the marginal nature of the eurosceptic movements that were mainly found amongst the fringe parties outside the

[14] 'Põhiseaduse 7. peatükk "Seadusandlus". Põhiseaduse Ekspertiisikomisjoni aruanne' [Expert Commission's report on Chapter 7 of the Constitution 'Legislation'], in *Expert Commission's Final Report on the Estonian Constitution* (1998), available in Estonian at www.just.ee

[15] L. Hänni in *Põhiseadus ja Põhiseaduse Assamblee* [Constitution and Constitutional Assembly] (Õigusteabe AS Juura, Tallinn, 1996), p. 530, cited in 'Põhiseaduse 7. peatükk'.

Table 7.3 *Public support for joining the EU*[a]

	1996–1997		2000–2001		2002	
	for (%)	against (%)	for (%)	against (%)	for (%)	against (%)
Romania	70–80	2–4	76–85	3–4	85–86	4
Bulgaria	49–57	4	70–80	4	61–73	7–14
Slovakia	46–62	9	65–76	10–16	68–69	10–27
Hungary	47–56	9–15	54–70	10–15	72–76	6–10
Poland	63–80	5–7	44–60	26	53–67	22–25
Slovenia	47–57	14–18	42–63	22	55–56	27–28
Czech Republic	43–49	11–15	38–54	14–22	41–51	17–36
Estonia	29–35	14–17	38–54	27–59	38–54	28–38
Latvia	34	13	38–53	31–37	37–42	38–43
Lithuania	35–40	6–13	47–50	20–21	50–57	17–25

[a] This table is based on public opinion surveys available at the Eurobarometer websites http://europa.eu.int/comm/public_opinion and http://europa.eu.int/comm/enlargement/opinion/ and national polls reported in the *RFE/RL Newsline* (www.rferl.org). Since the questions posed and methodology used vary and the national polls tend to show lower support rates, the table provides the lowest and highest rates reported during the given period, in order to give a general overview of the support rates.

Parliaments, public opinion in a number of countries did not subscribe to this enthusiasm. The picture varies in different countries (see Table 7.3), but there was a tendency for popular support to decrease the more people realised the economic and social cost of speedy adoption of EU obligations. In 2000–2001, support for EU entry was under or on the border of 50 per cent in six candidate countries: Estonia, Latvia, Lithuania, Poland, the Czech Republic and Slovenia, according to national public opinion surveys; it should be noted, however, that the Eurobarometer surveys and some national polls have shown higher support rates (see Table 7.3). The highest number of people against EU accession was recorded in Estonia in May 2001, when 59 per cent would have voted against EU accession. However, Estonia's victorious performance in the 2001 Eurovision song contest, and public enthusiasm surrounding the holding of the 2002 Eurovision contest in Tallinn, strikingly increased the support for the EU to 54 per cent by August 2001.[16] Since then, Latvia has taken up the position

[16] Reported respectively in *Postimees*, 19 May 2001 and *Postimees*, 25 August 2001.

of the most eurosceptic country: 43 per cent intended to vote against EU entry in 2001, had a referendum been held then. In the three Baltic countries and the Czech Republic, support for accession had also been consistently low in the preceding years. On the other hand, support rates have been constantly high in Bulgaria and Romania, countries further away from accession, as well as in Hungary and Slovakia. In Poland, euro-optimism decreased from 80 per cent in May 1996 to 55 per cent in June 1999, as the cost of adopting the EU environmental, technical and social standards became visible.[17]

With accession drawing closer, a shift towards a more 'euro-realist' or even eurosceptic stance also occurred amongst some more mainstream parties. For instance, Hungary's FIDESZ party, moving from government to opposition in the aftermath of the 2001 elections, started to highlight in its so-called 'yes, but' campaign problems accompanying the accession process. In Estonia, the Centre Party, one of the leading parties especially amongst the countryside population, voted in its annual congress in August 2003 against EU membership. The Czech Communist Party called on voters to reject EU accession outright,[18] and the same view was taken by the Socialist Party in Latvia.[19] In Poland, the position of the right-wing anti-EU parties Self-Defence and the League of Polish Families has consistently strengthened.

The reasons for euroscepticism vary in individual countries, but some common issues could be pointed out. These include the economic cost of speedy adoption of the EU's rather expensive environmental, technical and other standards; the fear of losing national identity and sovereignty (especially so in the Baltic countries); the rise of prices after accession; the fear of becoming second-class members, especially after the EU's proposal to grant just 25 per cent of the agricultural subsidies to the farmers of the acceding countries; the sensitive question of sale of land to foreigners; and the governments having to give priority to EU demands rather than financing some more urgent priorities, such as healthcare and education. In Estonia, euroscepticism has mainly formed a protest against the government's decade of ultra-liberal policies and, in addition, there are fears regarding the cost of harmonisation, the loss of Finnish mass tourism

[17] G. Blazyca and M. Kolkiewicz, 'Poland and the EU: Internal Disputes, Domestic Politics and Accession' (1999) 15 *Journal of Communist Studies and Transition Politics* 137.

[18] 'Czech Communists Call for "No" Vote in EU Referendum', *RFE/RL Newsline*, vol. 7, no. 79, Part II, 25 April 2003.

[19] 'Latvian Socialist Party Called People to Say No in Referendum', *BNS News*, 11 August 2003.

due to the abolition of tax-free shopping and the loss of low-cost import markets of raw materials due to the customs union.[20] The Lithuanians' concerns revolve particularly around the expected closure of the country's principal energy source, the nuclear power plant at Ignalina. In the Czech Republic, the EU is seen as 'overregulating, socialist and collectivist in comparison with Czech liberalism',[21] which also holds true for many circles in Estonia. The views of Czechs have also been influenced by consistent eurosceptic statements of President Vaclav Klaus who, albeit supporting the accession in general, regards EU membership as 'a marriage of convenience, but not of love'.[22] In some countries (e.g. Poland, Estonia, Latvia), it has also been pointed out that the EU's low reputation is partly due to the fact that governments have justified many unpopular and costly decisions by pleading EU requirements, even where the connection is rather tenuous or even non-existent. In fact, in the Baltic countries, the principal argument for EU membership has been their security with regard to Russia: according to a poll conducted in 2000, two-thirds of Estonians considered Russia to be a threat to Estonia's independence, and it was commented that the result of the referendum was dependent on developments in Russia.[23] On the other hand, the Slovenes have been primarily concerned about having to wait for the less prepared countries, while being themselves economically ready.

Accession referendums: procedural 'manoeuvres'

Notwithstanding the above concerns, the referendums on entry to the EU were overwhelmingly won, especially compared with EU referendums amongst the 'old' Member States. Indeed, approximately 92 per cent voted in favour in the Slovak referendum (16–17 May 2003), 91 per cent in Romania (18–19 October), 90 per cent in Slovenia (23 March) and Lithuania (10–11 May), 84 per cent in Hungary (12 April), 77 per cent in Poland (7–8 June) and the Czech Republic (14–15 June), 68 per cent in

[20] See for a wider discussion P. Ehin, 'Estonian Euroskepticism: A Reflection of Domestic Politics?' (2002/2003) 11/12 *East European Constitutional Review*, no. 4/1.

[21] C. Perron, *Views of Czech Local Politicians on European Integration* (European University Institute, Robert Schuman Centre Working Paper No. 2000/39, Florence, 2000), pp. 17–18.

[22] 'Czech President Says EU Accession is No "Marriage of Love"', *RFE/RL Newsline*, vol. 7, no. 73, Part II, 16 April 2003.

[23] J. Kivirähk, 'Eestlased kardavad Venemaad, muulased mitte' [Estonians are Afraid of Russia, Non-Estonians Not], *Eesti Päevaleht*, 29 March 2000, and M. Kirch, 'Eestlaste otsus tulevasel euroreferendumil sõltub Venemaast' [Estonians' Decision in the Euroreferendum Depends on Russia], *Eesti Päevaleht*, 28 March 2000.

Table 7.4 *EU accession referendums*[a]

Country	Type of referendum	Date (2003)	Turnout	'Yes'	'No'
Slovenia	Ordinary	23 March	60.3	89.6	10.4
Hungary	Ordinary	12 April	45.6	83.8	16.2
Lithuania	Ordinary	10–11 May	63.3	91	8.9
Slovakia	Ordinary	16–17 May	52.2	92.5	6.2
Poland	Ordinary	7–8 June	58.9	77.5	22.6
Czech Republic	New type: EU accession	13–14 June	55.2	77.3	22.7
Estonia	New type: accession and 'supplementing' of the Constitution	14 September	64	66.9	33
Latvia	New type: EU accession	20 September	72.5	67	32.3
Romania	On constitutional revision	18–19 October	55.7	91	8.9
Bulgaria	Not yet held	–	–	–	–

[a] This table is compiled on the basis of data available at www.euractiv.com

Estonia (14 September), and 67 per cent in Latvia (20 September). The results are also presented in Table 7.4.

However, this successful end-game was preceded by a few years of anxiety and political and procedural manoeuvring, due to the above-discussed minimum turnout requirements, high proportion of earlier unsuccessful referendums and relatively eurosceptic public opinion. To start with, a number of countries considered the option of not holding a referendum at all, even though recourse to referendums has otherwise been frequent, even in the case of relatively minor issues. In Poland, it has been reported that the government disliked the idea of holding a referendum given the slippage in pro-EU sentiment in the public opinion polls in 1999–2000,[24] and that a referendum was equally unlikely due to Parliament's concern about constantly low election rates.[25] In the Czech Republic, the government initially opposed a referendum on the EU, and it was preferred in many circles to accede by means of a parliamentary ratification of the Accession Treaty.[26] In Estonia, it was not clear until

24 Blazyca and Kolkiewicz, 'Poland and the EU', p. 141.

25 Czaplinski, 'L'Intégration européenne', p. 171.

26 Perron, *Views of Czech Local Politicians*, p. 20; D. Plichta, 'Czech Law Settles Referendum on EU-Membership', *Current Concerns*, no. 5, 26 November 2002, www.currentconcerns.ch/archive/20020309.php

2001 whether a referendum would be held at all; the then President Meri proposed to hold a referendum a few years after joining the EU, so that the people could decide whether they wanted to continue EU membership.[27] A political consensus among the Parliament's parties was finally achieved in March 2001,[28] on holding a referendum on the accession as an issue of national importance, as opposed to the more challenging constitutional amendment referendum. Objection to holding a referendum was also encountered in many of Lithuania's governing circles where ratification of the Accession Treaty by Parliament was favoured instead;[29] the Rapporteur of the constitutional amendment Working Group pointed to the difficulty of achieving a majority with 50 per cent turnout, given the low public support rates for the EU.[30] On the other hand, the Slovene government made it clear from the outset that a referendum would be held in the country prior to ratification of the Accession Treaty.

Amongst those countries where amendment of the constitution is subject to a referendum, a constitutional amendment referendum was only held in Romania. The Baltic countries, where a referendum is required for the amendment of sovereignty, interpreted the accession in a manner which did not find harm to sovereignty, and created instead new types of referendums for EU accession, involving a facilitation of procedural requirements. In Estonia, the Referendum Act was amended in October 2002 to permit holding together two types of referendums – on the 'supplementing' of the constitution and on an 'important national issue'. Thus, the people were asked in a single question whether they approved the supplementing of the constitution and accession to the EU. Initially, two separate questions had been envisaged, but there was a risk of a constitutional deadlock should one be answered in the affirmative and the other in the negative. In Latvia, the constitutional amendment Working Group found that the constitution did not provide for possibilities for

[27] H. Roonemaa, 'Meri: rahvas võiks aastate pärast hääletada euroliidust välja astumist' [Meri: the People Could Vote on Secession from the EU after a Few Years], *Eesti Päevaleht*, 5 May 2001.

[28] 'Erakonnad jõudsid euroreferendumi suhtes kokkuleppele' [The Parties Reached an Agreement with regard to Euroreferendum], *Eesti Päevaleht*, 17 March 2001.

[29] Reported by G. Vitkus, *Referendums on the Membership in the European Union: The History, Issues and Lessons for Lithuania: Summary* (2003), available at www.leidykla.vu.lt/inetleid/politol/25/s1.html

[30] V. Vadapalas, 'Lithuania: The Constitutional Impact of the Enlargement at National Level' in A. Kellermann, J. De Zwaan and J. Czuczai (eds.), *EU Enlargement: The Constitutional Impact at EU and National Level* (Asser Press, The Hague, 2001), p. 351; also 'Constitution Watch: Lithuania' (2002) 11 *East European Constitutional Review*, no. 3.

holding an EU referendum because accession would not harm sovereignty and independence. Therefore, a new type of referendum was created for EU issues, which has a reduced turnout requirement. In Lithuania, a new Referendum Law was adopted on 4 June 2002, which simplified the procedure.[31] The new Law dropped a clause requiring that one-third of all of the country's voters had to vote in favour in order to adopt a decision, although the 50 per cent minimum turnout requirement for the validity of a referendum was retained. However, the threshold majority was kept for referendums on joining international organisations that involve ceding of sovereign rights, where at least 30 per cent of the total electorate must still vote in favour. The new Referendum Law provides two types of referendums: binding and consultative. Binding referendums are to be held on the amendment of the constitution and on participation in international organisations when it involves a partial transfer of powers of state bodies; the latter was also used for the entry into the EU.

In most countries, wariness about meeting the turnout triggered some procedural manoeuvres or proposals to this effect. One of these was the lowering of the turnout requirement. As seen above, the turnout requirement was reduced in Latvia, Hungary having done so already in 1997 ahead of the NATO referendum. In Poland, Parliament adopted a statute that allowed it to ratify the accession agreement itself in case the turnout were to remain under 50 per cent. Some opposition members of the Sejm asked the Constitutional Tribunal to review the constitutionality of this law, but such a mechanism was found to be acceptable by the court.[32] In Lithuania, Prime Minister Algirdas Brasauskas recommended reducing the turnout requirement in January ahead of the referendum,[33] and the same was suggested in Romania by President Ion Iliescu.[34] Proposals were also repeatedly voiced to this effect in Slovakia. In the Czech Republic, the requirement for a minimum turnout of 50 per cent was one of the main reasons why the Referendum Law underwent several years of deliberations, along with disputes on whether there should be

[31] 'Constitution Watch: Lithuania' (2002) 11 *East European Constitutional Review*, no. 3; 'Lithuanian Parliament Passes New Referendum Law', *RFE/RL Newsline*, vol. 6, no. 104, Part II, 5 June 2002.

[32] Decision of 27 May 2003.

[33] 'Lithuanian Premier Wants to Lower the Bar in EU Referendum', *RFE/RL Newsline*, vol. 7, no. 13, Part II, 22 January 2003.

[34] 'Romanians Approve New Constitution', *RFE/RL Newsline*, vol. 7, no. 200, Part II, 21 October 2003.

a two-year prohibition period before repeating a referendum in case of failure.[35]

Another way of dealing with the issue of turnout has been the extension of the referendums over two days; the referendum laws were amended in this respect in Lithuania, Slovakia, the Czech Republic, Poland and Romania. Latvia's Parliament too considered this option, but extended instead the voting time by three hours.[36] In Romania, the extension was effected by amending the Referendum Law, which is an 'organic' law, by means of an ordinance; this move encountered criticism about its constitutionality.[37] Poland amended the Referendum Law once more on 10 May 2003, in order to allow the Central Election Commission to disclose the turnout after the first day of the referendum, with the aim of mobilising voters to show up on the second day.[38] A number of countries considered the option of holding a consultative rather than a binding referendum, including Estonia, Lithuania and Poland. For instance, in Lithuania, the Coordination Council of the Information Campaign for Entry to the EU recommended in February 2003 to downgrade the referendum to an advisory referendum, in order to avoid the minimum turnout requirement.[39] Later that spring, the Lithuanian Parliament adopted a Bill which allowed the removal from the list of approximately 200,000 persons who had travelled abroad and would thus be unlikely to participate in the referendum; however, this Bill was vetoed by the President in May shortly before the referendum.[40]

Recourse was made to various other devices in order to encourage turnout. In Poland, Pope John Paul II exhorted Poles to vote in favour of EU membership. This was followed by a letter, read aloud in Catholic churches throughout the country on 1 June, in which bishops called on the faithful to vote in the EU referendum.[41] Further, the government allowed

[35] 'Czech Senate Approves EU Referendum Legislation', *RFE/RL Newsline*, vol. 6, no. 178, Part II, 20 September 2002; Perron, *Views of Czech Local Politicians*, p. 20; Plichta, 'Czech Law Settles Referendum'.

[36] *RFE/RL Baltic States Report*, vol. 4, no. 29, p. 16.

[37] 'Extremist Party Criticizes Decision to Hold Two-day Referendum', *RFE/RL Newsline*, vol. 7, no. 195, Part II, 14 October 2003.

[38] 'Polish Parliament Changes Referendum Law to Boost EU Vote's Turnout', *RFE/RL Newsline*, vol. 7, no. 88, Part II, 12 May 2003.

[39] 'Is EU Vote to Be Downgraded to "Advisory" Referendum?', *RFE/RL Baltic States Report*, vol. 4, no. 7, 28 February 2003.

[40] 'Lithuania's Council of National Communities Supports EU Membership', *RFE/RL Newsline*, vol. 7, no. 85, Part II, 6 May 2003.

[41] 'Polish Roman Catholic Church Urges Faithful to Vote in EU Referendum', *RFE/RL Newsline*, vol. 7, no. 102, Part II, 2 June 2003.

students to vote in universities, as many of them would not have been able to travel home, and free rides to the polling stations were provided by Warsaw's taxis to the elderly.[42] In Romania, free football tickets were distributed to voters.[43] In Lithuania, the President and the Prime Minister made a dramatic appeal in the evening of the first day on national television to encourage people to vote. In addition, Catholic priests encouraged people at Sunday's mass to go from the churches to the polls, and a supermarket chain offered free bottles of beer and chocolate to those who had voted.[44] In many countries, the EU referendums were criticised for rather aggressive and one-sided campaigns. For instance, according to Lithuanian observers, a critical tone was almost absent in the country's media,[45] and the government in Hungary was accused of Communist-style propaganda.[46]

Finally, the timing of the referendums was carefully tailored. In the summer of 2002, the leaders of the Vishegrad countries proposed to coordinate their referendums, starting with the most pro-EU, Hungary, and moving then to more eurosceptic Poland and the Czech Republic. This aimed to benefit from the so-called 'domino theory', anticipating that 'yes' votes in countries that enjoyed firm public support for accession would help relieve the hesitations of the more sceptical publics.[47] This was also made use of in the Baltics – the referendums started in pro-EU Lithuania and ended with Latvia, where support for the EU had been the lowest. There were also proposals to hold referendums on days of symbolic importance, albeit to no avail. For instance, the Polish Prime Minister Leszek Miller proposed to hold the EU referendum in May 2003 because of the historical significance of this month commemorating the end of the Second World War, which led to the division of Europe.[48] The Baltic Assembly called

42 'Poola euroreferendumit ähvardas läbikukkumine' [Polish EU Referendum was Threatened by a Failure], *Postimees*, 9 June 2003.

43 M. Percival, 'Promoting the Highest Law in the Land . . . by Breaking the Law' in *Vivid* (Bucharest English language magazine), November 2003, also available at www.thinktankromania.ro/documents/Vivid%20Nov%2003%20(Link%2040).pdf

44 'Leedu hääletas nagu iseseisvust taastades' [Lithuania Voted as when Re-establishing Independence], *Postimees*, 13 May 2003; 'Lithuanians Overwhelmingly Approve EU Membership', *RFE/RL Newsline*, vol. 7, no. 88, Part II, 12 May 2003.

45 C. Ishkauskas, 'Esmatähtis on kartul, referendum tuleb pärast' [Potatoes are of Primary Importance, Referendum follows Afterwards], *Postimees*, 14 May 2003.

46 'As Finger-Pointing Follows Low Turnout', *RFE/RL Newsline*, vol. 7, no. 71, Part II, 14 April 2003.

47 Ehin, 'Estonian Euroskepticism'.

48 'Polish Premier Proposes to Hold EU Referendum in May 2003', *RFE/RL Newsline*, vol. 6, no. 169, Part II, 9 September 2002.

upon the three Baltic countries to hold simultaneous EU referendums on 23 August 2003, in order to celebrate the Baltic unity demonstrated in 1989, when two million people formed a chain from Vilnius to Tallinn in a call for independence, on the fiftieth anniversary of the Molotov-Ribbentrop Secret Pact.

Notwithstanding the above 'manoeuvres', the turnout still remained relatively modest in Hungary (42 per cent, which translates into support by just 38 per cent of eligible voters); Slovakia (52 per cent) and Romania (56 per cent). In Romania, Poland and Lithuania, anxiety was caused by the low participation on the first day – 14 per cent, 17 per cent and 23 per cent respectively. On the other hand, the Slovak turnout rate could be celebrated for it being the first successful referendum in the country.

The irregularities surrounding the referendums triggered in some countries challenges in the Constitutional Courts. In Estonia, altogether nine complaints were submitted to the National Court concerning the referendum; these were rejected on procedural grounds (e.g. passing of a deadline). These challenges were closely related to those brought against the 'supplementing' rather than 'amending' of the constitution, which were addressed in more detail in chapter 5. As regards those aspects pertaining specifically to the referendum, the following claims were made. The afore-mentioned eurosceptic leader Kalle Kulbok challenged the legality of the fusion of two types of referendums.[49] According to him, the question – 'Do you support accession to the European Union and the adoption of the Law on Supplementing the Estonian Constitution?' – was a multipart question, which left voters in confusion as to which question was to be answered. Further, he argued that 'supplementing' the constitution was void because the Referendum Law does not allow adoption of laws by means of a referendum on an 'important national issue', and that the accession referendum cannot be regarded as a mixture of a constitutional amendment referendum and a referendum on an 'important national issue', because the referendum outcomes enter into force at different times under article 63 of the Referendum Law. The claim by Helle Vilu and the Estonian Voters Union argued that the referendum question contained two mutually exclusive parts, since it was not possible to join the EU before the amendment of the constitution, and, in addition, it was not possible at the same time to keep Estonia's sovereignty and

[49] *Kulbok*, Decision No. 3-4-1-12-03, 29 September 2003, available at www.nc.ee. See also chapter 5 for discussion of this case.

independence, and grant part of it to the EU.[50] The claimants also argued that the constitution could only be 'amended' and not 'supplemented' by an independent act. Most of the remaining seven complaints concerned the unclear formulation of the multipart question, and alleged procedural breaches of the Referendum Law.

Amongst other countries, the far-right Justice and Life Party in Hungary claimed that Hungary's referendum question was worded ambiguously. The Supreme Court rejected this, finding the question to be in compliance with the law.[51] In Romania, the Greater Romania Party challenged the referendum results on the grounds of multiple voting, overuse of mobile balloting, and because of authorities' offering incentives to participate in the referendum in several localities.[52] The Constitutional Court refused to rule on grounds of lack of competence.[53] In Latvia, members of the Socialist Party challenged in the Constitutional Court the legitimacy of the EU referendum, pleading its illegality given that the country's non-citizen population (22 per cent) could not participate in the vote.[54]

What types of referendums were held in those countries that have not been mentioned? Besides Estonia, Latvia and Lithuania, new types of referendums were created in the Czech Republic and Slovenia. In the Czech Republic, the possibility of adopting a referendum law for entry into international organisations that involve a transfer of powers was envisaged in article 10a(2), which formed part of the EU-related constitutional amendments of 2001. Indeed, after rather long debates, the Referendum Law was finally adopted in November 2002. It did not set out a requirement for a minimum turnout, but prohibited repeating the referendum within two years should the outcome be negative. Slovene EU amendments of 2003 equally provided that before ratifying an international treaty involving a transfer of powers, Parliament may call a referendum, and is bound by its result (article 3a). Slovakia, Hungary, Poland and Romania all used the pre-existing types of referendums: referendum on 'important issues of public interest' in Slovakia (article 93(2) of the constitution); on 'any question falling within the competence of the Parliament' in Hungary

[50] *Vilu and Estonian Voters Union*, Decision No. 3-4-1-11-03, 24 September 2003, available at www.nc.ee. See also chapter 5 for discussion of this case.

[51] Decision of 26 March 2003, reported in 'Hungarian Supreme Court Rejects EU Referendum Challenge', *RFE/RL Newsline*, vol. 7, no. 59, Part II, 27 March 2003.

[52] 'Romanian Opposition Parties, NGOs Challenge Constitutional Referendum', *RFE/RL Newsline*, vol. 7, No. 202, Part II, 23 October 2003.

[53] Decision of 23 October 2003, reported in 'Romanian Constitutional Court Validates Referendum', *RFE/RL Newsline*, vol. 7, no. 203, Part II, 24 October 2003.

[54] Reported in *RFE/RL Baltic States Report*, vol. 5, no. 4, 10 February 2004.

(article 28B(1)); on ratifying the treaty on joining international organisations in Poland (article 90(3)); and on constitutional amendments in Romania (article 147(3)). As regards the referendum questions, these were worded in a relatively straightforward manner, with the afore-mentioned exception of fusing two questions into one in Estonia which caused a lot of confusion. In other countries, it was either simply asked whether the country should join the EU (e.g. Slovakia, Hungary), or a clause was added on joining 'on the conditions envisaged in the Accession Treaty' (e.g. the Czech Republic).

As concerns Bulgaria, President Georgi Parvanov has suggested holding a referendum on EU membership in 2006.[55] The Bulgarian referendum is equally likely to be successful, although it has been pointed out that support for the EU may decrease should the issue be linked to the closure of the controversial Kozloduy nuclear power plant, as demanded by the EU.

It may also be interesting to note that a number of referendum initiatives have been submitted with regard to various other aspects of EU entry, in particular land sales to foreigners and the closure of nuclear power plants. In Lithuania, a referendum on the sale of agricultural land to EU citizens was in fact held in 1996, but it failed due to an insufficient turnout. Another referendum on this issue has been requested since 2000 by left-wing opposition parties;[56] the issue was settled, as seen in chapter 5, by a constitutional amendment and a transition period. A referendum has also been requested in respect of the closure of the second reactor of the Ignalina nuclear power plant.[57] The issue of land sales to foreigners also led to calls for a referendum in Poland, where the League of Polish Families submitted in 2002 a motion for a referendum, which was later rejected by the Sejm.[58] In Hungary, a referendum on the sale of land to EU citizens was initially supposed to take place together with that on NATO in 1997. The opposition parties had collected signatures in this respect, but since the government proposed at the same time a referendum with its own set of questions on land sales and NATO, the opposition

[55] 'Bulgarian Foreign Minister Scolds President over EU-Referendum Proposal', *RFE/RL Newsline*, vol. 8, no. 15, Part II, 26 January 2004.

[56] 'Lithuanian Government, Opposition Agree on EU Action Plan', *RFE/RL Newsline*, vol. 2, Part II, 22 January 2001; 'Constitution Watch: Lithuania' (2002) 11 *East European Constitutional Review*, no. 1/2.

[57] 'Two Referendums to be Proposed in Lithuania', *RFE/RL Newsline*, vol. 6, no. 103, Part II, 4 June 2002.

[58] 'Polish Parliament Blocks Referendum on Land Sales', *EU Observer*, 14 November 2002, www.euobserver.com

made recourse to the Constitutional Court, which gave precedence to the former referendum as it had been initiated by citizens.[59] However, the referendum initiative was later dropped from the agenda, partly following the finding of the Parliament's Constitutional Committee that the proposed referendum would violate Hungary's treaty obligations, especially the GATT and the Europe Agreement, after the adoption of the new Referendum Law in February 1998. Nevertheless, this issue resurfaced in 2003, when Hajra Magyarorszag (Go, Hungary), a movement linked to the far-right Hungarian Justice and Life Party, gathered signatures in favour of such a referendum. The Constitutional Court rejected this initiative, due to a constitutional ban on referendums on commitments resulting from treaties.[60] In Bulgaria, various movements, including the Macedonian Revolutionary Organization, the opposition Socialist Party and the country's two largest trade unions, called in December 2002 for a referendum on the closure of two reactors of the Kozloduy nuclear power plant, which has been envisaged in the government's agreement with the EU.[61] In Estonia, the Social Democratic Labour Party and five other small, mainly eurosceptic parties deemed it necessary to hold two referendums, first on amending the constitution and second on joining the EU. They insisted on holding a referendum before the accession negotiations, in order to legitimise the pre-accession adaptations.

To borrow from a title of a presentation on the topic, the 'ghost of euroscepticism did not materialise'.[62] On the contrary, the referendums were eventually won by large margins. With procedural changes and rather aggressive campaigns, all countries secured positive results. These moves are understandable in the light of the high costs involved in remaining outside the EU, especially those related to geopolitical concerns, security and economy. Given the drastic history of Central and Eastern Europe,

[59] Decision No. 52/1997, 14 October 1997 *On Referendums*, in L. Solym and G. Brunner (eds.), *Constitutional Judiciary in a New Democracy: The Hungarian Constitutional Court* (Michigan University Press, 2000), pp. 371–8. See also 'Constitution Watch: Hungary' (1997) 6 *East European Constitutional Review*, no. 4.

[60] Decision of 23 September 2003, reported in 'Hungarian Constitutional Court Rules Against Referendum on Farmland Ownership', *RFE/RL Newsline*, vol. 7, no. 182, Part II, 24 September 2003.

[61] 'Protesters in Bulgarian Capital Demand Referendum on Kozloduy', *RFE/RL Newsline*, vol. 6, no. 225, Part II, 3 December 2002.

[62] V. Pettai, 'The Ghost that Didn't Materialize: Estonian Euroscepticism and the EU Referendum', paper presented at workshop 'Les référendums d'adhésion à l'Union européenne', organised by Groupe d'Analyses Electorales and Centre d'Etudes Politiques sur l'Europe du Nord, University of Lille, 13 October 2003, see www.afsp.msh-paris.fr/activite/groupe/gael/gaelje131003.html

the countries could simply not afford to risk remaining outside the EU, in a geopolitical 'grey zone'. However, some questions of legitimacy may remain and it would perhaps be a good occasion to consider facilitating procedural requirements for the future. For instance, some Lithuanian analysts have eloquently pointed out the 'ethica or moral stakes' concerning the referendum in their country,[63] or have disapproved changes in 'the rules of the game', as this may involve some degree of manipulation of the laws, and hence go against the principle of the rule of law, increasing public distrust in democratic values.[64] The above account of the tensions also complements our previous discussion of constitutional amendments, exemplifying the sensitivity of the wider context in which the debates regarding constitutional amendments for accession to the EU took place.

Implications for the EU treaty amendment procedure

It would be a mistake to regard the above-discussed procedural and political complications concerning referendums solely as an internal issue of the countries of Central and Eastern Europe. Since the amending of the Treaties in the EU requires approval by all countries under 'national constitutional procedures' (Article 48 TEU), these are likely to have a wider significance in the enlarged Union.[65] Although the issue of facilitating the treaty amendment procedure was under consideration in the Convention on the Future of Europe, the current procedure was largely left unmodified in the European Constitution, given that the requirement of ratification by all Member States has widely been perceived as a cornerstone for retaining sovereignty, as well as a defining element in characterising the EU's new basic document as a treaty rather than a constitution.[66] However, the fragility of this procedure was well demonstrated with the first Irish referendum on the Nice Treaty, where 33 per cent of the voters of a small country were able to block the Treaty's entry into force. The above sections show that enlargement does not increase the potential of paralysis just by virtue of a dramatic rise in the number of Member

[63] Reported by Vitkus, 'Referendums on Membership'.

[64] *Debates on a Referendum on Lithuania's Membership in the EU* (Lithuanian Free Market Institute, February 2003), see www.freema.org/Projects/Referendum.phtml

[65] This section draws on Albi, 'Referendums in the CEE Candidate Countries' and Albi, *Referendums in Eastern Europe*.

[66] See chapter 10 for changes in the amendment procedure of the Draft European Constitution.

States, but also because the 'national constitutional procedures' in the CEE countries, in particular referendums, do involve distinct procedural and political complications. In the case of the accession referendums, governments succeeded in mobilising the people for a positive outcome due to the paramount importance of the issue. However, this exercise may be rather more difficult should referendums be held on the European Constitution or its future amendments.[67] Indeed, the notoriously low turnout rates in the European Parliament elections of June 2004 strengthen the case for such concerns. The average turnout in the new Member States from Central and Eastern Europe was just 26.4 per cent, with the lowest results in Slovakia (16.7 per cent), Poland (20.5 per cent) and Estonia (26.7 per cent).

It is therefore likely that discussions on facilitating the amendment procedure of the European Constitution will resume in future. Therefore, it would be appropriate to consider which options have been considered so far for facilitating the procedure. In broad outline, the proposals proceeded from the division of the treaties into two parts.[68] The fundamental part would be amended infrequently and in accordance with 'national constitutional procedures'. The second part, which would comprise provisions of a technical, functional and implementing nature and would not directly affect the Member States' sovereignty, would be subject to an easier amendment procedure by EU institutions. The idea was first officially tabled by the so-called Dehaene Group in 1999.[69] It was then considered in 2000 by the Robert Schuman Centre of the European University Institute (EUI), which produced a Draft Basic Treaty, on the mandate of the European Commission,[70] followed by the Second Report examining the modalities of facilitating the amendment procedures.[71]

[67] We will come to referendums on the European Constitution in individual CEE countries in chapter 10.

[68] See in more detail B. De Witte, 'Entry into Force and Revision' in B. De Witte (ed.), *Ten Reflections on the Constitutional Treaty for Europe* (EUI-RSCAS/AEL, Florence, 2003), available at www.iue.it/RSCAS/Publications, pp. 203–20.

[69] R. Weizsäcker, J.-L. Dehaene and D. Simon, *The Institutional Implications of Enlargement: Report to the European Commission, Brussels* (18 October 1999), http://europa.eu.int/igc2000/repoct99_en.pdf

[70] *A Basic Treaty for the European Union: A Study of the Reorganisation of the Treaties* (European University Institute, Robert Schuman Centre, Florence, 15 May 2000), www.iue.it/RSC/Treaties.html

[71] *Reforming the Treaties' Amendment Procedures: Second Report on the Reorganising of the European Union Treaties* (European University Institute, Robert Schuman Centre, Florence, 31 July 2000), www.iue.it/RSC/Treaties.html

However, as regards retaining unanimity for the constitutional part, a number of other challenges have been pointed out besides the above-discussed risk of blockage resulting from unsuccessful referendums. For instance, Peter-Christian Müller-Graff has expressed scepticism about the effective decrease in the need for amendments, unless the Basic Treaty would be reduced to 'a minimum of undisputed and highly abstract principles', and he doubts that a final solution for the institutional structure could be found in view of the continuous contest between 'different forces of supranationality, national sovereignty and democracy'.[72] Further, the afore-mentioned Second Report of the European University Institute pointed out that the solutions in the Intergovernmental Conferences have often come down to the lowest common denominator, therefore frequently necessitating new Intergovernmental Conferences. The Report also pointed out that exceptions have to be formulated for individual Member States in a non-transparent manner, and that the unanimity requirement for amending the Treaties is rare in international organisations as well as in the constitutions of federal states.

Against the backdrop of these concerns, the following alternative mechanisms have been proposed. The EUI Report recommended a superqualified majority of four-fifths or nine-tenths of the Member States representing four-fifths of the population, with a blocking majority of at least two states. In addition, the EUI Report recommended a wider use of the autonomous amendment procedures by EU institutions for issues of a technical nature, and the introduction of the so-called 'negative ratification', a mode borrowed from international law according to which a treaty enters into force unless a notification of disagreement is submitted. Amongst other proposals, the President of the Convention, Valéry Giscard d'Estaing, has on several occasions called for holding an EU-wide referendum, which has been supported by a letter of ninety-six delegates of the Convention.[73] In practice, this is more likely to take the form of simultaneous referendums in those Member States that have a tradition of holding referendums, and parliamentary ratifications in the others. Amongst other proposals, the Commission has offered a controversial secession clause for non-ratifying countries in one of its drafts for

[72] P. C. Müller-Graff, 'The Future of the European Treaties: A Systematic Approach to a Basic Treaty' in A.Von Bogdandy, P. C. Mavroidis and Y. Meny (eds.), *European Integration and International Co-ordination: Studies in Transnational Economic Law in Honour of Claus-Dieter Ehlermann* (Aspen Publishers, The Hague, 2002), p. 344.

[73] 'Call for EU-wide Referendums on New Constitution', 13 June 2003, www.eubusiness.com

a constitutional treaty, known as the 'Penelope'. Proposals have also been put forward for creating special bodies for amending the secondary treaty, and for making a more frequent recourse to the mechanisms of enhanced cooperation and flexibility.

Although it is beyond the scope of this study to examine the amendment process further, one possibility to explore in future could be the use of national constituent bodies, perhaps to be called 'national conventions', in the process of ratification. These 'national conventions' could be composed of members of national Parliaments, as well as of representatives of regional and local governments and of civic society. The advantage of such expanded fora lies in providing a higher legitimacy than normal parliamentary ratification to future treaty amendments, which is important given the far-reaching constitutional implications of EU Treaties, in comparison with ordinary international treaties. A further advantage of such a mechanism is that it would help to avoid the well-known shortcomings of national referendums: populism, EU debates' being hijacked by domestic issues or even (un)popularity of national governments, as well as the constant threat of a new treaty being blocked by one or two countries.

8

Membership of NATO and other international organisations

NATO

In the wake of regime change, the countries of Central and Eastern Europe have also become members of various other international organisations. In terms of the strict protection of sovereignty in the CEE constitutions, the participation in the North Atlantic Treaty Organisation (NATO) is of particular interest. The Czech Republic, Hungary and Poland joined NATO in 1999; Slovakia, Slovenia, Romania, Bulgaria and the Baltic countries received their invitation to join in the autumn of 2002.

The main restrictions on a state's sovereign action by membership of NATO could be summarised as follows. As regards autonomy of external action, the state is constrained in making decisions upon war – it has to join in collective defence in the event of an aggression against one of the allied countries, under the North Atlantic Treaty concluded in 1949 in Washington. In terms of inviolability of state borders, a NATO member has to grant the right of passage or manoeuvre to certain foreign troops within its territory. In financial terms, a member country has an obligation to spend at least 2 per cent of its budget on defence. In addition, the need for fast decision-making effectively means that cumbersome and lengthy parliamentary decisions are to be replaced by the speedier decisions of domestic governments. Overall, however, membership of NATO has predominantly not been perceived as a restriction of sovereignty in the political rhetoric or constitutional theory of most CEE countries – on the contrary, it has formed a long-standing foreign policy goal and a key guarantee for the countries' security. There has been consistently high public support for joining NATO in most countries, in contrast to controversial sentiments in respect of accession to the EU. However, the situation was different in Slovenia, Slovakia and the Czech Republic, where public opinion has been less supportive of accession to NATO, especially as regards the financial burden on the state budget.

In CEE constitutional theory, debate has been scarce on membership of NATO's constitutional implications, compared with debates concerning EU membership. For instance, it has been reported that in the Czech Republic and Slovakia, membership of NATO has not been regarded as a constitutional problem, and this issue was not publicly addressed by Czech or Slovak scholars and officials.[1] This holds equally true for the three Baltic countries.

At the time the Vishegrad countries joined NATO in 1999, only the new Polish constitution contained a general clause on delegating powers to 'international organisations' (articles 90 and 91), which was aimed at both the EU and NATO. At the same time, all Vishegrad countries adapted their constitutions at an early stage with regard to some specific issues concerning NATO obligations. In Poland, the new constitution provides that the Sejm (the lower house of Parliament) may make a resolution on war 'when an obligation of common defence against aggression arises by virtue of international agreements' (article 116). Article 117 provides that the use of armed forces outside the state territory, and the presence and movement of foreign troops in Poland, shall be specified by a ratified international agreement or by a statute. This relates to the participation of Polish armed forces in NATO peace-keeping operations, such as the Bosnian mission, as well as the participation of NATO forces in common manoeuvres, and their stationing on Polish territory.[2] The Czech Republic adopted in 2000 the so-called 'peace-keeping amendment', which allowed the government to send Czech soldiers abroad without consulting Parliament. In 2001, this was complemented with the general clause on delegating powers to 'international organisations', which, introduced as part of the EU amendments, was also aimed at accommodating membership of NATO.[3] In Hungary, the NATO amendment was adopted in 2000. Articles 40B and 40C permit foreign armed forces to cross the country without the prior consent of Parliament, where this derives from international treaties or peace-keeping missions at the request of the United Nations. International treaties on defence matters require parliamentary

[1] M. Hoskova, 'Legal Aspects of the Integration of the Czech Republic and Slovakia into European Security and Economic Structures' (1994) 37 *German Yearbook of International Law* 86.

[2] See further A. Wasilkowski, 'International Law and International Relations in the New Polish Constitution of 2 April 1997' (1997–98) 23 *Polish Yearbook of International Law* 16.

[3] I. Slosarcik, 'The Reform of the Constitutional Systems of Czechoslovakia and the Czech Republic in 1990–2000' (2001) 7 *European Public Law* 544.

approval by a statute. Article 19(3) provides that Parliament decides on the deployment of armed forces abroad by a two-thirds majority of all deputies.

Hungary additionally held a referendum on NATO on 16 November 1997, being the only first-wave country to do so. Czech politicians decided against doing so, as an 'incorrect result' was feared by politicians.[4] As seen in the previous chapter, Hungary reduced the required minimum turnout by a constitutional amendment before the referendum. The newly established threshold majority – approval by 25 per cent of the total electorate – was met, as 49 per cent of voters participated, of whom 85 per cent approved accession. The issue of amending the constitution in respect of NATO came up again in 2003: the government submitted to Parliament an amendment proposal under which the Cabinet would be empowered to authorise the deployment of military forces for peace-keeping and humanitarian missions under the aegis of NATO, the United Nations and the EU.[5] Hungary has been recurrently criticised by NATO for being slow to commit troops abroad.[6]

Amongst the second-wave NATO accession countries, Slovenia, Slovakia and Romania have specifically amended their constitutions to authorise NATO membership. Slovakia's 2001 amendments authorise the accession to NATO in article 7(3), which provides that 'with the aim of maintaining peace, security and democratic order', Slovakia may join 'an organisation of mutual collective security'. The ratification of the pertinent treaty requires the consent of at least one-half of all deputies (article 84(3)). Furthermore, the 2001 amendments include new subparagraph (p) of article 119, which provides that the government decides on sending armed forces outside Slovakia 'within commitments ensuing from international treaties on common defence against an attack', for a maximum of sixty days and after notifying Parliament. Article 86 subsections (j), (k) and (l) enumerate the NATO-related competences of Parliament: adoption of decisions on the declaration of war and those resulting from commitments arising from international treaties on common defence; expression of consent to sending armed forces outside

[4] A. Stroehlein, 'Weaknesses of the Czech Media', *Central European Review*, 17 January 2000, www.ce-review.org/00/2/stroehlein2.html

[5] 'Hungarian Government Proposes Constitutional Amendment', *RFE/RL Newsline*, vol. 7, no. 143, Part II, 30 July 2003.

[6] 'Hungarian Opposition Wary of NATO Constitutional Amendment', *RFE/RL Newsline*, vol. 7, no. 151, Part II, 11 March 2003; 'Hungarian Politicking Delays Vote on NATO Deployment', *RFE/RL Newsline*, vol. 7, no. 181, Part II, 23 September 2003.

Slovakia and to the presence of foreign armed forces in the country. Article 119 further provides that the government's responsibility includes the following: sending armed forces outside Slovakia for the purposes of humanitarian aid, military manoeuvres or peace-keeping missions; and granting consent to the presence of foreign armies in Slovakia for the same purposes. In Slovenia, the package of 2003 amendments includes an authorisation to 'enter into a defence alliance' which is based on respect for human rights, democracy and the rule of law (article 3a). In Romania, new article 145.2, introduced in 2003, subjects the country's accession to NATO to a law, to be approved by two-thirds of the number of deputies and senators in a joint session. NATO membership is further regulated in article 117(1), which provides that the army shall contribute to 'collective defence in military alliance systems, and participate in peace keeping or peace restoring missions'. Paragraph 5 allows foreign troops to enter, carry out operations or pass through the country under the terms of the law or international treaties.

All three countries have additionally held referendums on NATO. Slovenia's referendum was held together with the referendum on the EU on 23 March 2003. As mentioned, public support in Slovenia for NATO has been rather cool, and the organisation was seen by the population as an unnecessary burden on the state budget. Eventually, just 66 per cent supported NATO membership in the referendum, compared with 90 per cent of the votes cast in favour of EU membership. In Romania, the referendum was held on 18–19 October 2003 on the constitutional amendments, central to which were the provisions both on the EU and NATO; 91 per cent of voters supported these amendments. In Slovakia, a NATO referendum had in fact been held in 1997, but it remained unsuccessful due to an insufficient turnout rate (9.5 per cent). A new referendum has been requested by various parties such as the Communist Party (opposed to NATO membership), the National Party, Vladimir Meciar's Movement for Democratic Slovakia, as well as by an initiative of thirty-eight Slovak writers, politicians and other prominent personalities.[7] However, the referendum proposal was rejected by Parliament in January 2003, for the reason that all other political parties backed NATO membership, and accession had formed a priority for every government in Slovakia since

[7] 'Slovak Communists Oppose Joining NATO', *RFE/RL Newsline*, vol. 6, no. 187, Part II, 3 October 2002; 'Prominent Slovak Personalities Back NATO Referendum', *RFE/RL Newsline*, vol. 7, no. 4, Part II, 8 January 2003.

the country's independence.[8] Public support for NATO membership has been rather modest: 34 per cent supported NATO and 52 per cent opposed membership in March 2003.[9]

In Bulgaria, President Georgi Parvanov asked the Constitutional Court on 2 January 2003 to determine whether the constitution required amendment for the country's entry into NATO, especially in respect of the provisions regulating the presence of foreign troops on Bulgarian territory, which require Parliament's permission on a case-by-case basis (article 84).[10] The Court ruled in February 2003 that the government is entitled to let foreign military forces use Bulgarian territory and to send Bulgarian troops abroad without Parliament's permission, provided that such actions are taken under the auspices of an international agreement.[11] The constitutional mechanisms for cooperation with NATO were earlier assessed by the Constitutional Court, in connection with the use of Bulgaria's airspace by NATO aircraft during the Kosovo conflict.[12]

In the Baltic countries, no specific steps were taken to legitimise NATO membership. The Lithuanian Constitution was the only one amongst the ten constitutions in question which contained from its adoption a provision permitting Lithuania to participate in international

[8] 'Slovak Parliament Rejects NATO Referendum Proposal', *RFE/RL Newsline*, vol. 7, no. 10, Part II, 16 January 2003.

[9] 'As Support for NATO Membership Wanes', *RFE/RL Newsline*, vol. 7, no. 60, Part II, 28 March 2003.

[10] 'Bulgarian Court to Decide if NATO Accession Necessitates Constitutional Amendment', *RFE/RL Newsline*, vol. 7, no. 1, Part II, 3 January 2003.

[11] 'Constitutional Court Rules in Favour of Foreign Troops on Bulgarian Soil', *Central European and Eurasian Law Initiative: Bulgaria* (February 2003), www.abanet.org/ceeli/countries/bulgaria/feb2003.html

[12] Decision No. 5/99, 22 April 1999, summary in English at www.infotel.bg/juen/resh/summaries99.htm. The Constitutional Court found that if a general provision were included in an international agreement ratified by Parliament, the courts' earlier interpretation of article 84(1), which required a separate authorisation for each entry of a foreign military aircraft, would not be applicable. As a result of this judgment, the Agreement between Bulgaria and NATO regarding Transit of NATO Aircraft was concluded, followed by ratification by Parliament. The opposition deputies challenged the Agreement in the Constitutional Court (Decision No. 6/99, 3 May 1999, summary in English at www.infotel.bg/juen/resh/summaries99.htm; 'Constitution Watch: Bulgaria' (1999) 8 *East European Constitutional Review*, no. 3), claiming that it would diminish Bulgaria's sovereignty and push the country towards a war. The Court held that the constitution explicitly provides for the transit of foreign troops via the country's territory. Parliament grants its permission by ratification of international instruments of a military nature. When Parliament exercises such power, there is no violation of the constitution or usurpation of sovereignty.

organisations, and, in addition, article 138 provides that Parliament ratifies and denounces treaties related to national defence. An amendment concerning the possibility of stationing foreign military troops on the territory of Lithuania has been under debate, but to no avail.[13] Problems may be additionally posed by articles 138(4) and 142, which respectively require a parliamentary decision for stationing Lithuania's armed forces abroad and for their use in fulfilling Lithuania's international obligations. In addition, article 137 may need amendment due to the prohibition on the stationing of weapons of mass destruction and foreign military bases on Lithuania's territory. In Estonia, the *travaux préparatoires* in the Constitutional Assembly envisaged that Estonia's accession, *inter alia*, to 'military unions of states' could only take place by amending article 1 by referendum.[14] However, ahead of accession, the constitutional impact of NATO was not specifically discussed amongst Estonian legal scholars and politicians. NATO entry was accommodated under article 121, which subjects treaties on joining international organisations to parliamentary ratification, by a majority of votes in favour. In addition, article 128 provides that Parliament decides on declaring war and on the use of the army in the fulfilment of Estonia's international obligations. As mentioned in chapter 5, there are plans to start work on the drafting of a new constitution, which is expected to include provisions regarding obligations deriving from NATO membership. In Latvia, the constitutional amendment of 2003 was addressed more broadly to 'international organisations', thus legitimising also membership of NATO. The Latvian Constitution is generally laconic and does not regulate defence matters. A referendum for accession to NATO has been under consideration only in Lithuania, but the initiative failed to gain the required 300,000 signatures.[15]

Other international organisations

Membership of other international organisations, such as the United Nations, International Criminal Court and World Trade Organisation, have been accommodated in CEE countries under broader constitutional provisions which regulate parliamentary ratification of international

[13] G. Steponavicius, 'Amending or Adjusting? Comments on Lithuania' in E. Smith (ed.), *The Constitution as an Instrument of Change* (SNS Förlag, Stockholm, 2003), p. 102.

[14] L. Hänni in *Põhiseadus ja Põhiseaduse Assamblee* [Constitution and Constitutional Assembly] (Õigusteabe AS Juura, Tallinn, 1996), p. 530.

[15] 'Initiative to Hold Referendum on NATO Membership Fails in Lithuania', *RFE/RL Newsline*, vol. 7, no. 6, Part II, 10 January 2003.

treaties pertaining to membership of international organisations (not involving a significant delegation of powers), as well as under the provisions on application of international law.

One of the organisations of major importance is the Council of Europe, which the CEE countries joined soon after the breakdown of Communism. By membership of the Council of Europe, the Member States undertake an obligation to respect the basic rights as established in the European Convention on Human Rights and Fundamental Freedoms (ECHR). In case of non-respect, the citizens of the Member States are entitled to bring a claim to the European Court of Human Rights in Strasbourg, provided that all domestic judicial resorts have been exhausted. Even though this system restricts to some degree the Member States' autonomous action, it has not been perceived so in CEE constitutional theory, and the question of sovereignty has not arisen with regard to the membership of the Council of Europe. This is because obligations deriving from membership of this organisation have rather been regarded as the application of international law. As discussed in chapters 3 and 5, the CEE constitutions are generally favourable and open towards international law; they provide in many cases expressly for direct applicability and supremacy of international law, and several make specific reference to the higher position of human rights treaties. The courts are readily applying the ECHR, whether directly or by using the interpretation given to certain provisions by the European Court of Human Rights. A more indirect means of influencing the constitutional systems of CEE is that in the process of joining the Council of Europe, the Commission of Venice on Democracy through Law has issued recommendations, which have become an integral part of the opinions of the Parliamentary Assembly of the Council of Europe. Under these, the countries wishing to join have had to make various adjustments, for instance in respect of the independence of the judiciary.[16] In terms of specific constitutional provisions, it has been reported that Bulgaria had to give a corrective interpretation to article 11(4) of the constitution that bans ethnic, racial and religious parties.[17]

[16] Reported in D. Maus, 'The Influence of Contemporary International Law on the Exercise of Constituent Power' in A. Jüränki (ed.), *National Constitutions in the Era of Integration* (Kluwer Law International, The Hague, 1999), pp. 52–3.

[17] *Ibid.*

9

Role of Constitutional Courts

Ultimate arbiter debate and CEE Constitutional Courts

One of the central constitutional disputes between the EU and its Member States has revolved around the issue of whether EU law takes precedence over national constitutions. As the European Court of Justice established in the cases of *Simmenthal* and *Internationale Handeslgesellschaft*, EC law is supreme even over fundamental norms of national constitutions.[1] This so-called EU-centred approach is based on the concerns of uniform application and effectiveness of Community law by national courts, as well as on the argument that, on the basis of the delegation clauses in the national constitutions, the Member States have delegated the power to strike down EC law to the ECJ. The national constitutional courts, although in principle recognising the supremacy of EC law, have, however, made reservations in respect of fundamental constitutional principles, and retain to themselves the right to review whether EU bodies exceed competences conferred upon them or violate fundamental constitutional principles. This state-centred view has been established most famously by the German Constitutional Court in the cases of *Solange I*[2] and *II*[3] and *Maastricht*,[4] the Italian Constitutional Court in the cases of *Granital*[5] and *Frontini*[6] and by the Danish Supreme Court in the *Maastricht* case.[7]

What will the advent of the courts of Central and Eastern Europe entail to the 'ultimate arbiter' debate? It has been pointed out that in the history of European integration, *Kompetenz-Kompetenz* disputes have arisen in those Member States which have Constitutional Courts, who

[1] Case 106/78, *Simmenthal* [1978] ECR 629; Case 11/70, *Internationale Handelsgesellschaft* [1970] ECR 1125 at 1134.

[2] *Solange I* BverfGE 37, 271 (1974). [3] *Solange II* BverfGE 73, 378 (1986).

[4] *Brunner* BVerfGE 89, 155 (1993), [1994] CMLR 57.

[5] *Granital*, Decision No. 170, 1984. [6] *Frontini*, Decision No. 183, 1973.

[7] *Carlsen* v. *Rasmussen*, judgment, 6 April 1998, [1999] CMLR 855.

have made the reception of supremacy contingent on certain conditions.[8] Unlike other high courts, the Constitutional Courts insist that it is the national constitutions, and not the ECJ or the EC Treaties, which mediate the relationship between EC law and national law.[9] This finding is of major importance in the context of EU enlargement, as the Constitutional Courts in the accession countries have a powerful status and a tradition of far-reaching judicial activism in rebuilding the independent legal systems.[10] As Wojciech Sadurski has said, '[o]ne of the most striking features of the ongoing transitions to democracy in these societies is the spectacular growth in the role and prominence of constitutional courts and tribunals in shaping the new constitutional order'.[11] The CEE Constitutional Courts are likely to continue their active input also after entry into the EU. This, however, may further exacerbate the tensions between EU law and national constitutions. In the worst case, there may be a risk of an anarchic situation which Matthias Kumm has called the 'Cassandra scenario',[12] where several Constitutional Courts quash EC legislation, based on their particular constitutional norms and values.

Another point to note is that unlike the constitutions of the 'old' Member States, most Central and Eastern European constitutions expressly establish the principle that the constitution is the highest legal source in the country,[13] and many also directly prohibit ratification of treaties that

[8] A. Stone Sweet, 'Constitutional Dialogues in the European Community' in A. M. Slaughter, A. Stone Sweet and J. H. H. Weiler (eds.), *The European Court and National Courts: Doctrine and Jurisprudence: Legal Change in its Social Context* (Hart, Oxford, 1998), p. 325.

[9] *Ibid.*

[10] It should be specified that in Estonia, constitutional review is exercised by the Chamber of Constitutional Review, which is a special chamber of the National Court. In Latvia, the Constitutional Court was established in 1996 by a relevant constitutional amendment. See further on the constitutional courts of Central and Eastern Europe, W. Sadurski (ed.), *Constitutional Justice, East and West: Democratic Legitimacy and Constitutional Courts in Post-Communist Europe in a Comparative Perspective* (Kluwer Law International, The Hague, 2002).

[11] W. Sadurski, 'Constitutional Justice, East and West: Introduction' in Sadurski, *Constitutional Justice*, p. 1.

[12] M. Kumm, 'Who is the Final Arbiter of Constitutionality in Europe? Three Conceptions of the Relationship between the German Federal Constitutional Court and the European Court of Justice and the Fate of the European Market Order of Bananas' (1999) 36 *Common Market Law Review* 360.

[13] e.g. article 8 of the Polish Constitution; article 153(1) of the Slovene Constitution; article 7 of the Lithuanian Constitution; article 5 of the Bulgarian Constitution; article 2(2) of the Slovakian Constitution; article 77(1) of the Hungarian Constitution; new article 1(5) of the Romanian Constitution (prior to 2003, article 51). In Estonia, supremacy is found to belong to the constitution under article 123(1) (prohibition to conclude treaties which are in conflict with the constitution), article 15 (courts declare unconstitutional acts which

are in conflict with the constitution. The supremacy of constitutions has also been reaffirmed in the case law of the Constitutional Courts across the region. For instance, the Constitutional Court of Slovenia has stated that the Slovene legal system 'does not recognize the primacy of international law over constitutional provisions'.[14] In Bulgaria, the Constitutional Court has held that as a consequence of articles 5, 85(3) and 149(1.4), there is no priority of international law over the constitution.[15] In Slovakia, the Constitutional Court has established that human rights instruments, under article 11, 'take precedence over the laws, but not over the Constitution'.[16] In Latvia, supremacy is not mentioned in the constitution, but according to the Constitutional Court, ratified treaties are subordinated to the constitution under article 13 of the Law on International Agreements.[17]

Furthermore, as seen in chapters 4 and 5, the Constitutional Courts of Hungary and Slovenia have warned that the constitutions may not be amended in a disguised way by ratification of treaties; the Parliaments must respect the more stringent constitutional amendment procedures.[18]

As regards the control of constitutionality of the treaties, all countries in question have established the preliminary review of treaties. In addition, in Poland, Hungary, Estonia and Bulgaria, the Constitutional Courts can exercise both preliminary and posterior review of treaties; the details were set out in chapter 5 in respect of the Accession Agreements. Where a treaty is found to be unconstitutional, such a finding does not entail consequences for the treaty itself in Poland, Hungary, Lithuania, Bulgaria and Slovenia, whereas the treaty may need to be renegotiated in Latvia and Estonia. In Lithuania, the Constitutional Court has stated that article 7 'in itself cannot invalidate a law or an international treaty, but it requires that the provisions thereof would not contradict the provisions of the Constitution'. A different conclusion, according to the Court, would obstruct the country in fulfilling its treaty obligations and thus violate the Vienna

conflict with the constitution) and article 152 (courts do not apply laws which conflict with the constitution, and are to initiate constitutional review proceedings).

[14] Decision No. RM-1/97, 5 June 1997, *Uradni list RS*, No. 40/97, *On Europe Agreement*, in English at www.us-rs.si/en/, para. 12.

[15] Decision No. 7, 2 July 1992, *Durzhaven Vestnik* 56/92, *on Interpretation of Articles 85(3) and 149(1.4) of the Constitution.*

[16] Decision No. 95/99, II, US 91/99, *on the Protection of Rights under Treaties*, summary in English at www.concourt.sk/A/a_index.htm

[17] Decision No. 04-02(99), 6 July 1999.

[18] e.g. *Magyar Közlöny*, Hungarian Constitutional Court Decision 30/1998 on the Europe Agreement (VI 25) AB, Slovene Constitutional Court Decision No. RM-1/97, 5 June 1997, *Uradni list RS*, No. 40/97, *On Europe Agreement*, in English at www.us-rs.si/en/, paras. 35–8.

Convention on the Law of Treaties. Instead, conformity with the constitution has to be secured in the process of conclusion, implementation and termination of a treaty.[19] In Hungary, the Constitutional Court has said that should it find a provision of a treaty to be unconstitutional, it establishes the unconstitutionality of the promulgating domestic legal rule; this does not influence Hungary's international commitments. However, by virtue of article 7(1) of the constitution, '[i]t is the task of the legislator to create harmony between the international obligation undertaken and the internal law'; until then the Court suspends taking its resolution as regards the date of annulment.[20] The Constitutional Court of Slovenia has held that where a conflict is found with the constitution, the Court may abrogate the law on ratification, but such a decision has effect only in the internal legal system and does not affect the state's obligations under international law.[21] According to the Bulgarian Constitutional Court, ratified and promulgated international instruments that have come into force are part of national legislation, and, as with other laws, are therefore subject to control for compliance with the constitution.[22] However, article 85(2) of the constitution expressly provides that treaties ratified by the National Assembly may be amended or denounced only by their built-in procedure, or in accordance with the universally acknowledged norms of international law.

On the other hand, in Latvia, article 32 of the Law on the Constitutional Court says that if the Constitutional Court has found any international agreement signed or entered into by Latvia to be incompatible with the constitution, the Cabinet of Ministers is immediately obliged to see to it that the agreement is amended, denounced, suspended or that accession to that agreement is reversed.[23] Similarly, in Estonia, the Law of Constitutional Review Procedure 2002 provides that where a treaty is found to be in conflict with the constitution, the National Court may suspend

[19] Decision No. 8/95 *On the Constitutionality of Law on International Treaties* (1997) 4 *East European Case Reporter of Constitutional Law* 253.

[20] *Magyar Közlöny*, Decision 30/1998 on the Europe Agreement (VI 25) AB, para. VI 2–VI 3, with reference to the Constitutional Court's Resolution No. 4/1997 (I.22) AB (ABH 1997, 41).

[21] Decision No. RM-1/97, 5 June 1997, *Uradni list RS*, No. 40/97, *On Europe Agreement*, in English at www.us-rs.si/en/, para. 13.

[22] Decision No. 8/99, 16 June 1999 on Cooperation Agreement with Turkey in Energy Sector, summary in English at www.infotel.bg/juen/resh/summaries99.htm

[23] Reported in A. Usaĉka, 'The Impact of the European Integration Process on the Constitution of Latvia' in A. Kellermann, J. De Zwaan and J. Czuçzai (eds.), *EU Enlargement: The Constitutional Impact at EU and National Level* (Asser Press, The Hague, 2001), p. 346.

the enforcement of the treaty (article 12), and it may declare invalid or unconstitutional a treaty or its provision (articles 14 and 15(1.3)). In this case, the state body which has concluded the treaty has to withdraw from the treaty and initiate its denunciation or modification so that it would be compatible with the constitution; treaties which are in conflict with the constitution are not internally applied (article 15).

As regards the issue of whether the Constitutional Courts of the post-enlargement CEE Member States will exercise control over conformity of EU law with fundamental constitutional principles, many commentators have preferred the Constitutional Courts to retain the right of review, rather than aligning with the ECJ's view. The Estonian Expert Commission's 1998 Report stated that the Estonian Constitutional Review Chamber should retain the ultimate *a posteriori* control over EU secondary legislation, to guarantee its conformity with the fundamental principles of the Estonian legal order and with the constitution.[24] In Latvia, the 1999 Report[25] has assigned to the Constitutional Court the responsibility of controlling future Community law in respect of potential violations of human rights or other constitutional rules.[26] A Hungarian commentator has proposed that the country's Constitutional Court should be granted powers to rule on the constitutionality of important steps taken by Community bodies or agreed collectively by the Member States, along the lines of the *Solange* and *Maastricht* cases.[27] The Polish Constitutional Court is likely to exercise some control, especially on the basis of article 90,

[24] *Võimalik liitumine Euroopa Liiduga ja selle õiguslik tähendus Eesti riigiõiguse seisukohalt* [Potential Accession to the European Union and its Consequences for Estonian Constitutional Law], Report of the Constitutional Amendment Expert Commission of Estonia (1998), in Estonian at www.just.ee/juridica2.html, pp. 10–11 and 20–1.

[25] *Constitutional and Administrative Facilitation of Effective Law Approximation and European Union Membership*, Report composed under the auspices of the European Integration Bureau and PHARE Technical Assistance to the Approximation of the Latvian Legislation to that of the European Communities (Riga, 1999).

[26] An example of a potential conflict could be the protection of national language. As seen in chapter 9, both the Latvian and Lithuanian Constitutional Courts have established that foreign names have to be written in accordance with the spelling rules of, respectively, the Latvian and Lithuanian language. This, however, appears to be at odds with the ECJ's ruling in Case C-168/91, *Konstantinidis* [1993] ECR I-1191. In that case, the ECJ found that mistranslation of a person's name violates the right of self-employed persons to non-discrimination on grounds of nationality.

[27] e.g. by B. Berke, 'Community Law and National Legal Order' in P. C. Müller-Graff (ed.), *East Central Europe and the European Union: From Europe Agreements to a Member Status* (Nomos, Baden-Baden, 1997), p. 62.

which permits only the transfer of 'some powers', but not all powers.[28] The limits for delegating powers would be twofold: the constitutional rules embodying the highest principles of government, essential to the very identity of Polish statehood (articles 1, 2, 3, 5 and 20), and those on human rights (Chapter II). Conflicts may arise, for instance, with regard to the equality of homosexual marriage or partnership (article 18), voting rights of EU citizens (article 62) and extradition of Polish nationals (article 55(1)).[29] On the other hand, Jan Barcz is of the view that the Constitutional Tribunal should search for pragmatic solutions and grant primacy to EU law, given the democratic legitimacy of the decision to join the EU taken in a referendum and due to the need to preserve the unity of EC law.[30]

It will remain to be seen which stance the Constitutional Courts of the accession countries will take. As seen in chapters 5 and 7, they have opted for a pragmatic approach in respect of various challenges to the legality of accession referendums, rejecting the claims on procedural grounds. The task of avoiding major clashes would be made easier for the Constitutional Courts by elimination of further conflicts with EU law from the constitutions, in addition to the initial minimal amendments.

Towards a 'European constitutional order'?

On the EU's side, enlargement, combined with the adoption of the European Constitution (to be discussed in the last chapter), appears to strengthen the case for a pluralist approach or even for an institutional solution to the 'ultimate arbiter' debate, given the advent of a number of activist Constitutional Courts, who have hitherto upheld values underlying the paradigm of sovereign nation-state.

The scholarly debate triggered by the *Maastricht* decision of the German Constitutional Court has led to a wider recognition[31] that 'national law

[28] W. Czaplinski, 'L'Intégration européenne dans la constitution polonaise de 1997' (2000) *Revue du Marché Commun et de l'Union Européenne* 172; S. Biernat, 'Constitutional Aspects of Poland's Future Membership in the European Union' (1998) 36 *Archiv des Völkerrechts* 405.

[29] Biernat, 'Constitutional Aspects', pp. 405–6; Czaplinski, 'L'Intégration européenne', p. 172.

[30] J. Barcz, 'Membership of Poland in the European Union in the Light of the Constitution of 2 April 1997' (1997–98) 23 *Polish Yearbook of International Law* 29 at p. 31.

[31] This section draws upon A. Albi and P. Van Elsuwege, 'EU Constitution, National Constitutions and Sovereignty: An Assessment of a "European Constitutional Order"' (2004) *European Law Review* (forthcoming).

and Community law can no longer be understood as completely separate legal spheres'.[32] Instead, the complex interdependence between the national constitutional framework on the one hand, and the developing process of European legal integration on the other, has increasingly been presented in pluralist terms: as a 'pluralistic legal order',[33] 'constitutional pluralism',[34] a system of 'multilevel constitutionalism',[35] etc. With some variations, it could be said that these concepts generally regard the national and European constitutional documents as no longer being the emanation of two hierarchically positioned independent legal systems, where the sovereign state is the ultimate source and centre of authority. Instead, the relationship between the orders 'is now horizontal rather than vertical – heterarchical rather than hierarchical'.[36] Each highest court within a subsystem – Constitutional Courts, European Court of Justice, as well as other adjudicating bodies such as the European Court of Human Rights and the WTO Dispute Settlement Body – derives authority and acts legitimately under its own basic documents,[37] retaining 'interpretative competence-competence'.[38] Essentially, 'no one has the final word: each legal system has, indeed, only the final word within its own sphere of competence'.[39] The focus here is on the prevention of conflicts through cooperation and interaction, both in a vertical (between the European Court of Justice and the national courts) and a horizontal (between the national courts of the Member States) direction. If conflicts

[32] J. Schwarze, 'The Birth of a European Constitutional Order' in J. Schwarze (ed.), *The Birth of a European Constitutional Order: The Interaction of National and European Constitutional Law* (Nomos, Baden-Baden, 2000), p. 545.

[33] N. MacCormick, *Questioning Sovereignty: Law, State, and Nation in the European Commonwealth* (Oxford University Press, 1999), p. 105; A. Verhoeven, *The European Union in Search of a Democratic and Constitutional Treaty* (Kluwer, 2002), pp. 291–304. A pluralist approach is also taken by Kumm, in 'Who is the Final Arbiter', and by M. Poiares Maduro in 'Contrapuntal Law: Europe's Constitutional Pluralism in Action' in N. Walker (ed.), *Sovereignty in Transition* (Hart, Oxford, 2003), pp. 523–4. Maduro offers an interesting concept of 'contrapuntal law', borrowing from musical terminology, where counterpoint denotes the method of harmonising different melodies that are not in a hierarchical relationship.

[34] N. Walker, 'The Idea of Constitutional Pluralism' (2002) 65 *Modern Law Review* 317.

[35] I. Pernice, 'Multilevel Constitutionalism and the Treaty of Amsterdam: European Constitution-Making Revisited' (1999) 36 *Common Market Law Review* 703 at p. 707.

[36] Walker, 'Idea of Constitutional Pluralism', p. 337.

[37] MacCormick, *Questioning Sovereignty*, ch. 7; N. Walker, 'Late Sovereignty in the European Union' in Walker, *Sovereignty in Transition*, pp. 3–32; Kumm, 'Who is the Final Arbiter', pp. 375–6.

[38] MacCormick, *Questioning Sovereignty*, p. 259.

[39] Verhoeven, *The European Union*, p. 302.

nevertheless occur, these should be solved on the basis of certain principles, taking account of the concrete constitutional context, time and practicalities,[40] or 'some political action' may be necessary to produce a solution.[41]

If, however, a matter of EU law has become overly sensitive for the national constitutional spheres, a final joint intervention mechanism by the Member States through the Intergovernmental Conference has proved effective.[42] The Intergovernmental Conference has amended the Treaties or added protocols with regard to the constitutionally sensitive issues decided by the European Court of Justice. For instance, this has been the case with Protocol No. 17 of the Maastricht Treaty which concerned the *Grogan* case on Irish abortion law, as well as with an amendment introduced to the EC Treaty by the Treaty of Amsterdam which concerned German discontent with a gender equality ruling given in the *Kalanke* case.[43] This mechanism appears to indicate a *de facto* move towards a recognition that one or a few Member States no longer seem to be able to reject further steps in European integration based on their particular constitutional provisions. This power rather belongs to a convincing majority of the Member States together, exercised in accordance with national constitutional procedures.

These developments could perhaps be characterised as a move towards a 'European constitutional order',[44] where the interaction between the Treaties and the national constitutions of the Member States reflects the Member States' collective agreement on how sovereign powers are exercised in the EU's legal space. The sovereign state is no longer the only source of authority: within the scope of EU law, the authority derives from the Treaties, adjudicated by the ECJ or, in borderline cases, by the Member States together through the Intergovernmental Conference. Such

[40] e.g. Kumm, 'Who is the Final Arbiter'.

[41] MacCormick, *Questioning Sovereignty*, p. 265.

[42] See also B. De Witte, 'Sovereignty and European Integration: the Weight of Legal Tradition' in Slaughter, Stone Sweet and Weiler, *The European Court and National Courts*, p. 304, and W. Van Gerven, 'Toward a Coherent Constitutional System within the European Union' (1996) 2 *European Public Law* 86.

[43] Respectively Cases C-159/90, *Grogan* [1991] ECR I-4685; Case C-450/93, *Kalanke* [1995] ECR I-3051, see J. H. H. Weiler, *The Constitution of Europe: 'Do the New Clothes Have an Emperor?' and Other Essays on the European Integration* (Cambridge University Press, 1999), p. 291 and T. Hartley, *Constitutional Problems of the European Union* (Hart, Oxford, 1999), pp. 54–6.

[44] This expression is borrowed from J. Schwarze, 'Introduction' in Schwarze, *Birth of a European Constitutional Order*, p. 14.

an approach appears to be reinforced by the Draft European Constitution, to be discussed in chapter 10.

At the same time, the practical effect of the EU's enlargement may render it more compelling to find a solid institutional solution to the ongoing polemics between the state-centred, EU-centred and pluralist views to the *quis iudicabit* problem. A partial solution envisaged in the European Constitution, as will be seen in the next chapter, is the new right of the national Parliaments to control whether the Commission proposals are in accordance with the principle of subsidiarity. However, perhaps more thought could have been given in the Convention to Joseph Weiler's widely discussed idea to establish a special European Constitutional Council, which would be composed of the representatives of the ECJ and of the Constitutional Courts and would review procedural aspects, competences and subsidiarity.[45]

[45] Weiler, *Constitution of Europe*, p. 350 *et seq.*

10

Implications of the European Constitution

EU's constitutional reform and involvement of candidate countries

One of the novelties of this enlargement is that for the first time, a major constitutional and institutional reform has been necessary on the part of the EU.[1] In fact, the requirement that the EU must adapt its institutions for enlargement constituted the fourth part of the Copenhagen Criteria, being addressed to the EU itself rather than to the candidate countries. The EU institutions were notably designed for six countries, and having been increasingly under strain with fifteen, a dramatic increase in the number of Member States was expected to be particularly challenging. Another reason for institutional reform was the advent of many small-sized countries or even micro-states: Malta and Cyprus have a population of respectively 400,000 and 800,000; Estonia 1.4 million; Slovenia 2 million; Latvia 2.4 million; Lithuania 3.7 million; Slovakia 5.4 million. Only Poland is a bigger player with 40 million people; Hungary and the Czech Republic each have a population of about 10 million. Although numerical adjustments for enlargement were made in the Treaty of Nice, these were widely considered to be a bare minimum, failing to respond to deeper challenges. Besides addressing the challenges of enlargement, the constitutional reform was also aimed at simplifying the current maze of treaties and making them more understandable to citizens, as well as increasing democracy and efficiency in the Union.

In order to address these challenges, the Laeken Declaration[2] established the Convention on the Future of Europe in 2001, which was charged with the production of a Basic Treaty for the EU. The Convention, which started its work in February 2002, brought together representatives of

[1] See in more detail B. De Witte, 'The Impact of Enlargement on the Constitution of the European Union' in M. Cremona (ed.), *The Enlargement of the European Union* (Oxford University Press, 2003), pp. 209–51.

[2] Laeken Declaration, Bull. EU, 2001–12, I.27.

Parliaments and governments both from the 'old' Member States and the then candidate countries, as well as from EU institutions. After eighteen months of heated deliberations, the Convention on 18 July 2003 presented the Draft Constitution for Europe to the European Council Presidency in Rome.[3] The Intergovernmental Conference notoriously failed to approve it in the Brussels Summit in December 2003, primarily due to the objections of Poland and Spain to giving up their favourable share of votes obtained in Nice. However, the change in the political climate after the dramatic events in Madrid in March 2003 paved the way for the approval of the Draft European Constitution on 18 June 2004.[4] After the expected signing of the document in Rome in October 2004, the European Constitution will be submitted to national ratifications in the Member States.

Before coming to the discussion of the nature of this new basic document, it would be appropriate to see what has been the stance of the candidate countries in this process. For the candidate countries, participation in the Convention was the first opportunity to take part in the EU's decision-making structures, although this was subject to the proviso that they were not to block any consensus that could have emerged amongst the Member States. Participation in the Convention was also a remarkable exercise in that, unlike previous enlargements, the accession countries of this wave found themselves in the middle of debates about the EU's future, not infrequently characterised by federal undertones. There had previously been very little debate on the 'Future of Europe' in the candidate countries, as the focus had been on accession negotiations and on the adoption of the *acquis*, especially in smaller candidate countries with a limited amount of EU specialists available. In general, federal visions of Europe caused uneasiness in the region where sovereignty had been newly established,[5] considering also negative experience with

[3] Draft Treaty establishing a Constitution for Europe, CONV 850/03, Brussels, 18 July 2003, http://european-convention.eu.int. Parts I and II of the Draft Treaty had been submitted to the European Council meeting in Thessaloniki on 20 June 2003.

[4] The changes made in the Draft Constitution by the Intergovernmental Conference are available in the Provisional Consolidated Version of the Treaty Establishing a Constitution for Europe, CIG 86/04, Brussels, 25 June 2004. However, this chapter will proceed from the numbering used in the Convention's Draft Constitution (Draft Treaty establishing a Constitution for Europe, CONV 850/03, Brussels, 18 July 2003, http://european-convention.eu.int), annotating the final changes where relevant. This is because of the provisional nature of the consolidated version, and because the Convention's version of the European Constitution has been widely published and referred to in scholarly studies.

[5] Also J. Motoc, 'Europe and its Teleology: Is there a Central-Eastern Vision?' in C. Joerges, Y. Meny and J. Weiler (eds.), *What Kind of Constitution for What Kind of Polity?* (Robert Schuman Centre of the European University Institute and Harvard Law School, 2001), p. 189.

federations in other contexts, such as the unequal status of the Hungarians and Romanians during the Habsburg Empire, of the non-Serb population in Yugoslavia and the Slovaks in Czechoslovakia.[6] Indeed, Joschka Fisher's famous speech on Europe's federal *finalité* encountered a negative reception in the candidate countries, and it was set aside as a utopian vision of a distant future.

These views were also echoed by CEE heads of state and top politicians in their speeches on the 'Future of Europe'.[7] In broad terms, they preferred to see a union of nation-states rather than a United States of Europe, and advocated a simplification of treaties rather than adoption of a constitution, or adoption of a constitutional treaty but with the emphasis on 'treaty'. For instance, the then Prime Minister of Hungary, Victor Orban, saw the EU's future as 'a union based on nations' instead of 'a European United States'.[8] According to the Polish President Aleksander Kwasniewski, 'a federation of nation-states' could appear perhaps in twenty years time.[9] In line with this, the top politicians supported incremental institutional reforms rather than a major overhaul. Overall, the speeches remained rather general and mainly approved of the need for reforms, rather than offering concrete proposals – it is indeed difficult to assess problems of a system in which one has not participated. The anti-federal positions were partly also influenced by the shadow of the then imminent accession referendums: several countries found it difficult to secure positive results due to eurosceptic public opinion and previous experience with insufficient turnout rates. A Union with federal undertones would have rendered this task even harder.

In the Intergovernmental Conference of 2003–2004, the accession countries predominantly stood for the continuation of some form of rotating presidency, for equal representation of all countries in the Commission, and for the rights of small countries. They also backed Poland in its quest for keeping its voting power in the Council on the favourable terms obtained in Nice. In addition, Slovakia, Poland, Hungary and the

[6] V. Mastny, 'The Historical Experience of Federalism in East Central Europe' (2000) 1 *East European Politics and Societies* 96, cited in Motoc, 'Europe and its Teleology', pp. 188–9.

[7] See for a study of speeches delivered by CEE politicians on the 'Future of the Union', A. Albi, *Referendums in Eastern Europe: The Effects on Reforming the EU Treaties and on the Candidate Countries' Positions in the Convention* (European University Institute, Robert Schuman Centre Working Paper, No. 2002/65, Florence, 2002), p. 15 *et seq*.

[8] Interview with V. Orban, *La libre Belgique*, 11 July 2001.

[9] A. Kwasniewski, 'Enlarged EU: Moving Towards a Political Union', speech delivered at the Stockholm School of Economics, 10 May 2001, www.europa.eu.int/futurum/documents/speech/sp100501_en.htm

Czech Republic insisted on a reference to God or Europe's Christian heritage and Hungary advocated a clause on the protection of minorities.

A constitution or a treaty?

The European Constitution has set off heated debates as to whether the new document constitutes a fundamental constitutional change or just another treaty of revision.[10] On the one hand, comparisons have notably been drawn with the Philadelphia Convention of 1787 at which the American Constitution was created,[11] and an EU-wide referendum has been called for this 'epoch-creating' move.[12] On the other hand, it has also been presented as a 'tidying-up exercise', especially by the UK government. The official title of the new document – 'Draft Treaty Establishing a Constitution for Europe' – does not provide a clear answer, combining both the terms, 'constitution' and 'treaty'.

The first scholarly studies appear to present the Convention's exercise more in terms of rationalisation and simplification, responding to the tasks set in Laeken rather than creating a genuine constitution.[13] For instance, Juliane Kokott and Alexandra Rüth consider it 'not an exercise of constitutionalization, but of constitutional rewriting and formalization'.[14] As a consequence, the new document has been termed a 'Constitutional

[10] Amongst some recent academic studies of the Draft European Constitution see M. Dougan, 'The Convention's Draft Constitutional Treaty: Bringing Europe Closer to its Lawyers' (2003) 28 *European Law Review* 763; J. Kokott and A. Rüth, 'The European Convention and its Draft Treaty Establishing a Constitution for Europe: Appropriate Answers to the Laeken Questions?' (2003) 40 *Common Market Law Review* 1315; K. Lenaerts and D. Gerard, 'The Structure of the Union according to the Constitution for Europe: the Emperor is Getting Dressed' (2004) 29 *European Law Review* 289; J. Schwarze, 'Guest Editorial: the Convention's Draft Treaty Establishing a Constitution for Europe' (2003) 40 *Common Market Law Review* 1037; J. Ziller, *La nouvelle Constitution européenne* (La Découverte, Paris, 2004); B. De Witte (ed.), *Ten Reflections on the Constitutional Treaty for Europe* (EUI-RSCAS/AEL, Florence, 2003), available at www.iue.it/RSCAS/Publications; K. Lenaerts and M. Desomer, 'New Models of Constitution-Making in Europe: The Quest for Legitimacy' (2002) 39 *Common Market Law Review* 1217.

[11] 'Giscard Wants to be Europe's Benjamin Franklin', *EU Observer*, 7 February 2002, www.euobserver.com; M. Rosenfeld, 'The European Convention and Constitution Making in Philadelphia' (2003) 1 *International Journal of Constitutional Law* 375.

[12] e.g. ninety-six delegates of the Convention in a joint call; see 'Call for EU-wide Referendums on New Constitution', 13 June 2003, www.eubusiness.com

[13] e.g. Kokott and Rüth, 'The European Convention'; Dougan, 'The Convention's Draft Constitutional Treaty'; Schwarze, 'Guest Editorial'; Ziller, *La nouvelle Constitution*, p. 25 *et seq*. However, for a view that the new document resembles a constitution see Lenaerts and Gerard, 'Structure of the Union'.

[14] Kokott and Rüth, 'The European Convention', p. 1320.

Treaty'[15] or even just another treaty.[16] The main reason why the document is found not to amount to a constitution lies in the fact that the mode of adoption has been retained: all Member States, as the 'Masters of the Treaties', have to approve and ratify it in the form of an international treaty, rather than by means of some sort of *pouvoir constituant européen*.[17] In addition to this, some commentators have found that the Constitutional Treaty is too long and detailed to form a genuine constitution, and that no substantially significant constitutional elements have been added so as to justify it being labelled a constitution.

However, the subsequent section will place the innovations in the Constitutional Treaty into the context of the criteria that were established by the German Constitutional Court back in 1993 for preserving sovereignty.[18] After outlining these criteria, it will be argued that in all the afore-mentioned respects, the new document does appear to entail some additional aspects which strengthen the case for speaking about its constitutional nature. After that, we will also consider those aspects of the Constitutional Treaty which, in contrast, consolidate the position of the Member States. We will then look at the first views towards the Constitutional Treaty in the Member States, and move thereafter to consider its impact upon the concept of sovereignty and upon national constitutions.

National constitutional limits to integration

About a decade ago, the ratification of the Treaty of Maastricht sparked an intensive debate as to how many powers a Member State may delegate without incurring the loss of its sovereignty. This question was referred to the highest courts in Germany, Denmark and France. In the German *Maastricht* case,[19] the plaintiff argued that the entry into force

[15] Schwarze, 'Guest Editorial', p. 1043.

[16] 'Editorial: The President's Tale' (2004) 29 *European Law Review* 1.

[17] e.g. Kokott and Rüth, 'The European Convention', p. 1320; 'Editorial: The President's Tale', p. 1.

[18] The following sections are based on A. Albi and P. Van Elsuwege, 'EU Constitution, National Constitutions and Sovereignty: An Assessment of a "European Constitutional Order"' (2004) *European Law Review* (forthcoming).

[19] *Brunner*, BVerfGE 89, 155 (1993), [1994] CMLR 57. See for comment e.g. M. Zuleeg, 'The European Constitution under Constitutional Constraints: The German Scenario' (1997) 22 *European Law Review* 19; K. Hailbronner, 'The European Union from the Perspective of the German Constitutional Court' (1994) 37 *German Yearbook of International Law* 93; S. Hobe, 'The German State in Europe after the Maastricht Decision of the German Constitutional Court' (1994) 37 *German Yearbook of International Law* 113; K. Meessen, 'Hedging European Integration: The Maastricht Judgement of the Federal Constitutional Court of Germany' (1994) 17 *Fordham International Law Journal* 511.

of the Maastricht Treaty threatened the 'existence of the Federal Republic of Germany as an independent sovereign State, something which under Article 79(3) of the Constitution . . . cannot be subject to constitutional amendment'.[20] The highest courts clarified the content of the delegation of the delimited powers, and established a number of criteria to assess the permissible level of integration, so that sovereignty would not be lost in an eventual membership of a European federal state. The *Maastricht* decision of the German Constitutional Court has become central to the EU's constitutional discourse, although some points were also repeated in the *Maastricht* decision of the Danish Supreme Court in 1998.[21] Both courts established that, through constitutional procedures, these countries have accepted to delegate some competences in order to exercise them in common with the other Member States. Such delegation has to remain strictly within the limits set by the Accession Treaty. In assessing the Maastricht Treaty, the courts found that the Treaty did not exceed these limits, nor did it involve a critical degree of delegation of competences.

The criteria under which these conclusions were reached were most thoroughly elaborated in the German *Maastricht* decision, and are partly also present in the Danish decision. Broadly speaking, seven criteria can be identified. First, the German Constitutional Court affirmed that the Member States remain the 'Masters of the Treaties' because each new delegation of competences is subject to their unanimous approval, combined with ratification under the national constitutional procedures.[22] The second main criterion for preserving sovereignty was that the so-called *Kompetenz-Kompetenz* remains with the Member States: the EU possesses no power over jurisdictional conflicts. Member States have transferred only limited individual powers, which have been specified in a sufficiently clear and foreseeable manner.[23] The Danish Supreme Court similarly made it clear that it cannot be left to international organisations to determine their own powers, but found the EU's activities to be delimited under the principle of conferred powers.[24] Thirdly, the German Constitutional Court pointed out that the EU's competences are

[20] *Brunner*, BVerfGE 89, 155 (1993), [1994] CMLR 75.

[21] *Carlsen* v. *Rasmussen*, judgment, 6 April 1998, [1999] CMLR 855. For a comment see e.g. H. Koch, 'The Danish Constitutional Order' in A. Kellermann, J. De Zwaan and J. Czuczai (eds.), *EU Enlargement: The Constitutional Impact at EU and National Level* (Asser Press, The Hague, 2001), pp. 109–16.

[22] *Brunner*, BVerfGE 89, 155 (1993), [1994] CMLR 84 at 91, 97.

[23] *Ibid.* at 89, 92 *et seq.*, 105.

[24] *Carlsen* v. *Rasmussen*, judgment, 6 April 1998, [1999] CMLR 858.

mainly limited to the economic field, whereas fundamental spheres of state sovereignty, such as defence, foreign policy and internal affairs, fall under the intergovernmental mode of cooperation, requiring unanimous consent of all Member States.[25] Fourthly, both courts found that the Maastricht Treaty did not exceed the extent to which new powers and functions of a state can be delegated, in that substantial powers still remain with national institutions.[26] Fifthly, the German Constitutional Court pointed out that democratic legitimacy is predominantly derived from the national level. It stems from the national authorisations for delegation of new powers, and from the accountability of governments *vis-à-vis* national Parliaments for their decision-making activity in the Council. The European Parliament's complementary role and the absence of a European people as such further exemplify the non-state character of the EU.[27] Sixthly, reference was made to the facts that the EU has no legal personality, and that Member States can withdraw from the Union.[28] Last but not least, both the German and Danish highest courts maintained that the ultimate supremacy lies in the national constitutions. In combination with the requirement of sovereignty, the German and Danish courts therefore ultimately remain responsible for controlling whether EU institutions act within the limits of powers conferred upon them by the Member States.[29]

A set of criteria, albeit of a somewhat different nature and in a different context, has also been established by the French Constitutional Council. Because of the system of preliminary rather than posterior constitutional review of treaties, enshrined in the French Constitution, the Constitutional Council has assessed the necessity of a constitutional amendment, rather than warning about the limits of permissible integration. This was also the case with the ratification of the Maastricht Treaty, where the Constitutional Council maintained its earlier formula that changes to the European Treaties may be acceptable provided that they do not undermine 'the essential conditions for the exercise of national sovereignty'.[30] These 'essential conditions' are the state's institutional structure, independence of the nation, territorial integrity and fundamental rights and

[25] *Brunner*, BVerfGE 89, 155 (1993), [1994] CMLR 80 at 90–1.

[26] *Ibid.* at 87–8; *Carlsen* v. *Rasmussen*, judgment, 6 April 1998, [1999] CMLR 862.

[27] *Brunner*, BVerfGE 89, 155 (1993), [1994] CMLR 85–8. [28] *Ibid.* at 91, 94.

[29] *Ibid.* at 89; *Carlsen* v. *Rasmussen*, judgment, 6 April 1998, [1999] CMLR 861.

[30] Decision No. 92–308 DC, 9 April 1992, www.conseil-constitutionnel.fr/decision/1992/92308dc.htm

liberties of nationals.[31] It found that these conditions were indeed affected by the provisions of the Maastricht Treaty concerning Monetary Union, the common visa policy and voting rights of EU citizens in local elections. Therefore, the French Constitution was supplemented by a new title on the EU (see chapter 2). A similar method was also applied before the ratification of the Amsterdam Treaty.[32] However, the idea that all sovereign powers ultimately belong to the people of the state continues to constitute the basis of the relationship between the national and European legal order.

'Constitutional' elements of the European Constitution

How does the European Constitution relate to the national constitutional criteria established at the time of Maastricht? To start with, an important element in the German *Maastricht* decision was the idea that the basic documents of the EU remain international treaties, of which the Member States are the 'Masters'. This is in line with the deeply entrenched understanding in national constitutional law that the notion of constitution is inherently bound to a nation-state, and its use is therefore inappropriate in the context of the European Union, to avoid connotations of the EU's federal statehood.

However, an increasing swell of post-national (or 'post-etatist')[33] literature is contesting this premise, arguing that constitutions do not necessarily presume a state, and may exist in non-state contexts, particularly in the EU as a new type of transnational polity.[34] The example of the ILO

[31] These criteria are, according to Jacques, contained in the Conseil Constitutionnel decision of 22 May 1985, see J.-P. Jacque, 'Commentaire de la décision du Conseil constitutionnel n 92–308 DC du 9 avril 1992: Traité sur l'Union européenne 1992' (1992) *Revue Trimestrielle du Droit Europeen* 256. See also J. Ziller, 'Sovereignty in France: Getting Rid of the Mal de Bodin' in N. Walker (ed.), *Sovereignty in Transition* (Hart, Oxford, 2003), p. 275.

[32] See S. Millns, 'The Treaty of Amsterdam and Constitutional Revision in France' (1999) 5 *European Public Law* 61.

[33] M. Aziz, 'Sovereignty Über Alles: (Re)Configuring the German Legal Order' in Walker, *Sovereignty in Transition*, p. 294.

[34] e.g. J. Shaw, 'Postnational Constitutionalism in the European Union' (1999) 6 *Journal of European Public Policy* 579; articles in J. H. H. Weiler and M. Wind (eds.), *European Constitutionalism Beyond the State* (Cambridge University Press, 2003); P. Craig, 'Constitutions, Constitutionalism and the European Union' (2001) 7 *European Law Journal* 138; U. Di Fabio, 'European Charter: Towards a Constitution for the Union' (2001) 7 *Columbia Journal of European Law* 164; R. Arnold, 'Peut-on définir le phénomène d'européanisation des droits constitutionnels nationaux?' in J. Ziller (ed.), *L'européanisation des droits constitutionnels à la lumière de la Constitution pour l'Europe* (L'Harmattan, Paris, 2003),

Constitution of 1919 has often served to illustrate the use of a constitution in a non-state context. That a constitution no longer necessarily signals a polity's transition into statehood is the first departure point for our subsequent analysis of the EU's new basic document.

Alongside this post-national approach to the notion of a constitution, the second starting-point for our analysis is the fact that the Treaties in the current form are treated as a 'constitutional charter' in terms of their nature. This fact was established in 1986 by the European Court of Justice,[35] and it has generally been endorsed in scholarly writing.[36] Amongst manifold similarities with the role of constitutions, the following have usually been highlighted in particular: the Treaties determine the EU's governing institutions, their powers and the system of checks and balances, their relations with each other and with Member States; they stipulate decision-making procedures, which involve a directly elected parliamentary assembly; they create various direct links between EU institutions and individuals. Furthermore, a set of constitutional principles has been developed by the ECJ, such as supremacy, direct effect and the protection of fundamental rights. The consolidation and strengthening of the 'constitutional charter' into a single and more readily accessible document should therefore presumably reinforce the case for speaking about a constitution. As pointed out by Koen Lenaerts and Damien Gerard:

> [t]here is a general agreement on the fact that the basic Treaties forming the current Union already display the minimal content of a Constitution. The Convention has given an additional dimension to the Union through a complete re-foundation of its legitimacy, impacting on both formal and substantial constitutional aspects.[37]

The third point of departure for our subsequent assessment of the European Constitution is that it should not be considered in isolation. While the European Constitution taken alone does not create revolutionary changes, it clearly goes beyond ordinary international treaties when taken together with previous steps of integration, including the Treaties

p. 85; M. Brand, *Affirming and Refining European Constitutionalism: Towards the Establishment of the First Constitution for the European Union* (European University Institute, Law Department, Working Paper No. 2004/02, Florence, 2004), www.iue.it/PUB/law04-2.pdf, p. 17.

35 Case 294/83, *Les Verts* [1986] ECR 1339, para. 23.

36 Amongst recent articles on the subject, Paul Craig has demonstrated that the EU has indeed transformed into a constitutional order, and that arguments to the contrary are not convincing. See Craig, 'Constitutions, Constitutionalism', p. 128 *et seq.*

37 Lenaerts and Gerard, 'Structure of the Union', p. 321.

of Maastricht, Amsterdam and Nice. The point is that European integration has usually taken place by incremental, piecemeal steps, by means of new treaties and case law of the European Court of Justice. Traditional international treaties deal with a limited field of regulation, and are predominantly addressed to states rather than creating direct links with individuals. European integration, by contrast, has evolved to the extent that very few areas are still entirely unaffected by the EU's activity, and there are manifold and increasing direct forms of interaction with citizens. As is well known, the ECJ has established that the European Communities form a new legal order, for the benefit of which the Member States have limited their sovereign rights and the law of which is supreme and directly applicable, taking precedence even over national constitutions. In 1994, the Maastricht Treaty dramatically deepened the integration process: it established the European Union; created the Monetary Union which has led to a common currency in twelve Member States; introduced EU citizenship; endowed the EU with competences in the field of foreign and defence policy and judicial and home affairs; expanded the use of qualified majority voting; and significantly strengthened the role of the European Parliament. The Treaties of Amsterdam and Nice further pushed the national constitutional limits, strengthening the EU's role in foreign and defence policy and justice and home affairs, moving a part of the Third Pillar under the First Pillar, strengthening the European Parliament's role and bringing new fields of decision-making under qualified majority voting. In 2000, the proclamation of the Charter of Fundamental Rights reinforced the constitutional character of the EU. Notwithstanding the originally non-binding character of this document, the solemn form of its adoption by the Convention process, its manifestation of an agreement over shared values and rights and its role in the debate about a European Constitution, have been considered to accord it a privileged[38] or even a constitutional status.[39] As a result of this piecemeal integration, the EU has evolved into a highly integrated

[38] See Opinion of Advocate-General Leger of 10 July 2001 in Case C-353/99, *Hautala* [2001] ECR I-9565, paras. 80–3, and Opinion of Advocate-General Mischo of 20 September 2001, in Joined Cases C-20 and 64/00, *Booker Acquaculture and Hydro Seafood* [2003] ECR I-07411, para. 126 *et seq.*

[39] See S. Douglas-Scott, 'The Charter of Fundamental Rights as a Constitutional Document' (2004) *European Human Rights Law Review* 42; see also G. De Burca and J. B. Aschenbrenner, 'The Development of European Constitutionalism and the Role of the EU Charter of Fundamental Rights' (2003) 9 *Columbia Journal of European Law* 380.

supranational organisation, the membership of which entails the most far-reaching effects upon sovereignty in the contemporary world.

These three broader starting-points should be kept in mind in our subsequent analysis of those arguments that find the new document not to be a constitution.

We will start with the argument about the form of adoption. Although the final word indeed belongs to the Intergovernmental Conference and national ratifying bodies, it should be pointed out that the Convention has formed the crux of the overall process.[40] According to Juliane Kokott and Alexandra Rüth, even though designed as 'a consultative, not a constituent, assembly, its symbolic significance for the elaboration of a "Constitution" is undeniable'.[41] Bolder parallels with the Philadelphia Convention have been drawn by Michael Rosenfeld, who points out the 'open and public nature' of the European Convention, by contrast with the secret operation in Philadelphia.[42] As regards openness, the Convention process has indeed been characterised as the most transparent constitution-making exercise ever undertaken;[43] furthermore, its 2,000 working documents remain available online until 2008. The involvement of the Convention mechanism is also envisaged for the future amendment proceedings. In addition, a minor but potentially significant exception to the adoption procedure is that the matter will be referred to the European Council, should the ratification of the constitution be completed in four-fifths of the Member States but encounter difficulties in the remaining states.

The Convention mechanism is also of a major importance in that, for the first time, the 'people' element is brought to the procedure of adopting a new treaty. While it is often thought that there can be no constitution without a people, constitutions themselves can have an instrumental role in demos-building. For instance, Rosenfeld has shown that, contrary to the common belief, the American constitution preceded the people.[44] We will explore later in more detail the debate about the existence of a European demos, and the impact of the EU's constitutional process upon its reinforcement.

[40] See for the constitutional role of the Convention also Lenaerts and Gerard, 'Structure of the Union', p. 298.

[41] Kokott and Rüth, 'The European Convention', p. 1316.

[42] Rosenfeld, 'The European Convention', pp. 375–6.

[43] Ziller, *La nouvelle Constitution*, p. 81.

[44] Rosenfeld, 'The European Convention', pp. 375–6.

With regard to the argument about the excessive length of the EU's new basic document, it should be pointed out that this is not unprecedented for a constitution: the Constitution of India consists of 395 articles; the Constitution of Portugal of 299 articles and the Constitution of Brazil of 246 articles. In addition, the intention of the Convention was probably not without significance: rather than choosing merely to simplify and reorganise the Treaties – the options initially on the table – the Convention decided to draft a 'Constitution for Europe'.

Besides the above innovations in the formal aspects of the EU's new basic document, the European Constitution equally introduces some substantive changes which, adding to the already existing 'constitutional charter', appear to go further beyond what is normally associated with a treaty. Detailed accounts of the content of the Draft European Constitution have been presented elsewhere;[45] we will focus on some issues which may be relevant to the afore-mentioned national constitutional limits.

First, the new supremacy clause in article 10 has already provoked sensitive national reactions. It provides that '[t]he Constitution, and law adopted by the Union institutions in exercising their competences conferred on it, shall have primacy over the law of the Member States'. Although supremacy is well established in the case law of the European Court of Justice, the national courts have maintained that instead of deriving from the nature of Community law itself – as established by the ECJ – the direct effect and supremacy of EC law are based on the delegation of powers through the provisions of national constitutions, which they view as the ultimate basis for supremacy. With the codification of the principle of supremacy into the EU's Constitution, supremacy will now clearly derive from the EU level, even though disputes concerning the ultimate supremacy and the limits of delegation are likely to endure. Another significant change is that the depillarisation of the EU appears to extend the principle of supremacy across the full range of policy titles contained in Part III of the European Constitution.[46]

Secondly, the national constitutional limits are challenged by article 6, which expressly endows the EU with a legal personality. Although some academic commentators have found that, implicitly, the EU already possesses a legal personality, the absence of the EU's legal personality was

[45] See Dougan, 'The Convention's Draft Constitutional Treaty'; Kokott and Rüth, 'The European Convention'.

[46] Dougan, 'The Convention's Draft Constitutional Treaty', p. 64.

identified in the German *Maastricht* decision as one of the guarantees for Member States' sovereignty.

Thirdly, the European Constitution reduces in many new areas the possibility of using a veto right, sharpening thereby the tensions in respect of another aspect of sovereignty deemed vital by the highest courts. As of 2009, qualified majority voting will become the rule (article 24), limiting unanimity voting to the few most sensitive areas.

Another challenge to national constitutional limits may be found in the piecemeal but nevertheless tangible strengthening of the EU's role in Common Foreign and Security Policy. The European Constitution creates the post of the European Council President (article 21), the post of the EU Minister for Foreign Affairs (article 27), and foresees the establishment of a common diplomatic service – the European External Action Service (article III-197). In the field of defence, the European Constitution enables the establishment of closer cooperation in mutual defence amongst a group of countries interested in doing so (article III-213), and foresees the creation of the European Armaments, Research and Military Capabilities Agency. Although the CFSP continues to function under the intergovernmental mode, these reforms, combined with the introduction of the EU's legal personality and earlier reforms in Amsterdam and Nice, signal a move towards the Union's stronger presence in foreign and defence policy. The retention of these core areas of sovereign statehood under the national sphere was considered crucial for sovereignty by the German Constitutional Court.

The same holds true for justice and home affairs, another core area of sovereignty. The reforms gradually strengthen the EU's presence: the post of European Public Prosecutor is envisaged (article III-175), and unanimity will be replaced by qualified majority voting in matters concerning asylum, immigration and some aspects of criminal law and law enforcement.

As regards the reforms in the EU's democratic construction, the European Parliament's complementary role in the Union's democratic architecture, compared with national modes of democratic legitimisation, was regarded by the German Constitutional Court as a sign that the EU was not evolving into a federal state. In this respect, it may be of some significance that the Draft European Constitution strengthens the European Parliament, by making the co-decision procedure a rule and endowing the Parliament with the right to elect the Commission President (articles 33 and 19). Another innovation strengthening direct democratic links between the EU and citizens is the new right of one million European citizens to initiate a petition asking the Commission to present a proposal on a subject relevant to the constitution (article 46(4)). The democratic dimension is also reflected in the introduction of double majority voting, which reinforces the principle of dual, people-based and state-based legitimacy. According to the final agreement in the Intergovernmental Conference, the passing of acts will require, as of 2009, the representation of at least 55 per cent of the states, and 65 per cent of the EU's population.[47]

Next, although an issue not raised by the highest national courts, it may be of relevance that two modes of direct national participation in the governance of the EU have been downgraded to some extent: the system of rotating presidency of the European Council is abolished and rotation in Commission membership is anticipated as of 2014 (article 25). The former has presented an opportunity for national governments to design the EU's strategic agenda at certain intervals, as well as bringing Europe 'home'. As concerns the reform of the Commission, although the role of this institution lies in representing European rather than the national interest, the importance of equal national presence in the Commission was well illustrated by the fierce resistance to this reform by small countries and accession countries.

Last but certainly not least, the European Constitution incorporates the Charter and endows it with binding effect. On the one hand, improvements in the protection of fundamental rights at the EU level have been welcomed by the Constitutional Courts; on the other hand, the Charter's parallels to a 'Bill of Rights' may renew the 'federal question'.[48] Placing 'the individual at the heart of its activities' (Preamble), the Charter reinforces direct links between the EU and individuals, and forms a central building block for the 'Constitutional Treaty'.

The above considerations indicate that Europe's new basic document is more than what is generally associated with a treaty: although not amounting to a fully-fledged constitution, it can certainly be characterised as a 'Constitutional Treaty', with an emphasis on the 'constitutional'.

[47] According to the clauses added by the Intergovernmental Conference, qualified majority voting (QMV) is subject to the clause that decisions are approved by at least fifteen Member States, the blocking minority being at least four states. When three-quarters of the Member States or the population necessary to form a blocking minority indicate their opposition to the Council adopting an act by QMV, the Council shall discuss the issue in order to find a satisfactory solution.

[48] P. Eeckhout, 'The EU Charter of Fundamental Rights and the Federal Question' (2002) 39 *Common Market Law Review* 946. See for further comments on the constitutional role of the Charter the articles mentioned above n. 39.

Changes consolidating the position of Member States

Whereas the above changes challenge to some extent the limits set in the decisions of the national Constitutional Courts, there are also those which strengthen the position of the Member States: the Convention and the IGC have introduced or left out critical provisions which the national courts and political rhetoric have deemed important for preserving sovereignty.

For instance, article 5(1) explicitly states that 'the Union shall respect the national identities of the Member States, inherent in their fundamental structures, political and constitutional' and '[i]t shall respect their essential State functions, including those for ensuring the territorial integrity of the State, and for maintaining law and order and safeguarding internal security'. The principle of conferred competences is declared in article 1 and reiterated in article 9: 'the limits of Union competences are governed by the principle of conferral' and 'competences not conferred upon the Union in the Constitution remain with the Member States'. Furthermore, the European Constitution establishes the right to secede from the Union (article 59). The continuation of the current treaty amendment procedure (Article 48 TEU), denoting the status of the Member States as the 'Masters of the Treaties', is another important safeguard for national constitutional law, although it involves some new constitutional dimensions outlined above.

Amongst other points where Member States' interests have been paid tribute to is the keeping of the veto right in crucial areas of state sovereignty, such as tax, foreign and defence policy. Moreover, the Intergovernmental Conference added a so-called 'emergency brake system' in the field of social security and in judicial cooperation in criminal matters: when a Member State is of the opinion that fundamental aspects of its social security system or criminal justice system are at stake, it may request that a draft framework law be referred to the European Council. In this case, the decision-making process will be suspended. On the other hand, the European Constitution makes it possible to move certain fields from unanimity voting to qualified majority voting, thus escaping the cumbersome procedure of ratification under the national constitutional requirements (article 24(4)). According to the final changes made in the Intergovernmental Conference, this so-called 'passerelle' mechanism requires unanimity in the European Council, the consent of the European Parliament and the absence of opposition from national Parliaments. The role of national Parliaments is also increased by the so-called 'early warning' mechanism: the European Constitution accords them a right of information and an opportunity to challenge Commission proposals should these infringe the principle of subsidiarity. On behalf of the national Parliaments, the Member States' governments may pursue the Commission before the European Court of Justice on the grounds of alleged violations of this principle.[49] Further, the European Constitution does not entail a transfer of significant new competences to the EU level. Finally, it is also noteworthy that references to the 'United States of Europe' and to a division of competences on 'a federal basis', proposed in earlier drafts, were left out from the final version.

National responses

Although a number of key safeguards have been secured for the Member States, the above considerations indicate that the EU's new basic document is more than what is generally associated with a treaty: although not amounting to a fully-fledged constitution, it can certainly be characterised as a 'Constitutional Treaty', with an emphasis on its 'constitutional' nature. While research on the impact of the Draft European Constitution on national constitutions is still relatively scarce at the time of writing,[50] the discussions on the political level are revealing a great degree of sensitivity. Several Member States have considered the document to be of such an importance as to necessitate the holding of a referendum, including Denmark, Ireland, Spain, Portugal, Luxembourg, the United Kingdom and even the Netherlands, a country where no nation-wide referendums have been held before.[51] In Denmark, legal experts have suggested that the country will not be able to ratify the European Constitution without first undergoing the arduous procedure of amending the Danish

[49] Protocol on the role of national Parliaments in the European Union, and Protocol on the application of the principles of subsidiarity and proportionality, CONV 850/03, 226–31.

[50] See for a preliminary examination of the topic at time when the text of the Draft European Constitution was not yet available, e.g. J. Schwarze, 'The Birth of a European Constitutional Order' in J. Schwarze (ed.), *The Birth of a European Constitutional Order: The Interaction of National and European Constitutional Law* (Nomos, Baden-Baden, 2000); Lord Slynn of Hadley and M. Andenas (eds.), *FIDE XX Congress London 30 October–2 November 2002*, vol. 1, *National Reports: European Union Law and National Constitutions* (BIICL, London, 2002), and P. Steinberg, 'A Tentative Survey of the Innovations of the Constitution for Europe that Might Impact Upon National Constitutions' in J. Ziller (ed.), *L'européanisation des droits constitutionnels à la lumière de la Constitution pour l'Europe* (L'Harmattan, Paris, 2003).

[51] 'Referenda on EU Constitution', *EurActive Portal*, 24 June 2004, www.euractive.com

Constitution.[52] Discussions on holding a referendum are underway elsewhere, including Belgium, France and Finland. Germany, a country where the constitution does not permit referendums at the federal level, nonetheless faced calls for a referendum by the Christian Social Union and Liberal Democratic Party. A referendum was eventually ruled out, however, by the German Parliament in November 2003.

Amongst the accession countries, the prevailing view has been that the new document is just an international treaty, partly to avoid having to hold new referendums shortly after the accession referendums. However, the Czech Republic and Poland have recently decided to have recourse to a referendum. In the former, the notoriously eurosceptic President Klaus has characterised the European Constitution as 'a radical document with big consequences for national sovereignty', as 'the EU will no longer derive its power from its member countries but from its own constitution'.[53] In Estonia, the governing view has dismissed the need for a referendum, as the new document is perceived as an international treaty rather than a constitution, and it will change nothing in the Estonian legal order.[54] However, after the United Kingdom's decision to hold a referendum, proposals have emerged in favour of holding a referendum. In Poland, both the former Prime Minister Leszek Miller and President Aleksander Kwasniewski indicated in March 2004 that the country is likely to hold a referendum, possibly together with the presidential elections of 2005, in order to safeguard a high turnout.[55] Slovakian Prime Minister Mikuláš Dzurinda rejected the need for a referendum with the argument that the Slovakian Constitution requires a referendum only if the country is to join 'a new state formation'.[56] In Latvia, President Vaira Vike-Freiberga, in consultation with top politicians, has found no reason for holding a referendum on the European Constitutional Treaty. This was because the accession referendum has only just been held and the country 'cannot

[52] See *EU Observer* reports 'Danish Leader Affirms "Constitution Guarantee"' (6 June 2003) and 'Denmark under Pressure to Alter Constitution' (30 May 2003), www.euobserver.com

[53] 'Czech President Calls European Constitution "A Radical Document"', *RFE/RL Newsline*, vol. 7, no. 180, Part II, 22 September 2003.

[54] e.g. U. Reinsalu, Chairman of the Parliament's Constitutional Commission, in 'Põhiseadus säilitab euroliidu tänase näo' [The Constitution Retains the European Union's Current Face], *Eesti Päevaleht*, 15 July 2003.

[55] 'Poland Ready for Referendum on Constitution', *EU Observer*, 25 March 2004, www.euobserver.com

[56] 'Slovak Premier Opposes Referendum on EU Constitution', *RFE/RL Newsline*, vol. 7, no. 116, Part II, 20 June 2003.

hold referendums every day on technical matters and on issues the people [have] already . . . voted for'.[57]

Altogether, the Treaty establishing a Constitution for Europe is reviving the longstanding debate on potential conflicts between national constitutions and EU membership. Again, the postulate of national sovereignty will have to be reconciled with further steps in the process of European integration. It is likely that in some Member States, the Constitutional Courts may have to pronounce on the compatibility of the European Constitution with the national constitutions and with the principle of sovereignty, which may revive the criteria articulated in the *Maastricht* decisions. In fact, this question has already been raised in Estonia as part of an afore-mentioned case against the legality of the accession referendum: a claimant argued that the EU is in the process of transforming into a federal state, especially in view of the work towards adopting a European Constitution. According to this argument, article 1 of the Estonian Constitution, by declaring Estonia's independence and sovereignty to be eternal and inalienable, prohibits becoming a part of such a Union.[58] The claimant invoked in support of his argument the above-discussed Report of the Estonian Constitutional Expert Commission, where such reasoning had also been used.[59] The Court rejected the claim on procedural grounds, but similar challenges are likely to recur across Europe.

Incremental transition towards sovereignty of 'the peoples of Europe'?

The previous sections showed that the Treaty establishing the Constitution for Europe, combined with previous steps of integration introduced in the Treaties of Maastricht, Amsterdam and Nice, may to some extent further defy the critical thresholds established by the Constitutional Courts. However, beyond an academic exercise, it would be rather impracticable to speculate about the precise future end-point of sovereignty, especially given that sovereignty plays a vital role in the Constitutional Courts' potential future decisions on European integration, and considering that

[57] 'Senior Officials See No Need for Referendum on European Constitution', *RFE/RL Baltic States Report*, vol. 4, no. 33, 13 September 2003.

[58] *Kulbok*, Decision No. 3–4–1–12–03, 29 September 2003, available at www.nc.ee

[59] *Võimalik liitumine Euroopa Liiduga ja selle õiguslik tähendus Eesti riigiõiguse seisukohalt* [Potential Accession to the European Union and its Consequences for Estonian Constitutional Law], Report of the Constitutional Amendment Expert Commission of Estonia (1998), in Estonian at www.just.ee/juridica2.html

future steps of integration may need approval by citizens in referendums. Moreover, discussions about an eventual end-point would overlook the fact that sovereignty has been a fluid concept since its creation, adapting over the course of history to a changing social context and new modes of governance, from the absolute sovereignty of a monarch to the idea that sovereignty is vested in the people.[60]

Indeed, the need for another revision of the concept of sovereignty was forcefully brought to the fore by the influential wave of literature that has been sparked off by the German *Maastricht* decision.[61] In broad terms, this line of literature criticised the German Constitutional Court for failing to characterise adequately the multifaceted EU, and for setting limits to further integration on the basis of constitutional concepts of the nineteenth century. In a more global context, this is because most fields of contemporary life have become internationalised. The task of providing for the common good has shifted from the national to transnational level, supreme authority is now dispersed between numerous regulatory and judicial entities on international, supranational and national levels (e.g. the EU, United Nations, the Council of Europe, NATO, WTO), and territorial boundaries have been overlaid with the functional competence boundaries of international organisations.[62]

In the context of the European Union, the interference with various elements of sovereignty has been considerably more far-reaching. For instance, Stephen Hobe, assessing the EU in the light of standard textbook criteria for sovereign statehood – supreme power, government, territory, population and capacity for international action – has demonstrated a degree of erosion in all four respects. For instance, the EU has fairly efficient governing institutions which issue more than half of the Member States' legislation; EC law is supreme over national law; a state's territory is blurred due to the abolition of border controls; the Union has a multinational people defined by EU citizenship; and the EU has a relatively

[60] See for the evolution of the concept, e.g. R. Jackson, 'Sovereignty in World Politics: A Glance at the Conceptual and Historical Landscape' (1999) 47 *Political Studies* 435.

[61] See e.g. J. Habermas, 'The European Nation-State and the Pressures of Globalization' (1999) *New Left Review*, no. 235, 40–59; B. De Witte, 'Sovereignty and European Integration: The Weight of Legal Tradition' in A. M. Slaughter, A. Stone Sweet and J. H. H. Weiler (eds.), *The European Court and National Courts: Doctrine and Jurisprudence: Legal Change in its Social Context* (Hart, Oxford, 1998); Hobe, 'The German State', pp. 113–35; N. MacCormick, *Questioning Sovereignty: Law, State, and Nation in the European Commonwealth* (Oxford University Press, 1999); N. Walker, 'Late Sovereignty in the European Union' in N. Walker (ed.), *Sovereignty in Transition* (Hart, Oxford, 2003), pp. 3–32.

[62] See on the last points especially Walker, 'Late Sovereignty', pp. 22, 26.

broad capacity for international action.[63] One could add elements such as the common currency; the EU's varying degree of powers in core areas of sovereignty, such as foreign and defence policy and home affairs; the constitutional character of the Treaties; and manifold direct links between the EU institutions and citizens. As seen earlier, these aspects are further strengthened by the European Constitution.

In fact, the EU's effects upon sovereign governance seem so profound that it is no longer contested that the Member States do not possess full sovereignty – the view of shared, pooled, divided or commonly exercised sovereignty is by now well accepted in European and national, judicial and academic circles alike. Instead, the focus has shifted to the question of whether the EU is in the process of becoming a federal state. Therefore, the highest courts in the *Maastricht* decision, as well as legal scholars, have been focusing instead on 'the conservatory elements of statehood'.[64] For instance, the German Constitutional Court acknowledged the delegation of part of sovereignty, and devoted most of the judgment instead to elaboration of its view of why the EU was not a federal state. An influential analysis by Jean-Claude Piris similarly concludes that the Member States are no longer fully sovereign, although the EU is not a state.[65]

Considering these various challenges to sovereignty, several new ways have been proposed for looking at sovereignty in the EU. For instance, Stephen Hobe has advocated the concept of 'open statehood', which regards openness to international cooperation as a new element of statehood rather than a threat to sovereignty.[66] In the contemporary world, he says, 'most of the tasks, aims and purposes of the State, like e.g. security, safety, defence and welfare are characterized by a specific international

[63] See in more detail, Hobe, 'The German State', pp. 130–2, 142.

[64] Term borrowed from A. Dashwood, who uses it in a wider context of EU constitutional order; see A. Dashwood, 'States in the European Union' (1998) 23 *European Law Review* 201.

[65] J.-C. Piris, 'Does the European Union have a Constitution? Does it Need One?' (1999) 24 *European Law Review* 569. His article points out similar issues as mentioned above by the German Constitutional Court in the *Maastricht* decision, adding some further areas where Member States have retained most, although not full, control. These include the EU's lack of capacity to 'make war and peace', the dependence on national administrations and courts in implementation and enforcement, the absence of a head of state and of coercive powers (police, army, prisons), and the small size of the total staff of EU institutions and of the EU's budget. See for some similar points, also Dashwood, 'States in the European Union', pp. 209–13.

[66] See Hobe, 'The German State', pp. 113–35; S. Hobe, 'Statehood at the End of the 20th Century: The Model of the "Open State": A German Perspective' (1997) *Austrian Review of International and European Law* 125.

element; one can even go so far as to describe the openness of the State to international cooperation as a central aim of statehood'.[67] Others locate sovereignty in the peoples of the EU together through the Intergovernmental Conference.[68] Yet others even doubt sovereignty's explanatory currency, speaking of 'late sovereignty',[69] or 'post-sovereignty' and governance 'beyond the sovereign state'.[70] Since the latter approaches bring us eventually back to the question about the end-point of sovereignty, the former options seem more readily applicable from the point of view of national constitutional law.

A few years ago, Bruno De Witte sketched at the end of his insightful article on sovereignty the following question: 'Could it be that sovereignty lies with the peoples of the European Union taken together, rather than with each of those peoples separately?'. In his view, Article 48 TEU, which lays down the treaty amendment procedure, shows that 'ultimate authority lies with the Intergovernmental Conference of the Member States of the Union and the national constitutional bodies that must ratify their operation'.[71] He pointed out that constitutions of other countries, such as the Russian Constitution of 1993, show that 'it can make constitutional sense to attribute sovereignty to a *multinational* people'.[72] Amaryllis Verhoeven has developed a similar idea: 'Clearly, sovereignty can no longer be fused with or embodied in the organisational order of the state (and, within the state, in one representative organ, the parliament), be it at the national or European level. European integration compels us, rather, to remand sovereignty to its rightful "owners": the people, or rather peoples, of Europe.'[73]

These views deserve further consideration, as they appear to find support in the increasing recognition of a European demos, as well as gaining strength from the developments in the EU's constitutional process. As discussed in chapter 6, the concept of a European demos has increasingly gained ground as a result of the debate sparked off by the German *Maastricht* decision, where the German Constitutional Court famously took an ethno-cultural approach to democracy. Building upon influential writings by Weiler and Habermas, it is now widely acknowledged that,

[67] Hobe, 'Statehood at the End of the 20th Century', p. 150.
[68] De Witte, 'Sovereignty and European Integration', p. 304.
[69] Walker, 'Late Sovereignty', p. 19.
[70] MacCormick, *Questioning Sovereignty*, e.g. at pp. 95, 126, 133, 137.
[71] De Witte, 'Sovereignty and European Integration', p. 304. [72] *Ibid.*
[73] A. Verhoeven, *The European Union in Search of a Democratic and Constitutional Treaty* (Kluwer, 2002), p. 292.

existing in parallel to national identity, European identity is based on common, transcending cultural and political values.[74]

The fundamental developments in the EU's constitutional reform are likely to reinforce this line of thinking, as the process alludes in many respects to a further strengthening of the content of a European demos. As discussed above, the Convention process has manifold similarities with a constituent assembly, and the EU's direct links with citizens are strengthened by the incorporation of the Charter, the right of initiative of EU citizens, and by strengthening of the European Parliament. Both the European Constitution and the Charter set out the Union's common values, such as respect for human dignity, democracy, equality, the rule of law and human rights, which are 'common to the Member States in a society of pluralism, tolerance, justice, solidarity and non-discrimination' (article 2).[75] In addition, the European Constitution mentions that the European peoples are 'united ever more closely' (Preamble). The dual legitimacy – people-based and state-based legitimacy – of the EU is further recognised by reference to the will of both 'the citizens and the States of Europe' (Preamble and article 1,1), and by the above-mentioned introduction of double majority voting in the Council.

Indeed, during the work of the Convention, a number of commentators have mentioned, in some form or other, the possibility of the *pouvoir constituant* lying with the European peoples collectively.[76] However, it is

[74] J. H. H. Weiler, 'Does Europe Need a Constitution? Demos, Telos and the German Maastricht Decision' (1995) 1 *European Law Journal* 233 at p. 238; J. H. H. Weiler, *The Constitution of Europe. 'Do the New Clothes have an Emperor?' and Other Essays on the European Integration* (Cambridge University Press, 1999); J. Habermas, 'The European Nation State: Its Achievements and its Limitations: On the Past and Future of Sovereignty and Citizenship' (1996) 9 *Ratio Juris* 125; Habermas, 'The European Nation-State and the Pressures of Globalization'.

[75] See on values in more detail S. Millns, 'Unravelling the Ties that Bind: National Constitutions in the Light of Values, Principles and Objectives of the Constitution for Europe' in Ziller, *L'européanisation des droits constitutionnels*, pp. 97–120.

[76] e.g. Convention President Giscard d'Estaing on multiple occasions when calling for an EU-wide referendum. In academia, see e.g. A. Von Bogdandy, 'The Preamble' in De Witte, *Ten Reflections*, p. 5; Verhoeven, *The European Union*, p. 302; A. Føllesdal, 'Drafting a European Constitution: Challenges and Opportunities' (2002) Constitutionalism Web-Papers, ConWEB, http:// les1.man.ac.uk/conweb, p. 8; K. Nicolaidis, 'Our European Demoi-cracy: The New Constitution is on the Right Track', paper presented at the conference 'Towards a Federal Europe', European University Institute, Florence, 2 March 2003, to be published in (2005) *Journal of European Public Policy* (forthcoming); R. Arnold, 'Fundamental Rights Charter for the European Union' (2001) 15/16 *Tulane European and Civil Law Forum* 49; Lenaerts and Desomer, 'New Models of Constitution-Making', pp. 1251–2 ('peoples and the Member States of the European Union act as a constituent authority').

relevant to stress here that the European demos is regarded as implying European *peoples* rather than a single European *people*. As argued by Joseph Weiler in an article against a European Constitution, a single European people indeed does not exist in the EU.[77] However, it is precisely the European *peoples* collectively rather than a single European people that the above authors speak about.[78] The examples of South Africa, India, Russia and Brazil have often been used to indicate the feasibility of a plurality of nations and languages instead of a homogeneous people. According to Kalypso Nicolaidis, the EU as a new kind of political community rests on the plurality of its component peoples forming a 'demoi-cracy', which is based on sharing of identities, a community of shared projects and objectives and multicentred governance.[79] Udo Di Fabio speaks about '*Demoi* of multi-level democracy'.[80] Common belongingness has also been associated with the notion of a 'European social contract', which, according to Ingolf Pernice, has been created by the peoples of the Member States under national procedures, in order to transfer power and legitimising thereby the actions of European institutions.[81] It should be underscored here that legitimacy deriving from the EU level does not, of course, replace the national modes of legitimisation, but exists alongside it.

These developments in academic pages may, in fact, be indicative of the instrumental role of the constitutions themselves in demos-building.[82] The American experience informs us that 'We the people' behind the US Constitution 'did not connote the existence of American nation in 1787 in the sense that there was a French nation at the eve of the 1789 French Revolution'.[83] According to Michael Rosenfeld, 'whereas the people of the European Union are not yet united, the people behind the 1787 American constitution were profoundly divided and, for the most part, not yet formed'.[84] Jeffrey Goldsworthy also points out that for decades, passionate debates endured on whether the American Constitution was enacted

[77] J. H. H. Weiler, *Federalism and Constitutionalism: Europe's Sonderweg* (Jean Monnet Working Paper No. 10, 2000), www.jeanmonnetprogram.org

[78] Also Andreas Føllesdal in his response to Weiler; Føllesdal, 'Drafting a European Constitution', p. 8.

[79] Nicolaidis, 'Our European Demoi-cracy'.

[80] Di Fabio, 'European Charter', pp. 168, 169.

[81] I. Pernice, 'Multilevel Constitutionalism and the Treaty of Amsterdam: European Constitution-Making Revisited' (1999) 36 *Common Market Law Review* 710 at pp. 717–18, 720–2.

[82] See also Brand, 'Affirming and Refining European Constitutionalism', pp. 44–5; Lenaerts and Gerard, 'Structure of the Union', p. 322.

[83] Rosenfeld, 'The European Convention', p. 375.

[84] *Ibid.*

by 'the sovereign people of a single nation, or a compact between the sovereign peoples of independent states?'.[85] Paul Craig has also pointed out that the empirical and normative foundation for the claim that constitutions must go back to an act attributed to the people are not readily apparent.[86]

Indeed, the belief in an organic, natural nature of the national identity and nation-states has often been proved to be a myth: numerous nation-states have been created by various forms of force by non-representative elites and homogeneity is rare in the light of ubiquitous ethnic minorities and growing immigration movements.[87] The EU, on the contrary, has been developed incrementally, peacefully and democratically, as a voluntary pact.[88] Habermas has pointed out the key role of the writings of intelligentsia, scholars and mass media in the construction of national identity: the transformation of the *Adelsnation* into a *Volksnation* was a constructed artefact, a result of a deep change effected in the consciousness of the general population.[89] In the EU context, EU citizenship – with accompanying political, economic and social rights – has been regarded as a major building block for a European identity, playing an important role in the decoupling of state and nation, citizenship and national identity.[90]

To add an empirical dimension, the Eurobarometer survey of 2003 shows that 57 per cent of the citizens feel themselves European to some degree (with the highest proportion in Italy and Luxembourg and the lowest in the United Kingdom), even though an overwhelming part of the citizens (47 per cent) perceive themselves first as citizens of their own country and then as citizens of Europe.[91] Although beyond the scope

[85] J. Goldsworthy, 'The Debate About Sovereignty in the United States: A Historical and Comparative Perspective' in Walker, *Sovereignty in Transition*, p. 424, see also p. 425 *et seq.*

[86] Craig, 'Constitutions, Constitutionalism', p. 137.

[87] See e.g. G. Kirsch, 'The New Pluralism: Regionalism, Ethnicity, and Language in Western Europe' in K. Knop, S. Ostry, R. Simeon and K. Swinton (eds.), *Rethinking Federalism: Citizens, Markets, and Governments in a Changing World* (University of British Columbia Press, Vancouver, 1995), p. 66; J. R. Llobera, 'The Role of the State and the Nation in Europe' in S. Garcia (ed.), *European Identity and Search for Legitimacy* (Pinter, London, 1993), pp. 77–8.

[88] Llobera, 'Role of the State', pp. 77–8.

[89] Habermas, 'The European Nation State: Its Achievements and its Limitations', pp. 127,130, 132.

[90] This conclusion has been reached by all writers discussed in J. Shaw, *Citizenship of the Union: Towards Post-national Membership?* (Jean Monnet Working Paper No. 6/97, 1997), www.law.harvard.edu/programs/JeanMonnet/papers/97/97-06-.html, p. 45.

[91] *Eurobarometer 60*, February 2004, http:// euro.eu.int/comm/public_opinion/archives/eb/eb60/eb60_rapport_standard_en.pdf, p. 20.

of this study, it would be interesting to ask whether any role may be attributable to projects associated with an identity-fostering dimension, such as EU citizenship, the Erasmus programme, and the common currency.

In parenthesis, it may also be interesting to point out that at the time of the United States Constitution in 1787, there was no rail connection (the first passenger railway was opened in 1827 in Baltimore), and the journey from one part of the country to another could take several months, costing many lives. The first telegraph line within the USA was sent in 1844. Furthermore, the country was fraught by civil war in 1861–1865. Europeans, by contrast, regularly hop between European cities by low-cost airlines or even own holiday-homes in another country, exchange messages within seconds by email and Internet and war amongst them would be unimaginable.

To speak about a gradual and continuous move from sovereignty of individual countries to sovereignty of European peoples may pose problems from the point of view of traditional constitutional law, once again encapsulated well in the German *Maastricht* decision, where peoplehood was seen as intrinsically linked to a state, and hence the emergence of a European people would denote the EU's transition into a federal state. However, as with the above-discussed decoupling of the notion of a constitution from statehood, an emergence of European *demoi* need not necessarily be conductive to the statal character of a polity. This is yet another area where traditional constitutional categorisations appear to become outdated – the EU is rather a novel and unique combination of supranational and intergovernmental structures to which nation-states remain central, and where democratic legitimacy emanates from multiple levels.

To avoid the federal implications which so often seem to hamper a free discussion concerning constitutionalism and demos, it is perhaps better to search for a novel, non-statal label for the EU. Thoughtful alternatives have indeed been proposed, such as a 'European *Commonwealth*',[92] a 'system of multilevel governance',[93] or an organisation whose functioning resembles a new form of federalism such as an 'integrative federalism'[94] or

[92] MacCormick, *Questioning Sovereignty*; R. Bellamy and D. Castiglione, 'Building the Union' (1997) 16 *Law and Philosophy* 421.

[93] A standard term in political science.

[94] K. Lenaerts, 'Federalism: Essential Concepts in Evolution: the Case of the European Union' (1998) 21 *Fordham International Law Journal* 746.

a 'supranational federation'.[95] The German Constitutional Court offered a promising term 'Staatenverbund', which however has proved difficult for adequate translation into other languages without facing the federation-confederation dilemma. In practical terms, the EU is perhaps still best characterised as a 'supranational organisation *sui generis*': this term has proved relatively uncontroversial in respect of national constitutional sensitivities, being at the same time capable of embracing new facets of integration.

Overall, there seems to be increasingly grounds for speaking about an incremental and continuous shift in the crux of the concept of sovereignty from the sovereignty of individual states to the sovereignty of the European peoples – or peoples and Member States – together, who exercise it in common and jointly hold the supreme power. This move, perhaps accompanied by a novel, non-statal approach to the EU, entails several practical and conceptual advantages. European integration has developed so dramatically that it is practically meaningless to discuss which point of future integration would deprive a Member State of its internal or external sovereignty, as traditionally understood. At the same time, it would neither be practicable nor justified to speak about the end of sovereignty, at least beyond academic circles. Against this background, the proposed new approach has the advantage of letting us also continue the use of the concept of sovereignty after future transfers of powers, which is crucial in order to secure future national authorisations for new steps of integration. This, in turn, preserves the credibility of the national constitutions, to which sovereignty is, explicitly or implicitly, a central concept.

A crucial prerequisite for a credible re-examination of sovereignty, and for a move towards a genuine European constitutional order, is a more significant recognition of the EU's role on governance in the national constitutions. Many of them – both in the 'old' Member States and accession countries – still accommodate the transfer of powers to the EU under elusive norms on international organisations or, indeed, have minimal provisions or are completely silent on any aspect of EU membership. The absence of a clear authorisation for delegation of powers to the EU upholds the traditional views on sovereignty, and sustains the potential for destructive clashes based on national constitutional limits to delegation. Updating the constitutions with a view to the effects of EU

[95] A. Von Bogdandy, 'The European Union as a Supranational Federation: A Conceptual Attempt in the Light of the Amsterdam Treaty' (2000) 6 *Columbia Journal of European Law* 27.

membership – ideally on the model of Germany, France, Portugal and, amongst the current and future accession countries, Slovakia and Romania – would, *inter alia*, have the advantage of allowing national constitutions to live up to their rationale, as well as bringing citizens closer to the European venture. The provisions that the constitutions could contain with regard to EU membership were explored in chapter 6 alongside some broader observations about the role of the national constitutions in the process of European integration. The European Constitution strengthens the case for a wider presence of the European Union in national constitutions.

EPILOGUE: 'TAKING CONSTITUTIONS SERIOUSLY' IN THE PROCESS OF EUROPEAN INTEGRATION

This book shows a remarkable journey of Central and Eastern European countries from regaining sovereignty to delegating part of it, a little more than a decade later, to one of the most highly integrated organisations in the world. While the constitutional lawyers in the 'old' Member States have had time to adapt incrementally to and absorb new steps of integration, the accession of the CEE countries represents a major 'constitutional leap', in the sense that they are joining at a time when the EU is preparing a Constitution which for many involves federal connotations. A central element of this 'constitutional leap' was the revision of the CEE constitutions, where the *pouvoir constituant* has entrenched a complex set of guarantees for sovereignty and independence. This proved a rather challenging and controversial exercise, resulting in most countries in minimal amendments prior to the accession referendums. Indeed, many of them have preferred to continue the amendment process in a politically more relaxed post-referendum environment, as well as in the light of new challenges posed by the European Constitution. Having explored throughout the book the complex and multifaceted process of constitutional revision, perhaps six broader conclusions could be drawn.

To start with, the constitutional developments both in the 'old' and 'new' Member States have raised the question about the role of national constitutions in the context of ever deeper integration. Amongst the 'old' Member States, nearly half of the constitutions contain minimal references to the European Union, or even none at all, and have been commented on as suffering from a 'European deficit'. In the accession countries of Central and Eastern Europe, the solutions also remained relatively minimal, with the exception of Slovakia and Romania (the latter still being a candidate country). The minimalism finds expression in the amendments being addressed to 'international organisations', and/or limiting the revision to a minimum, compared with the constitutional conflicts the elimination of which had initially been deemed necessary. In the Baltic countries, we additionally witnessed procedural minimalism, in that the rigid amendment procedures, requiring a referendum for amending the provisions of sovereignty, were rather liberally interpreted. Although the comparative experience is diverse and lends support to such solutions, the book drew attention to some distinct dimensions of CEE constitutions which justify a wider range of EU amendments. First, in reaction to the propagandist and political nature of the Communist constitutions, the new constitutions of Central and Eastern Europe are distinctly clear, up-to-date and detailed documents, which enjoy a prominent position in the respective national legal orders. They appear to be 'taken more seriously' than perhaps in some Western European countries with long traditions of stable statehood, and therefore changes in the distribution of powers between domestic institutions of governance have usually been preceded in CEE constitutions by prior constitutional revision rather than broad interpretation. Further, CEE constitutions have what the book has termed a 'souverainist' character, in that they protect sovereignty through various safeguards and were until recently closed towards delegating powers to international organisations. Also, these constitutions clearly establish the principle of supremacy of the constitutions, and some constitutional courts have expressly warned the Parliaments against amending the constitutions in a disguised way by ratifying international treaties. It is against this background that the EU amendments in most countries remain modest. The book discussed a number of issues that deserve reflection in the constitutions, in order to keep the constitutions meaningful in respect of the actual exercise of powers. Adequate amendments would additionally endow participation in the European construction with a higher legitimacy, avoid unnecessary challenges to the supremacy of Community law, as well as bringing the European venture closer to citizens.

Secondly, the examination of the amendment process demonstrated the impact of factors such as procedures, referendums and the level of public support for European integration upon the content of the amendments. With some variations, a pattern could be discerned that the amendments were more far-reaching in those countries where the constitutions could be amended by a relatively flexible parliamentary procedure (Slovakia) and where accession benefited from firm public support (Slovakia, Romania).[1] By contrast, the amendment process was fraught with difficulties, and the results remained minimal, in the Baltic countries, where the constitutional amendment procedures are rather rigid and euroscepticism was the highest amongst the candidate countries. Further,

[1] Although the Romanian Constitution has a rigid amendment procedure.

the then imminent referendums left a strong imprint on the amendments in most countries: due to concerns about high minimum turnout requirements, low public support levels for EU accession and the sensitivity of the issue of delegating sovereignty, it was important not to reflect too much of the EU's impact upon sovereign governance in the national constitutions, as this could have become a dangerous tool in the hands of the eurosceptic movements. Besides minimal constitutional amendments, the risk of failure of the accession referendums also led to a variety of procedural manoeuvres, which eventually secured an overwhelming 'yes' to EU membership in all accession countries.

This leads us to the third point – the relevance of CEE referendum practice in the enlarged Union. The amendment of the treaties in the EU is subject to the approval by all Member States under their 'national constitutional procedures' (Article 48 TEU), and this procedure has largely been retained in the European Constitution. The fragility of this procedure has well been exemplified by the Danish and Irish referendums, and enlargement will put this procedure under further strain. Chapter 7 showed that this is not just by virtue of an increase in the number of Member States, but also because the 'national constitutional procedures' in the accession countries involve several procedural and practical complications: there is a tradition of holding referendums frequently; referendums usually require a minimum of 50 per cent turnout; the majority of recent referendums have been invalid due to a failure to meet the minimum turnout requirements; and unsuccessful referendums may not be re-initiated within one to four years in a number of countries.

Fourthly, besides the above-mentioned factors, the content of the constitutional amendments has also been influenced by the constitutional theory in CEE countries. While Western Europe has been revising the concept of sovereignty, the countries of Central and Eastern Europe operated until recently in the traditional language of sovereignty, independence, ethnically defined nation-state and national self-determination. Awareness of the EU's constitutional impact has registered in CEE literature only towards the very end of the 1990s, as constitutional research, after the fall of the Iron Curtain, has been predominantly focused on the re-establishing of sovereignty and the impact of public international law upon it. Proceeding from the traditional concept of sovereignty, as well as from the constitutionally entrenched distinction between independence and sovereignty, legal theory in the accession countries appears to adhere to the view that a part of sovereign powers (internal sovereignty) may be delegated to the European Union, whereas independence, in the meaning of statehood or external sovereignty, must be retained. The European Union has generally been portrayed in the constitutional amendment discussions as an international organisation, which does not significantly impact upon sovereignty. However, entry into the Union, especially at a time when the EU has been engaged in the 'Future Debate', is triggering a major change in the traditional nation-state-centred paradigm of sovereignty and democratic legitimacy, paving the way to exploring theories of supranational governance and post-national democracy.

Fifthly, the book pointed out some issues in terms of legitimacy of the pre-accession adaptations, in view of the strict protection of sovereignty in the CEE constitutions (except Poland where a new constitution was adopted in 1997). Since the early 1990s, the CEE countries have been engaged in a gigantic task of harmonising their law with EU law. Besides about 80,000 pages of *acquis*, this involves some core functions of statehood, such as foreign and internal security policy, as well as areas that are not binding on all Member States, such as Schengen and EMU, and even some areas beyond the EU's domestic competences, such as social system reform and nuclear safety. Meanwhile, unlike the EEA countries, the candidate countries did not have significant opportunities to participate in the creation of EU law, even as regards those acts which were in the drafting process. Therefore, more sovereignty paradoxically might have been surrendered during the pre-accession period, some of it being regained upon accession through the countries' inclusion in the EU's decision-making process. The Hungarian Constitutional Court's insightful observations about the legitimacy of judicial harmonisation in its *Europe Agreement* decisions are of particular interest here.

Finally, some broader implications of the Draft European Constitution for national constitutions and sovereignty were considered. While the prevailing view characterises the Union's new basic document as a treaty rather than as a constitution, it was argued in the final chapter that, taken together with relatively far-reaching steps of integration introduced in the previous treaties, the European Constitution appears to go beyond what is normally associated with a treaty, giving ground for speaking of a 'Constitutional Treaty', with an emphasis on the 'constitutional'. This is based on the premise that, as pointed out in an increasing amount of post-national literature, constitutions are no longer inextricably linked to statehood. The conclusion about the 'constitutional character' of the new basic document, coupled with some innovations in its content, appears to challenge in some respects the criteria for preserving sovereignty, which had been elaborated by the German Constitutional Court in the *Maastricht* decision back in 1993 and have been widely invoked in national constitutional literature. Hence, the Draft European Constitution strengthens the case for revising the concept of sovereignty, as was proposed by many scholars in the wake of the German *Maastricht* decision. This is especially so given that it would neither be practicable to speak about an eventual future end-point of sovereignty, nor would it be consistent with the historically fluid and socially conditioned nature of this concept. Amongst the plethora of new approaches to sovereignty, the view that sovereignty might be in a gradual and continuous process of transition from the individual Member States to the peoples of the Member States – or peoples and Member States – collectively deserves further consideration, due to the increasing recognition of the concept of a European demos and its reinforcement by the EU's constitutional process.

Overall, the above developments indicate that the notion of 'constitution' itself appears to be 'in transition'. Laying down the foundations of sovereign governance in a nation-state, constitutions have traditionally been associated with states. The increasingly intensifying challenges to this by various external organisations have caused the 'opening up' of constitutions to accommodate international and European governance. The ongoing process of adopting a European Constitution is triggering another major change of the paradigm, in that the notion of 'constitution' is being decoupled from statehood and used in the context of a novel, *sui generis* transnational polity such as the EU.

BIBLIOGRAPHY

Articles, monographs and edited volumes

Agh, A., 'The Role of ECE Parliaments in the Pre-Accession Strategy' in Z. Mansfeldová and M. Klíma (eds.), *The Role of the Central European Parliaments in the Process of European Integration: Proceedings of International Conference, Prague, 12–14 September 1997* (Academy of Sciences, Prague, 1998), p. 116

Albi, A., 'Estonia's Constitution and the EU: How and to What Extent to Amend It?' (2002) *Juridica International, Law Review of Tartu University* 39

Referendums in Eastern Europe: The Effects on Reforming the EU Treaties and on the Candidate Countries' Positions in the Convention (European University Institute, Robert Schuman Centre Working Paper No. 2002/65, Florence, 2002)

'Post-modern Versus Retrospective Sovereignty: Two Different Sovereignty Discourses in the EU and Candidate Countries?' in N. Walker (ed.), *Sovereignty in Transition* (Hart, Oxford, 2003), pp. 401–22

'Referendums in the CEE Candidate Countries: Impact on EU Treaty Amendment Procedure' in C. Hillion (ed.), *EU Enlargement: A Legal Approach* (Hart, Oxford, 2004), pp. 57–76

'Common Currency and National Constitutions' in C. Zilioli and F. Torres (eds.), *Governing EMU: Legal, Political, Economic and Historical Aspects* (European University Institute, Florence, forthcoming 2004)

Albi, A. and P. Van Elsuwege, 'EU Constitution, National Constitutions and Sovereignty: An Assessment of a "European Constitutional Order"' (2004) *European Law Review* (forthcoming)

Arnold, R., 'Fundamental Rights Charter for the European Union' (2001) 15/16 *Tulane European and Civil Law Forum* 43

'Peut-on définir le phénomène d'européanisation des droits constitutionnels nationaux?' in J. Ziller (ed.), *L'européanisation des droits constitutionnels à la lumière de la Constitution pour l'Europe* (L'Harmattan, Paris, 2003), pp. 85–96

Arnold, R. and M. Nedelka, 'Different Models of Adjusting to European Integration with a View to the Implementation and Enforcement of the Europe Agreements' in P. C. Müller-Graff (ed.), *East Central Europe and the European*

Union: From Europe Agreements to a Member Status (Nomos, Baden-Baden, 1997), pp. 357–67

Auer, A. and M. Bützer (eds.), *Direct Democracy: The Eastern and Central European Experience* (Ashgate, Aldershot, 2001)

Aziz, M., 'Sovereignty Lost, Sovereignty Regained? Some Reflections on the *Bundesverfassungsgericht*'s Bananas Judgment' (2002) 9 *Columbia Journal of European Law* 109

'Sovereignty Über Alles: (Re)Configuring the German Legal Order' in N. Walker (ed.), *Sovereignty in Transition* (Hart, Oxford, 2003), pp. 280–304

Balas, V., 'Legal and Quasi-legal Thresholds of the Accession of the Czech Republic to the EC' in A. Kellermann, J. De Zwaan and J. Czuczai (eds.), *EU Enlargement: The Constitutional Impact at EU and National Level* (Asser Press, The Hague, 2001), pp. 267–78

Barcz, J., 'Membership of Poland in the European Union in the Light of the Constitution of 2 April 1997' (1997–98) 23 *Polish Yearbook of International Law* 21

Bartole, S., *Riforme costituzionali nell'Europa centro-orientale* (Bologna, 1993)

Bellamy, R. and D. Castiglione, 'Building the Union' (1997) 16 *Law and Philosophy* 421

Berke, B., 'Community Law and National Legal Order' in P. C. Müller-Graff (ed.), *East Central Europe and the European Union: From Europe Agreements to a Member Status* (Nomos, Baden-Baden, 1997)

'Implementation of the Association Agreement, Approximation of Laws, Eventual Accession: Some Constitutional Implications' in F. Mádl (ed.), *On the State of the EU Integration Process: Enlargement and Institutional Reforms* (ELTE University, EU Centre for Research and Documentation, Budapest, 1997), pp. 323–41

Besselink, L., 'The Separation of Powers under Netherlands Constitutional Law and European Integration' (1997) 3 *European Public Law* 311

Biernat, S., 'Constitutional Aspects of Poland's Future Membership in the European Union' (1998) 36 *Archiv des Völkerrechts* 398

'The Openness of the Constitution of the Republic of Poland Towards European Integration' in G. Amato, G. Braibant and E. Venizelos (eds.), *The Constitutional Revision in Today's Europe* (Esperia Publications, London, 2002), pp. 439–51

Blazyca, G. and M. Kolkiewicz, 'Poland and the EU: Internal Disputes, Domestic Politics and Accession' (1999) 15 *Journal of Communist Studies and Transition Politics* 131

Bonnie, A., 'The Constitutionality of Transfers of Sovereignty: The French Approach' (1998) 4 *European Public Law* 517

Botelho Moniz, C., 'The Portuguese Constitution and the Participation of the Republic of Portugal in the European Union' (1998) 4 *European Public Law* 465

Brand, M., *Affirming and Refining European Constitutionalism: Towards the Establishment of the First Constitution for the European Union* (European University Institute, Law Department, Working Paper No. 2004/02, Florence, 2004), www.iue.it/PUB/law04-2.pdf

Bugge, P., *Czech Perceptions of the Perspective of EU Membership: Havel vs Klaus* (European University Institute, Robert Schuman Centre, Working Paper No. 2000/10, Florence, 2000)

Buka, A. and K. Jarinovska, 'Will Referendum on Accession to the EU Take Place in Latvia?' (in Latvian) (1999) *Likums und Tiesibas*, no. 1

Cerar, M., 'Slovenia: From Elite Consensus to Democratic Consolidation' in J. Zielonka and A. Pravda (eds.), *Democratic Consolidation in Eastern Europe*, vol. 1, *Institutional Engineering* (Oxford University Press, 2001), pp. 378–405

Chirico, A., *La soveranita monetaria tra ordine giuridico e processo economico* (CEDAM, Padova, 2003)

Ciobanu-Dordea, A., 'Constitutional Problems of Accession in Romania' in A. Kellermann, J. De Zwaan and J. Czuczai (eds.), *EU Enlargement: The Constitutional Impact at EU and National Level* (Asser Press, The Hague, 2001), pp. 311–14

Craig, P., 'Constitutions, Constitutionalism, and the European Union' (2001) 7 *European Law Journal* 125

Cremona, M. (ed.), *The Enlargement of the European Union* (Oxford University Press, 2003)

'Introduction' in M. Cremona (ed.), *The Enlargement of the European Union* (Oxford University Press, 2003), pp. 1–8

Czaplinski, W., 'The Relationship between International Law and Polish Municipal Law in the Light of the 1997 Constitution and Jurisprudence' (1999) *Droit Polonais Contemporain* 19

'L'Intégration européenne dans la constitution polonaise de 1997' (2000) *Revue du Marché Commun et de l'Union Européenne* 168

Czuczai, J., 'The Constitutional Challenges of Accession in Central and East European Countries: A Comparative Study on Hungary, Poland and Czech Republic' in A. Kellermann, J. De Zwaan and J. Czuczai (eds.), *EU Enlargement: The Constitutional Impact at EU and National Level* (Asser Press, The Hague, 2001), pp. 411–23

'National Preferences in Light of the Constitutional Adaptation Process to the EU Accession Acquis: The Hungarian Experiences in a Comparative Dimension of Central and Eastern Europe' in *Europe 2002* (Budapest, March 2004), vol. V/1, pp. 49–56

Dashwood, A., 'States in the European Union' (1998) 23 *European Law Review* 201

De Burca, G. and J. B. Aschenbrenner, 'The Development of European Constitutionalism and the Role of the EU Charter of Fundamental Rights' (2003) 9 *Columbia Journal of European Law* 355

De la Sierra, S. and F. Domínguez-García, 'The Treatment of European Law in the Study of Constitutional Law: Has an Effective Europeanisation of Constitutional Law Already Taken Place?' in J. Ziller (ed.), *L'européanisation des droits constitutionnels à la lumière de la Constitution pour l'Europe* (L'Harmattan, Paris, 2003), pp. 53–68

Desny, P., 'The Harmonisation of the Legislation of the Czech Republic with European Union Law' (1997) 8 *Perspectives* 45

De Witte, B., 'Pays-Bas' in J. Rideau (ed.), *États Membres de l'Union Européenne: Adaptations, mutations, résistances* (LGDJ, Paris, 1997), pp. 367–90

'Sovereignty and European Integration: The Weight of Legal Tradition' in A. M. Slaughter, A. Stone Sweet and J. H. H. Weiler (eds.), *The European Court and National Courts: Doctrine and Jurisprudence: Legal Change in its Social Context* (Hart, Oxford, 1998), pp. 277–304

'Constitutional Aspects of European Union Membership in the Original Six Member States: Model Solutions for the Applicant Countries?' in A. Kellermann, J. De Zwaan and J. Czuczai (eds.), *EU Enlargement: The Constitutional Impact at EU and National Level* (Asser Press, The Hague, 2001), pp. 65–80

'Entry into Force and Revision' in B. De Witte (ed.), *Ten Reflections on the Constitutional Treaty for Europe* (EUI-RSCAS/AEL, Florence, 2003), available at www.iue.it/RSCAS/Publications, pp. 203–20

'The Impact of Enlargement on the Constitution of the European Union' in M. Cremona (ed.), *The Enlargement of the European Union* (Oxford University Press, 2003), pp. 209–51

Ten Reflections on the Constitutional Treaty for Europe (EUI-RSCAS/AEL, Florence, 2003), available at www.iue.it/RSCAS/Publications

Dick, I. and A. E. Howard (eds.), *Constitution Making in Eastern Europe* (Woodrow Wilson Centre Press, Washington, 1993)

Di Fabio, U., 'European Charter: Towards a Constitution for the Union' (2001) 7 *Columbia Journal of European Law* 159

Dougan, M., 'The Convention's Draft Constitutional Treaty: Bringing Europe Closer to its Lawyers' (2003) 28 *European Law Review* 763

Douglas-Scott, S., 'The Charter of Fundamental Rights as a Constitutional Document' (2004) *European Human Rights Law Review* 37

Dubois, L., 'France' in J. Rideau (ed.), *États Membres de l'Union Européenne: Adaptations, mutations, résistances* (LGDJ, Paris, 1997), pp. 215–37

Duculescu, V., 'La réforme constitutionnelle en Roumanie et les exigencies de l'intégration europóene' (2004) *Revue Internationale de Droit Comparé* 193

'Editorial: The President's Tale' (2004) 29 *European Law Review* 1

Eeckhout, P., 'The EU Charter of Fundamental Rights and the Federal Question' (2002) 39 *Common Market Law Review* 945

Ehin, P., 'Estonian Euroskepticism: A Reflection of Domestic Politics?' (2002/2003) 11/12 *East European Constitutional Review*, no. 4/1

Evans, A., *The Integration of the European Community and Third States in Europe* (Clarendon Press, Oxford, 1996)

'Voluntary Harmonization in Integration between the European Community and Eastern Europe' (1997) 22 *European Law Review* 201

Evtimov, E., 'Die Bulgarische Verfassung und das Europarecht: Spannungsfelder und Lösungsansätze' (2001) 47 *Osteuropa Recht* 394

Føllesdal, A., 'Drafting a European Constitution: Challenges and Opportunities', 2002, Constitutionalism Web-Papers, ConWEB, http://les1.man.ac.uk/conweb

Gallagher, M. and P. V. Uleri (eds.), *The Referendum Experience in Europe* (Macmillan, Basingstoke, 1996)

Ganev, V., 'Bulgaria: The (Ir)Relevance of Post-Communist Constitutionalism' in J. Zielonka and A. Pravda (eds.), *Democratic Consolidation in Eastern Europe,* vol. 1, *Institutional Engineering* (Oxford University Press, 2001), pp. 186–211

Gelazis, N., 'Institutional Engineering in Lithuania: Stability through Compromise' in J. Zielonka and A. Pravda (eds.), *Democratic Consolidation in Eastern Europe,* vol. 1, *Institutional Engineering* (Oxford University Press, 2001), pp. 165–85

Goldsworthy, J., 'The Debate About Sovereignty in the United States: A Historical and Comparative Perspective' in N. Walker (ed.), *Sovereignty in Transition* (Hart, Oxford, 2003), pp. 423–48

Gomula, J., 'Dispute Settlement under Association Agreements with Central and Eastern European States' (1995–1996) 22 *Polish Yearbook of International Law* 107

Grabbe, H., *A Partnership for Accession? The Implications of EU Conditionality for the Central and East European Applicants* (European University Institute, Robert Schuman Center, Working Paper No. 99/12, Florence, 1999)

Grabbe, H. and K. Hughes (eds.), *Eastward Enlargement of the European Union* (The Royal Institute of International Affairs, London, 1998)

'Central and East European Views on EU Enlargement: Political Debates and Public Opinion' in K. Henderson (ed.), *Back to Europe* (UCL Press, London, 1999)

Griller, S., 'Introduction to the Problems in the Austrian, the Finnish and Swedish Constitutional Order' in A. Kellermann, J. De Zwaan and J. Czuczai (eds.), *EU Enlargement: The Constitutional Impact at EU and National Level* (Asser Press, The Hague, 2001), pp. 147–81

Grimm, D., 'Does Europe Need a Constitution?' (1995) 1 *European Law Journal* 282

Grozavescu, I., 'International Agreements in the Legal Orders of the Candidate Countries: Romania' in A. Ott and K. Inglis (eds.), *Handbook on European Enlargement* (T. M. C. Asser Press, The Hague, 2002), pp. 309–21

Grzelak, A., 'Poland' in *Criminal Law in the European Union: A Giant Leap or A Small Step? FIDE 2004 National Reports*, www.fide2004.org/reports/mc/mc17b.pdf

Györi, E., 'Parliaments and the European Union: The Involvement of the Hungarian National Assembly in the Process of European Integration' in Z. Mansfeldová and M. Klíma (eds.), *The Role of the Central European Parliaments in the Process of European Integration: Proceedings of International Conference, Prague, 12–14 September 1997* (Academy of Sciences, Prague, 1998), pp. 75–90

Habermas, J., 'The European Nation State: Its Achievements and its Limitations: On the Past and Future of Sovereignty and Citizenship' (1996) 9 *Ratio Juris* 125

'The European Nation-State and the Pressures of Globalization' (1999) 235 *New Left Review* 40

Hailbronner, K., 'The European Union from the Perspective of the German Constitutional Court' (1994) 37 *German Yearbook of International Law* 93

Harmathy, A., 'Constitutional Questions of the Preparation of Hungary to Accession to the European Union' in A. Kellermann, J. De Zwaan and J. Czuczai (eds.), *EU Enlargement: The Constitutional Impact at EU and National Level* (Asser Press, The Hague, 2001), pp. 315–26

Hartley, T., *Constitutional Problems of the European Union* (Hart, Oxford, 1999)

Hesse, J., 'Introduction. Constitutional Policy and Change in Europe: The Nature and Extent of the Challenges' in J. Hesse and N. Johnson (eds.), *Constitutional Policy and Change in Europe* (Nuffield European Studies, Oxford University Press, 1995), pp. 3–22

Hiller, K., 'Neue Verfassung für Ungarn?' (1998) 2 *Recht in Ost und West* 74

Hillion, C., 'Cases C-63/99 *Gloszczuk*; C-235/99 *Kondova*; C-257/99 *Barkoci and Malik*; Case C-268/99 *Jany*; Case C-162/00 *Pokrzeptowicz-Meyer*' (2003) 40 *Common Market Law Review* 465

'Enlargement of the European Union: A Legal Analysis' in T. Arnull and D. Wincott (eds.), *Accountability and Legitimacy in the European Union* (Oxford University Press, 2003), pp. 401–18

(ed.), *EU Enlargement: A Legal Approach* (Hart, Oxford, 2004)

Hobe, S., 'The German State in Europe after the Maastricht Decision of the German Constitutional Court' (1994) 37 *German Yearbook of International Law* 113

'Statehood at the End of the 20th Century: The Model of the "Open State": A German Perspective' (1997) *Austrian Review of International and European Law* 125

Hoffmeister, F., E. Evtimov, V. Tyc, *et al.*, 'International Agreements in the Legal Orders of the Candidate Countries' in A. Ott and K. Inglis (eds.), *Handbook on European Enlargement* (T. M. C. Asser Press, The Hague, 2002), pp. 209–348

Hofmann, M., 'The Right to Establishment for Nationals of the European Union Associated Countries in the Recent Jurisprudence of the European Court of Justice' (2001) 44 *German Yearbook of International Law* 469

Hogan, G., 'Ireland and the European Union: Constitutional Law and Practice' in A. Kellermann, J. De Zwaan and J. Czuczai (eds.), *EU Enlargement: The Constitutional Impact at EU and National Level* (Asser Press, The Hague, 2001), pp. 89–108

Hoskova, M., 'Legal Aspects of the Integration of the Czech Republic and Slovakia into European Security and Economic Structures' (1994) 37 *German Yearbook of International Law* 68

Inglis, K., 'The Europe Agreements Compared in the Light of their Pre-accession Reorientation' (2000) 37 *Common Market Law Review* 1175

Jackson, R., 'Sovereignty in World Politics: A Glance at the Conceptual and Historical Landscape' (1999) 47 *Political Studies* 431

Jacobs, F., 'The Constitutional Impact of the Forthcoming Enlargement of the EU: What Can be Learnt from the Experience of the Existing Member States?' in A. Kellermann, J. De Zwaan and J. Czuczai (eds.), *EU Enlargement: The Constitutional Impact at EU and National Level* (Asser Press, The Hague, 2001), pp. 183–94

Jacque, J.-P., 'Commentaire de la décision du Conseil constitutionnel n 92-308 DC du 9 avril 1992. Traité sur l'Union européenne 1992' (1992) *Revue Trimestrielle du Droit Européen* 251

Jüränki, A., 'Transferring Powers of a Nation-State to International Organisations: The Doctrine of Sovereignty Revisited' in A. Jüränki (ed.), *National Constitutions in the Era of Integration* (Kluwer Law International, The Hague, 1999), pp. 61–85

Justynski, J., 'The Impact of the European Integration Process on the Creation of the Broad Lines of the Constitution of the Republic of Poland and on the Political Practices of the Country' in A. Kellermann, J. De Zwaan and J. Czuczai (eds.), *EU Enlargement: The Constitutional Impact at EU and National Level* (Asser Press, The Hague, 2001), pp. 279–90

Kellermann, A., 'Constitutional Aspects for Bulgaria of the Integration Process to the EU: Pre-accession Effect of Association Agreement?', paper presented at seminar 'The Impact of (Future) Accession to the European Union on the National Legal Systems', organised by T. M. C. Asser Instituut and Centre for the Study of Democracy, Sofia, 16–17 April 2004

Kellermann, A., J. De Zwaan and J. Czuczai (eds.), *EU Enlargement: The Constitutional Impact at EU and National Level* (Asser Press, The Hague, 2001)

Kennedy, D. and D. E. Webb, 'The Limits of Integration: Eastern Europe and the European Communities' (1993) 32 *Common Market Law Review* 1095

Kirsch, G., 'The New Pluralism: Regionalism, Ethnicity, and Language in Western Europe' in K. Knop, S. Ostry, R. Simeon and K. Swinton (eds.), *Rethinking Federalism: Citizens, Markets, and Governments in a Changing World* (University of British Columbia Press, Vancouver, 1995), pp. 59–74

Koch, H., 'The Danish Constitutional Order' in A. Kellermann, J. De Zwaan and J. Czuczai (eds.), *EU Enlargement: The Constitutional Impact at EU and National Level* (Asser Press, The Hague, 2001), pp. 109–16

Kokott, J. and A. Rüth, 'The European Convention and its Draft Treaty Establishing a Constitution for Europe: Appropriate Answers to the Laeken Questions?' (2003) 40 *Common Market Law Review* 1315

Konstantinov, E., 'The Implementation of International Treaty Obligations in the National Legal Order: The Answer of the Bulgarian Constitution' (1995) 2 *Journal of Constitutional Law in Eastern and Central Europe* 62

Kopecky, P., 'The Czech Republic: From the Burden of the Old Federal Constitution to the Constitutional Horse Trading among Political Parties' in J. Zielonka and A. Pravda (eds.), *Democratic Consolidation in Eastern Europe*, vol. 1, *Institutional Engineering* (Oxford University Press, 2001), pp. 319–46

Korkelia, K., 'New Trends Regarding the Relationship between International and National Law (with a Special View towards the States of Eastern Europe)' (1997) 23 *Review of Central and East European Law* 227

Kumm, M., 'Who is the Final Arbiter of Constitutionality in Europe? Three Conceptions of the Relationship between the German Federal Constitutional Court and the European Court of Justice and the Fate of the European Market Order of Bananas' (1999) 36 *Common Market Law Review* 351

Kunova, V., 'Constitutional Aspects of the Accession of the Slovak Republic to European Union' in A. Kellermann, J. De Zwaan and J. Czuczai (eds.), *EU Enlargement: The Constitutional Impact at EU and National Level* (Asser Press, The Hague, 2001), pp. 327–36

Küpper, H., 'Integration mit Hindernissen – Die "Europa-Entscheidung" des ungarischen Verfassungsgerichts' (1998) *Recht in Ost und West* 333

Laffranque, J., 'Influence of European Community Law on Estonian Law and, in Particular, Law-Making' (1999) 4 *Juridica International, Law Review of Tartu University* 86

'Constitution of the Republic of Estonia in the Light of Accession to the European Union' (2001) *Juridica International, Law Review of Tartu University* 207

Lazowski, A., *Adaptation of the Polish Legal System to European Union Law: Selected Aspects* (Sussex European Institute Working Paper No. 45, Brighton, 2001)

'International Agreements in the Legal Orders of the Candidate Countries: Poland' in A. Ott and K. Inglis (eds.), *Handbook on European Enlargement* (T. M. C. Asser Press, The Hague, 2002), pp. 299–307

Lehti, M., *Sovereignty Redefined: Baltic Co-operation and the Limits of National Self-determination* (Working Paper of COPRI, Copenhagen, 1999)

Lenaerts, K., 'Federalism: Essential Concepts in Evolution: The Case of the European Union' (1998) 21 *Fordham International Law Journal* 746

Lenaerts, K. and M. Desomer, 'New Models of Constitution-making in Europe: The Quest for Legitimacy' (2002) 39 *Common Market Law Review* 1217

Lenaerts, K. and D. Gerard, 'The Structure of the Union according to the Constitution for Europe: The Emperor is Getting Dressed' (2004) 29 *European Law Review* 289

Lesage, M. (ed.), *Constitutions d'Europe Centrale, Orientale et Balte* (La documentation Française, Paris, 1995)

'Introduction: Transition vers la démocratie et l'Etat de droit et changement constitutionnel' in M. Lesage (ed.), *Constitutions d'Europe Centrale, Orientale et Balte* (La documentation Française, Paris, 1995)

Letowska, E., 'A Constitution of Possibilities' (1997) 6 *East European Constitutional Review*, no. 2/3

Lissauer, G., 'The Potential Impact of European Union Membership on Hungary's Constitution', LLM Thesis, University of Kent at Canterbury (Canterbury, 1999)

Llobera, J. R., 'The Role of the State and the Nation in Europe' in S. Garcia (ed.), *European Identity and Search for Legitimacy* (Pinter, London, 1993), pp. 64–80

Loeber, D. A., 'Regaining Independence: Constitutional Aspects: Estonia, Latvia, Lithuania' (1998) 24 *Review of Central and East European Law* 1

Ludwikowski, R., *Constitution-Making in the Region of Former Soviet Dominance* (Duke University Press, Durham and London, 1996)

Luthers-Thümmel, D., 'International Agreements in the Legal Orders of the Candidate Countries: Latvia' in A. Ott and K. Inglis (eds.), *Handbook on European Enlargement* (T. M. C. Asser Press, The Hague, 2002), pp. 267–80

Lutz, D., 'Towards a Theory of Constitutional Amendment' (1994) 88 *American Political Science Review* 355

Mabaka, P., 'L'Europe dans le droit constitutionnel positif des Etats' in J. Ziller (ed.), *L'européanisation des droits constitutionnels à la lumière de la Constitution pour l'Europe* (L'Harmattan, Paris, 2003), pp. 25–38

MacCormick, N., *Questioning Sovereignty: Law, State, and Nation in the European Commonwealth* (Oxford University Press, 1999)

Malenovsky, J., 'Résumé: Projet commenté des articles de la Constitution de la République tchèque régissant ses rapports au droit international' (1999) 5 *Pravnik* 403

Malova, D. and E. Lastic, 'The Gradual Amending of the Slovak Constitution: Combating the Ambiguous Rules in 1992–2001' (2001) 2 *Central European Political Science Review* 103

Mansfeldová, Z. and M. Klíma (eds.), *The Role of the Central European Parliaments in the Process of European Integration: Proceedings of International Conference, Prague, 12–14 September 1997* (Academy of Sciences, Prague, 1998)

Maresceau, M., '"Europe Agreements": A New Form of Cooperation between the European Community and Central and Eastern Europe' in P. C. Müller-Graff (ed.), *East-Central European States and the EC: Legal Adaptations to the Market Economy* (Nomos, Baden-Baden, 1993), pp. 209–33

'Pre-Accession' in M. Cremona (ed.), *The Enlargement of the European Union* (Oxford University Press, 2003), pp. 9–42

Maresceau, M. (ed.), *Enlarging the European Union: Relations Between the EU and Central and Eastern Europe* (Longman, London and New York, 1997)

Maresceau, M. and E. Montaguti, 'The Relations between the European Union and Eastern Europe: A Legal Appraisal' (1995) 32 *Common Market Law Review* 1327

Masiokas, J., 'Status of Lithuanian and European Union Nationals under the Association Agreement' (1998) 11 *Revue Baltique* 23

Mathernova, K., 'Czecho?Slovakia: Constitutional Disappointments' in I. Dick and A. E. Howard (eds.), *Constitution Making in Eastern Europe* (Woodrow Wilson Center Press, Washington, 1993), pp. 57–92

Maus, D., 'The Influence of Contemporary International Law on the Exercise of Constituent Power' in A. Jüränki (ed.), *National Constitutions in the Era of Integration* (Kluwer Law International, The Hague, 1999), pp. 45–57

Meessen, K., 'Hedging European Integration: The Maastricht Judgement of the Federal Constitutional Court of Germany' (1994) 17 *Fordham International Law Journal* 511–30

Meintapoulos, S., 'Le droit constitutionnel polonais face à l'adhésion à l'Union Européenne' (1999) 45 *Osteuropa Recht* 18

Merusk, K. and R. Narits, *Constitutional Law: Estonia* (Kluwer Law International, The Hague, 1999)

Mik, C., 'State Sovereignty and European Integration: Public International Law, EU Law and Constitutional Law in the Polish Context' in N. Walker (ed.), *Sovereignty in Transition* (Hart, Oxford, 2003), pp. 367–400

Millns, S., 'The Treaty of Amsterdam and Constitutional Revision in France' (1999) 5 *European Public Law* 61

'Unravelling the Ties that Bind: National Constitutions in the Light of Values, Principles and Objectives of the Constitution for Europe' in J. Ziller (ed.), *L'européanisation des droits constitutionnels à la lumière de la Constitution pour l'Europe* (L'Harmattan, Paris, 2003), pp. 97–120

Motoc, J., 'Europe and its Teleology: Is there a Central-Eastern Vision?' in C. Joerges, Y. Meny and J. Weiler (eds.), *What Kind of Constitution for What Kind of Polity?* (Robert Schuman Centre of the European University Institute and Harvard Law School, 2001), pp. 181–94

Müller-Graff, P. C., 'East Central Europe and the European Union: From Europe Agreements to Member Status' in P. C. Müller-Graff (ed.), *East Central Europe and the European Union: From Europe Agreements to Member Status* (Nomos, Baden-Baden, 1997), pp. 17–22

'Legal Framework for Relations between the European Union and Central and Eastern Europe: General Aspects' in M. Maresceau (ed.), *Enlarging the*

European Union: Relations Between the EU and Central and Eastern Europe (Longman, London and New York, 1997), pp. 27–31

'The Future of the European Treaties: A Systematic Approach to a Basic Treaty' in A. Von Bogdandy, P. C. Mavroidis and Y. Meny (eds.), *European Integration and International Co-ordination: Studies in Transnational Economic Law in Honour of Claus-Dieter Ehlermann* (Aspen Publishers, The Hague, 2002), pp. 329–48

Müller-Graff, P. C. (ed.), *East Central Europe and the European Union: From Europe Agreements to a Member Status* (Nomos, Baden-Baden, 1997)

Müllerson, R., M. Fitzmaurice and M. Andenas (eds.), *Constitutional Reform and International Law in Central and Eastern Europe* (Kluwer Law International, The Hague, 1998)

Nello, S. and K. Smith, *The European Union and Central and Eastern Europe: The Implications of Enlargement in Stages* (Ashgate, Aldershot, 1998)

Nicolaides, P., 'Preparing for Accession to the European Union: How to Establish Capacity for Effective and Credible Application of EU Rules' in M. Cremona (ed.), *The Enlargement of the European Union* (Oxford University Press, 2003), pp. 43–78

Nicolaidis, K., 'Our European Demoi-cracy: The New Constitution is on the Right Track', paper presented at the conference 'Towards a Federal Europe', European University Institute, Florence, 2 March 2003, to be published in (2005) *Journal of European Public Policy* (forthcoming)

Ojala, M., *The Competition Law of Central and Eastern Europe* (Sweet & Maxwell, London, 1999)

Ott, A. and K. Inglis (eds.), *Handbook on European Enlargement* (T. M. C. Asser Press, The Hague, 2002)

Peers, S., 'An Ever Closer Waiting Room? The Case for Eastern European Accession to the European Economic Area' (1995) 32 *Common Market Law Review* 187

Pernice, I., 'Multilevel Constitutionalism and the Treaty of Amsterdam: European Constitution-making Revisited' (1999) 36 *Common Market Law Review* 703

Perron, C., *Views of Czech Local Politicians on European Integration* (European University Institute, Robert Schuman Centre Working Paper No. 2000/39, Florence, 2000)

Piontek, E., 'Towards Membership of the European Union' (1994) *Droit Polonais Contemporain* 5

Piris, J.-C., 'Does the European Union have a Constitution? Does it Need One?' (1999) 24 *European Law Review* 557

Pisuke, H., 'Estonia and the European Union: European Integration in Estonia' (1996) *Juridica International, Law Review of Tartu University* 2

Pogany, I., 'Constitutional Reform in Central and Eastern Europe: Hungary's Transition to Democracy' (1993) 42 *International and Comparative Law Quarterly* 332

Põhiseadus ja Põhiseaduse Assamblee [Constitution and Constitutional Assembly] (Õigusteabe AS Juura, Tallinn, 1996)

Poiares Maduro, M., 'Contrapunctual Law: Europe's Constitutional Pluralism in Action' in N. Walker (ed.), *Sovereignty in Transition* (Hart, Oxford, 2003), pp. 501–39

Preuss, U. K., 'Patterns of Constitutional Evolution and Change in Eastern Europe' in J. Hesse and N. Johnson (eds.), *Constitutional Policy and Change in Europe* (Nuffield European Studies, Oxford University Press, 1995), pp. 95–128

'Problems of a Concept of European Citizenship' (1995) 1 *European Law Journal* 267

Raba, K., 'Estonia' in *Criminal Law in the European Union: A Giant Leap or A Small Step? FIDE 2004 National Reports*, www.fide2004.org/reports/mc/mc06b.pdf

Racz, A., 'Major Phases of Constitutional Development' in A. Harmathy (ed.), *Introduction to Hungarian Law* (Kluwer Law International, The Hague, 1998)

Rapaczynski, A., 'Constitutional Politics in Poland: A Report on the Constitutional Committee of the Polish Parliament' in I. Dick and A. E. Howard (eds.), *Constitution Making in Eastern Europe* (Woodrow Wilson Centre Press, Washington, 1993), pp. 93–132

Rideau, J. (ed.), *États Membres de l'Union Européenne: Adaptations, mutations, résistances* (LGDJ, Paris, 1997)

Roosma, P., 'Amending or Adjusting? Comments on Estonia' in E. Smith (ed.), *The Constitution as an Instrument of Change* (SNS Förlag, Stockholm, 2003), pp. 104–10

Rosas, A., 'Finland's Accession to the European Union: Constitutional Aspects' (1995) 1 *European Public Law* 166

Rosenfeld, M., 'The European Convention and Constitution Making in Philadelphia' (2003) 1 *International Journal of Constitutional Law* 373

Rosner, N., 'The Constitutional Limits to the Application of European Union Law', LLM Thesis No. 1998/7, Central European University, Law Department, (Budapest, 1998)

Sadurski, W., 'Conclusions: On the Relevance of Institutions and the Centrality of Constitutions in Post-Communist Transitions' in J. Zielonka and A. Pravda (eds.), *Democratic Consolidation in Eastern Europe*, vol. 1, *Institutional Engineering* (Oxford University Press, 2001), pp. 455–73

'Constitutional Justice, East and West: Introduction' in W. Sadurski (ed.), *Constitutional Justice, East and West: Democratic Legitimacy and Constitutional Courts in Post-Communist Europe in a Comparative Perspective* (Kluwer Law International, The Hague, 2002), pp. 1–20

Sadurski, W. (ed.), *Constitutional Justice, East and West: Democratic Legitimacy and Constitutional Courts in Post-Communist Europe in a Comparative Perspective* (Kluwer Law International, The Hague, 2002)

Saraviita, I., 'European Economic Integration in the Framework of the EEA Treaty and its Impact on the Sovereignty of the EFTA Countries' (1993) 35 *Acta Juridica Hungarica* 237

Scheinin, M. and T. Ojanen, 'Finland' in J. Rideau (ed.), *États Membres de l'Union Européenne: Adaptations, mutations, résistances* (LGDJ, Paris, 1997), pp. 185–213

Schwarze, J., 'The Birth of a European Constitutional Order' in J. Schwarze (ed.), *The Birth of a European Constitutional Order: The Interaction of National and European Constitutional Law* (Nomos, Baden-Baden, 2000)

'Guest Editorial: The Convention's Draft Treaty Establishing a Constitution for Europe' (2003) 40 *Common Market Law Review* 1037

Schwarze, J. (ed.), *The Birth of a European Constitutional Order: The Interaction of National and European Constitutional Law* (Nomos, Baden-Baden, 2000)

Schweisfurth, T. and R. Alleweldt, 'The Position of International Law in the Central and Eastern European Countries' (1997) 40 *German Yearbook of International Law* 164

Shaw, J., *Citizenship of the Union: Towards Post-national Membership?* (Jean Monnet Working Paper No. 6/97, 1997), www.law.harvard.edu/programs/JeanMonnet/papers/97/97-06-.html

'Postnational Constitutionalism in the European Union' (1999) 6 *Journal of European Public Policy* 579

Simons, W. B. (ed.), *The Constitutions of the Communist World* (Sijthoff & Noordhoff, Alphen, 1980)

Slosarcik, I., 'The Reform of the Constitutional Systems of Czechoslovakia and the Czech Republic in 1990–2000' (2001) 7 *European Public Law* 529

Slosarcik, I. and S. Klouckova, 'Czech Republic' in *Criminal Law in the European Union: A Giant Leap or A Small Step? FIDE 2004 National Reports*, www.fide2004.org/reports/mc/mc04b.pdf

Slynn, Lord, of Hadley and M. Andenas (eds.), *FIDE XX Congress London 30 October–2 November 2002*, vol. 1, *National Reports 'European Union Law and National Constitutions'* (BIICL, London, 2002)

Smith, E., 'The Constitution as an Instrument of Change: Introduction' in E. Smith (ed.), *The Constitution as an Instrument of Change* (SNS Förlag, Stockholm, 2003), pp. 11–20

'The Constitution between Politics and Law' in E. Smith (ed.), *The Constitution as an Instrument of Change* (SNS Förlag, Stockholm, 2003), pp. 21–54

Smith, K., 'The Evolution and Application of EU Membership Conditionality' in M. Cremona (ed.), *The Enlargement of the European Union* (Oxford University Press, 2003), pp. 105–40

Sokolewicz, W., 'The Relevance of Western Models for Constitution-Building in Poland' in J. Hesse and N. Johnson (eds.), *Constitutional Policy and*

Change in Europe (Nuffield European Studies, Oxford University Press, 1995), pp. 243–77

Solym, L. and G. Brunner (eds.), *Constitutional Judiciary in a New Democracy: The Hungarian Constitutional Court* (Michigan University Press, 2000)

Sprudzs, A., 'Rebuilding Democracy in Latvia: Overcoming a Dual Legacy' in J. Zielonka and A. Pravda (eds.), *Democratic Consolidation in Eastern Europe*, vol. 1, *Institutional Engineering* (Oxford University Press, 2001), pp. 139–64

Staciokas, S., 'Democracy and Sovereignty (The Lithuanian Experience)' in *Philosophy and Democracy* (Vilnius, 1996), p. 99

Stein, E., 'International Law in Internal Law: Toward Internationalization of Central-Eastern European Constitutions?' (1994) 88 *American Journal of International Law* 427

Steinberg, P., 'A Tentative Survey of the Innovations of the Constitution for Europe that Might Impact Upon National Constitutions' in J. Ziller (ed.), *L'européanisation des droits constitutionnels à la lumière de la Constitution pour l'Europe* (L'Harmattan, Paris, 2003), pp. 139–56

Steponavicius, G., 'Amending or Adjusting? Comments on Lithuania' in E. Smith (ed.), *The Constitution as an Instrument of Change* (SNS Förlag, Stockholm, 2003), pp. 101–3

Stone Sweet, A., 'Constitutional Dialogues in the European Community' in A. M. Slaughter, A. Stone Sweet and J. H. H. Weiler (eds.), *The European Court and National Courts: Doctrine and Jurisprudence: Legal Change in its Social Context* (Hart, Oxford, 1998), pp. 305–30

Tanchev, E., 'National Constitutions and EU Law: Adapting the 1991 Bulgarian Constitution in the Accession to the European Union' (2000) 6 *European Public Law* 229

'Constitutional Amendments Due to Bulgarian Full EU Membership' in A. Kellermann, J. De Zwaan and J. Czuczai (eds.), *EU Enlargement: The Constitutional Impact at EU and National Level* (Asser Press, The Hague, 2001), pp. 301–10

Tatham, A., 'Constitutional Judiciary in Central Europe and the Europe Agreement: Decision 30/1998 (VI.25) AB of the Hungarian Constitutional Court' (1999) 48 *International and Comparative Law Quarterly* 913

Taube, C., *Constitutionalism in Estonia, Latvia and Lithuania: A Study in Comparative Constitutional Law* (Iustus Förlag, Uppsala, 2001)

Triska, J. F. (ed.), *Constitutions of the Communist Party-States* (The Hoover Institution on War, Revolution and Peace, Stanford University, 1986)

Tyc, V., 'Czech Republic' in A. Ott and K. Inglis (eds.), *Handbook on European Enlargement* (T. M. C. Asser Press, The Hague, 2002), pp. 229–37

Usaĉka, A., 'The Impact of the European Integration Process on the Constitution of Latvia' in A. Kellermann, J. De Zwaan and J. Czuczai (eds.), *EU Enlargement:*

The Constitutional Impact at EU and National Level (Asser Press, The Hague, 2001), pp. 337–46

Vachudova, M. A., 'Strategies for Democratization and European Integration in the Balkans' in M. Cremona (ed.), *The Enlargement of the European Union* (Oxford University Press, 2003), pp. 141–60

Vadapalas, V., 'Lithuania: The Constitutional Impact of the Enlargement at National Level' in A. Kellermann, J. De Zwaan and J. Czuczai (eds.), *EU Enlargement: The Constitutional Impact at EU and National Level* (Asser Press, The Hague, 2001), pp. 347–68

'Lithuania' in *Criminal Law in the European Union: A Giant Leap or A Small Step? FIDE 2004*, www.fide2004.org/reports/mc/mc13b.pdf

Vadapalas, V. and I. Jarukaitis, 'International Agreements in the Legal Orders of the Candidate Countries: Lithuania' in A. Ott and K. Inglis (eds.), *Handbook on European Enlargement* (T. M. C. Asser Press, The Hague, 2002), pp. 281–9

Van Gerven, W., 'Toward a Coherent Constitutional System within the European Union' (1996) 2 *European Public Law* 81

Van Ham, P., *The EC, Eastern Europe and Unity: Discord, Collaboration and Integration since 1949* (Pinter, London, 1993)

Varhely, O., 'International Agreements in the Legal Orders of the Candidate Countries: Hungary' in A. Ott and K. Inglis (eds.), *Handbook on European Enlargement* (T. M. C. Asser Press, The Hague, 2002), pp. 257–65

Vehar, P., 'Constitutional Problems in the Period of Pre-Accession in the Republic of Slovenia' in A. Kellermann, J. De Zwaan and J. Czuczai (eds.), *EU Enlargement: The Constitutional Impact at EU and National Level* (Asser Press, The Hague, 2001), pp. 369–74

Vereshchetin, V. S., 'New Constitutions and the Old Problem of the Relationship between International Law and National Law' (1996) 7 *European Journal of International Law* 29

Verheiren, T., *Constitutional Pillars for New Democracies: The Cases of Bulgaria and Romania* (PSWO Press Leiden University, 1995)

Verhoeven, A., *The European Union in Search of a Democratic and Constitutional Treaty* (Kluwer, 2002)

Vitkus, G., *Referendums on the Membership in the European Union: The History, Issues and Lessons for Lithuania: Summary* (2003), available at www.leidykla.vu.lt/inetleid/politol/25/s1.html

Vodicka, K., 'Unaufhebbare Grundprinzipien der tschechischen Verfassungsordnung' (1996) 42 *Osteuropa Recht* 225

Volkai, J., *The Application of the Europe Agreement and European Law in Hungary: The Judgement of an Activist Constitutional Court on Activist Notions* (Jean Monnet Working Paper No. 8/99, Harvard, 1999), www.law.harvard.edu/Programs/JeanMonnet/papers/99/ 990801.html

Von Bogdandy, A., 'The European Union as a Supranational Federation: A Conceptual Attempt in the Light of the Amsterdam Treaty' (2000) 6 *Columbia Journal of European Law* 27

'The Preamble' in B. De Witte (ed.), *Ten Reflections on the Constitutional Treaty for Europe* (EUI-RSCAS/AEL, Florence, 2003), available at www.iue.it/RSCAS/Publications, pp. 3–10

Walker, N., 'The Idea of Constitutional Pluralism' (2002) 65 *Modern Law Review* 317

'Late Sovereignty in the European Union' in N. Walker (ed.), *Sovereignty in Transition* (Hart, Oxford, 2003), pp. 3–32

Wasilkowski, A., 'The Future Polish Constitution in the Perspective of Poland's Membership of the European Union' (1993) *Droit Polonais Contemporain* 5

'International Law and International Relations in the New Polish Constitution of 2 April 1997' (1997–8) 23 *Polish Yearbook of International Law* 7

Weiler, J. H. H., 'Does Europe Need a Constitution? Demos, Telos and the German Maastricht Decision' (1995) 1 *European Law Journal* 219

The Constitution of Europe: 'Do the New Clothes have an Emperor?' and Other Essays on the European Integration (Cambridge University Press, 1999)

Federalism and Constitutionalism: Europe's Sonderweg (Harvard Jean Monnet Working Paper No. 10, 2000), www.jeanmonnetprogram.org

Weiler, J. H. H. and M. Wind (eds.), *European Constitutionalism Beyond the State* (Cambridge University Press, 2003)

Wojtowicz, K., 'Proposed Changes in the Polish Constitution of 1997 ahead of Poland's Accession to the European Union' (2001) 25 *Polish Yearbook of International Law* 27

Wyrzykowski, M., 'The Constitutions of the Eastern European Countries in the Structure of European Constitutionalism' in R. Bieber and P. Widmer (eds.), *L'Espace Constitutionnel Européen* (Schulthess Polygraphischer Verlag, Zürich, 1995), pp. 151–64

Zajc, D., 'The Responsibilities of a Central European Parliament in the Process of European Integration: The Case of the Parliament of Slovenia and its Commission for European Affairs' in Z. Mansfeldová and M. Klíma (eds.), *The Role of the Central European Parliaments in the Process of European Integration: Proceedings of International Conference, Prague, 12–14 September 1997* (Academy of Sciences, Prague, 1998), pp. 91–9

Zemanek, J., 'The Amendments of the Czech Constitution for the Accession to the European Union' in A. Kellermann, J. De Zwaan and J. Czuczai (eds.), *EU Enlargement: The Constitutional Impact at EU and National Level* (Asser Press, The Hague, 2001), pp. 423–34

Zielonka, J. and A. Pravda (eds.), *Democratic Consolidation in Eastern Europe*, vol. 1, *Institutional Engineering* (Oxford University Press, 2001)

Ziemele, I., 'Incorporation and Implementation of Human Rights in Latvia' in M. Scheinin (ed.), *International Human Rights Norms in the Nordic and Baltic Countries* (Kluwer Law International, Dordrecht, 1996), pp. 73–91

Zikmane, Z., 'Latvia' in *Criminal Law in the European Union: A Giant Leap or a Small Step? FIDE 2004 National Reports*, www.fide2004.org/reports/mc/mc12b.pdf

Ziller, J., 'Sovereignty in France: Getting Rid of the Mal de Bodin' in N. Walker (ed.), *Sovereignty in Transition* (Hart, Oxford, 2003), pp. 261–77

La nouvelle Constitution européenne (La Découverte, Paris, 2004)

Žilys, J., 'The New Constitution of the Republic of Lithuania in the Context of the European Law System' in T. Jundzis (ed.), *The Baltic States at Historical Crossroads: Problems in the Context of International Cooperation on the Doorstep of the 21st Century* (Academy of Sciences of Latvia, Riga, 1998), pp. 232–47

Zukova, G., 'Uniform Interpretation and Application of International Agreements in the European Union' in G. Zukova, *Legal Aspects of Trade in Goods between the EU and its Candidate States: The Case of Latvia* (Latvias Vestnesis, Riga, 2004), pp. 207–26

Zuleeg, M., 'The European Constitution under Constitutional Constraints: The German Scenario' (1997) 22 *European Law Review* 19

Documents, reports and speeches

A Basic Treaty for the European Union: A Study of the Reorganisation of the Treaties (European University Institute, Robert Schuman Centre, Florence, 15 May 2000), www.iue.it/RSC/Treaties.html

Accession Partnerships with individual countries, available at the European Commission's website, www.europa.eu.int/comm.enlargement

Agenda 2000: For a Stronger and Wider Union, Bulletin of the European Communities. Supplement 5/97, www.europa.eu.int/comm/enlargement/agenda 2000/

Comments on Lithuanian draft amendments by F. Frowein, P.-C. Müller-Graff, I. Pernice and others in *Stojimas I Europos Sajunga Ir Konstitucija. Seminaro Medziaga 29–30 June 1999* (Eugrimas, Vilnius, 2000)

'Constitution of the Republic of Hungary (Draft)' (1997) 38 *Acta Juridica Hungarica, Hungarian Journal of Legal Studies* 5

Constitutional and Administrative Facilitation of Effective Law Approximation and European Union Membership, Report composed under the auspices of the European Integration Bureau and PHARE Technical Assistance to the Approximation of the Latvian Legislation to that of the European Communities (Riga, 1999)

Constitutions of 'old' and 'new' Member States are available at website 'Consolidating European Public Law', European University Institute, Florence, www.iue.it/OnlineProjects/LAW/conseulaw/

Debates on a Referendum on Lithuania's Membership in the EU (Lithuanian Free Market Institute, February 2003), www.freema.org/Projects/Referendum.phtml

Eurobarometer public opinion surveys, available at http://europa.eu.int/comm/public_opinion and http://europa.eu.int/comm/enlargement_opinion/

'Eurobarometer 60', February 2004, http://euro.eu.int/comm/public_opinion/archives/eb/eb60/ eb60_rapport_standard_en.pdf

European Commission's Opinion on Romania's Application for EU Membership, Brussels, July 1997

European Commission's Regular Report on Slovakia, 2000, www.politika.host.sk/Prispevky/dokument_slovensko_EU2_politicalcriteria.htm

Kwasniewski, A., 'Enlarged EU: Moving Towards a Political Union', speech delivered at the Stockholm School of Economics, 10 May 2001, www.europa.eu.int/futurum/documents/speech/sp100501_en.htm

'Õiguskantsleri arvamus Justiitsministeeriumis välja töötatud eelnõu "Põhiseaduse rakendamine Euroopa Liidu liikmeks oleku tingimustes" kohta' [Legal Chancellor's Opinion on the Ministry of Justice Draft Law 'Implementation of the Constitution in the Conditions of European Union Membership'], 16 April 2002, unpublished document

Opinions of foreign experts L. Lopez Guerra, M. Niemivuo, J. Gardner, G. Carcassone, and H. Beemelmans on amending of the Constitution of Estonia, available in the collection *Põhiseaduse Juriidilise Ekspertiisi Komisjoni Tegevuse Aruande Lisa 'Välisekspertiisid'* [Appendix 'Foreign Expert Opinions' to the Report on the Activity of the Constitutional Expert Commission] (Justiitsministeerium, Tallinn, 1998)

'Organisational Structure of Accession Negotiations in Poland' in *Accession Negotiations: Poland on the Road to the European Union* (Chancellery of the Prime Minister of the Republic of Poland, Warsaw, October 2000), pp. 19–27

Parliament of Estonia, transcripts of the sessions are available in Estonian at www.riigikogu.ee

'Põhiseaduse 7. peatükk "Seadusandlus". Põhiseaduse Ekspertiisikomisjoni aruanne' [Expert Commission's report on Chapter 7 of the Constitution 'Legislation'] in the *Expert Commission Final Report on the Estonian Constitution* (1998), www.just.ee

'Predlog za začetek postopka za spremembe ustave Republike Slovenije' [Proposal to initiate the Procedure of Amendments to the Constitution of the Republic of Slovenia] in *Poročevalec – Državnega zbora Republike Slovenije*, 6 August 2001, p. 4

'Project Proposal: The Constitutional Impact of Accession at the National Level of the Candidate Countries' in A. Kellermann, J. De Zwaan and J. Czuczai (eds.), *EU Enlargement: The Constitutional Impact at EU and National Level* (Asser Press, The Hague, 2001), pp. 590–2

Reforming the Treaties' Amendment Procedures: Second Report on the Reorganising of the European Union Treaties (European University Institute, Robert Schuman Centre, Florence, 31 July 2000), www.iue.it/RSC/Treaties.html

'Republic of Lithuania Constitutional Law on the Amendment of Articles 136 and 138 of the Constitution of the Republic of Lithuania: Draft of the Working Group established under the Seimas Chancellery' in *Stojimas I Europos Sajunga Ir Konstitucija. Seminaro Medziaga 29–30 June 1999* (Eugrimas, Vilnius, 2000), p. 138

The Theoretical Foundation of the Amendments to Satversme Proposed by the Working Group (Ministry of Justice, Riga, November 2001)

'Ühispöördumine seoses nn. Põhiseaduse Kolmanda akti riigiõiguslike probleemidega' [Joint Statement concerning the Constitutional Problems of the Third Constitutional Act], by A. Albi, M. Gallagher, I. Koolmeister, R. Maruste, L. Mälksoo and P. Roosma (2002) 5 *Juridica* 352

Võimalik liitumine Euroopa Liiduga ja selle õiguslik tähendus Eesti riigiõiguse seisukohalt [Potential Accession to the European Union and its Consequences for Estonian Constitutional Law], Report of the Constitutional Amendment Expert Commission of Estonia (1998), in Estonian at www.just.ee/juridica2.html

Weizsäcker, R., J.-L. Dehaene and D. Simon, *The Institutional Implications of Enlargement: Report to the European Commission* (Brussels, 18 November 1999), http://europa.eu.int/igc2000/repoct99_en.pdf

White Paper, *Preparation of the Associated Countries of Central and Eastern Europe for Integration into the Internal Market of the Union*, COM (95) 163 final

Selected newspaper articles

'Interview with Victor Orban', *La libre Belgique*, 11 July 2001

Ishkauskas, C., 'Esmatähtis on kartul, referendum tuleb pärast' [Potatoes are of Primary Importance, Referendum Follows Afterwards], *Postimees*, 14 May 2003

Jõks, A., 'Põhiseadus muutuste künnisel' [Constitution at the Doorstep of Changes], *Postimees* 17 April 2002

Kirch, M., 'Eestlaste otsus tulevasel euroreferendumil sõltub Venemaast' [Estonians' Decision in the Euroreferendum Depends on Russia], *Eesti Päevaleht*, 28 March 2000

Kivirähk, J., 'Eestlased kardavad Venemaad, muulased mitte' [Estonians are Afraid of Russia, Non-Estonians Not], *Eesti Päevaleht*, 29 March 2000

Maruste, R., 'Eesti enne euro-otsustust' [Estonia before the EU Decision], *Postimees*, 16 December 2001

'Põhiseadust tuleks siiski muuta' [The Constitution Should Still be Amended], *Postimees*, 30 January 2002

'Eesti vajaks uut põhiseadust' [Estonia Needs a New Constitution], *Eesti Päevaleht*, 26 March 2004

Mattheus, Ü., 'Põhiseaduse muutjad Eesti suveräänsuse kahjustamist ei karda' [The Amenders of the Constitution are not Afraid of Harming Estonia's Sovereignty], *Raadio Vaba Euroopa Online*, 16 May 2002, www.vabaeuroopa.org

Mite, V., 'Latvia Adjusts Language Laws, but the Issue Remains Divisive', *RFE/RL Newsline*, vol. 6, no. 93, Part II, 20 May 2002

Percival, M., 'Promoting the Highest Law in the Land . . . by Breaking the Law' in *Vivid* (Bucharest English language magazine), November 2003, also available at www.thinktankromania.ro/documents/Vivid%20Nov%2003%20(Link%2040).pdf

Plichta, D., 'Czech Law Settles Referendum on EU Membership', *Current Concerns*, no. 5, 26 November 2002, www.currentconcerns.ch/archive/20020309.php

Reiljan, J., 'Rahvas põhiseaduse kaitsjana' [People as the Guardian of the Constitution], *Postimees*, 15 July 2002

Reinsalu, U., 'Põhiseadus säilitab euroliidu tänase näo' [The Constitution Retains the European Union's Current Face], *Eesti Päevaleht*, 15 July 2003

'Eesti põhiseadus 21. sajandil' [Estonian Constitution in the 21st Century], *Postimees*, 30 January 2004

Roonemaa, H., 'Meri: rahvas võiks aastate pärast hääletada euroliidust välja astumist' [Meri: the People Could Vote on Secession from the EU After a Few Years], *Eesti Päevaleht*, 5 May 2001

Stroehlein, A., 'Weaknesses of the Czech Media', *Central European Review*, 17 January 2000, www.ce-review.org/00/2/stroehlein2.html

Selected news sources

Baltic States Report, email news provided by Radio Free Europe/Radio Liberty, www.rferl.org

Central European and Eurasian Law Initiative, www.abanet.org/ceeli/

Constitution Watch: Country Updates, *East European Constitutional Review*; the *Review* is available both as hard copy and online, at www.law.nyu.edu/eecr/

Current Concerns, www.currentconcerns.ch

Delfi (online news portal in Estonia), www.delfi.ee

Direct Democracy, http://c2d.unige.ch/

Eesti Päevaleht (Estonian daily newspaper), www.epl.ee

EU Business, www.eubusiness.com

EU Observer, www.euobserver.com

EurActive portal, Euractive.com

Postimees (Estonian daily newspaper), www.postimees.ee
Raadio Vaba Euroopa [Radio Free Europe, Estonia], www.vabaeuroopa.org
Radio Free Europe /Radio Liberty, www.rferl.org
RFE/RL Newsline, daily email news provided by Radio Free Europe/Radio Liberty, www.rferl.org
Slovak News, www.slovensko.com

APPENDIX

Table A1 *Constitutional amendment procedures*

	Initiative	Parliamentary procedure	Referendum	Other remarks
Estonia	President; 1/5 of the Parliament membership	Initially 3 readings with 4 months total minimum interval, then three options: (1) two successive Parliament memberships, if so decided by 3/5 majority of the Parliament membership (2) urgency procedure: the amendment proposal requires 4/5 and the Amendment Act 2/3 majority of the Parliament membership; (3) referendum, if so decided by 3/5 of the Parliament membership	Obligatory for fundamental provisions and for amending the amendment procedure, optional for ordinary amendments; no minimum turnout; referendum can take place within 3–6 months from Parliament decision	Independence and sovereignty are timeless and inalienable. In case of an unsuccessful referendum, no re-initiating within 1 year; Parliament dissolved
Latvia	Parliament; 1/10 of electorate	3 readings in the presence of 2/3 deputies, with 2/3 majority approval	Obligatory for amending fundamental provisions and amendment procedure; optional for ordinary amendments; minimum turnout is 50%	–

Lithuania	1/4 of the Parliament membership; 300,000 voters	2/3 majority of Parliament membership on two votes, with 3 months interval	Obligatory for amending fundamental provisions and the amendment procedure; amendment of article 1 requires approval by 3/4 of total electorate; other referendums require a minimum turnout of 50%	If the amendment or referendum fails, no re-initiating within 1 year
Romania	President on proposal of government; 1/4 of all deputies or senators; 500,000 citizens	2/3 membership of both chambers or, if no agreement, 3/4 approval in joint session of both chambers	Obligatory for all amendments; minimum turnout is 50%	Prohibition to amend the national and independent character of state
Poland	1/5 of the Parliament membership; Senate; President	Successive approval by 2/3 of the Lower House with half of deputies present, and absolute majority of half of the Senate; 60 days interval between parliamentary readings to amend Chapter I	Optional for amending fundamental provisions and amendment procedure; no minimum turnout	If the referendum fails, no re-initiating within 4 years
Slovenia	20 deputies; government; 30,000 voters	Proposal requires 2/3 of the deputies present and voting, amendment requires 2/3 majority of all deputies	For all amendments, if demanded by 30 deputies; minimum turnout is 50%	Right of self-determination is timeless and inalienable

(cont.)

Table A1 (*cont.*)

	Initiative	Parliamentary procedure	Referendum	Other remarks
Bulgaria	1/4 of the Parliament membership; President	Ordinary constitutional amendments are carried out by Parliament, by 3/4 of all deputies on three different days If amendments concern certain fundamental issues, 2/3 of all deputies decide to elect the Grand National Assembly (GNA). GNA is elected 3 months after Parliament's resolution. It decides on amendment within 2nd to 5th month of its election by 2/3 majority of all members, on three different days	No referendums allowed for amending the constitution	–
Slovakia	Committees or deputies of Parliament; government	3/5 majority of all deputies	Referendums not provided for amending the constitution	–
Czech Republic	Deputies; Senate; government; representatives of a higher territorial self-governing entity	3/5 majority of all deputies and 3/5 of senators present (quorum 1/3)	Referendums not provided for amending the constitution	Changes of fundamental attributes of the democratic law-observing state are inadmissible
Hungary	President; Parliament's deputies and committees; government	4/5 of all deputies (until 1995 3/4 majority)	Referendums not provided for amending the constitution	–

Table A2 *Amendments of the CEE constitutions (other than those pertaining to EU accession)*[a]

	Year	Amendments	Major unsuccessful amendment proposals other than EU-related
Slovakia	1998	Division of powers	Replacement of 'we the Slovak nation' with 'we the citizens of Slovakia'
	1999	Direct presidential elections; restriction of President's prerogatives	
	2001	Package of 85 amendments, including creation of ombudsman, separation of powers, local government reform, judicial reform	
Lithuania	1996	Acquisition of non-agricultural land by EU citizens under Europe Agreement (article 47)	Enhancing of presidential powers; determining prosecutors' powers; non-intervention of Parliament into the work of judges; right to free healthcare and education; reducing the size of Parliament
	2001	Extension of term of office of local councils (article 119)	
Slovenia	1997	Sale of real estate to EU citizens under Europe Agreement (article 68)	Not available
	2000	Electoral system	
Hungary	1995	Constitutional amendment procedure	Extending the term of office of judges; direct presidential elections
	1997	Referendum; status of ministers; change of court system, etc.	

(cont.)

Table A2 (*cont.*)

	Year	Amendments	Major unsuccessful amendment proposals other than EU-related
	2000	Use of Hungarian airspace by foreign troops and participation of foreign troops in military exercises in Hungary by government approval	
Czech Republic	1997	Reform of self-governing territories	Abolition of Senate; direct presidential elections; restriction of the immunity of MPs and of Constitutional Court judges; increase of powers of Senate; replacement of proportional representation with majoritarian; reform of judiciary
	2000	Peace-keeping	
Latvia	1994	Voting age lowered from 21 to 18 (article 8)	Change of the proportional election with a mixed system; direct election of president
	1996	Introduction of Constitutional Court (article 85)	
	1997	Extension of Parliament's and President's term of office (articles 10 and 35); exclusion of dual citizenship for presidential candidates (article 37); technical amendments on Parliament and President (articles 10, 11, 13, 30, 35, 39 and 45); endowing government with a right to adopt regulations in cases of urgent necessity during parliamentary recesses (article 81); responsibility of judges (articles 84 and 85)	

	1998	New Chapter VIII on human rights (articles 89–116); new provision that Latvian is the state language (article 4), technical amendments (articles 77 and 82)	
	2001	Reinforcement of the Latvian language as the official procedural language in Parliament and local elected offices	
Poland		New constitution adopted in 1997, not amended	Abolition of the Senate; time of holding elections
Bulgaria	2003	Judiciary	Extension of Parliament's powers until the convening of new Parliament; mandate of interim government; granting President a power to issue legislation and to strengthen his position as political arbiter; introduction of ombudsman; introduction of citizens' direct right to resort to Constitutional Court
Romania	2003	A large package of amendments, including amplification of the scope of human rights protection; improvement of judiciary; protection of private property	Replacement of article 1 that Romania is a 'national and unitary state'; division of powers between two houses; changing the electoral system of the Senate; abolition of direct presidential elections
Estonia	2003	Prolongation of the term of office of local councils	Direct presidential elections; presidential powers; right of public initiative to amend the constitution

[a] Note that this list may be incomplete. The information is mainly based on country reports in the *East European Constitutional Review* and *RFE/RL Newsline*, www.rferl.org

Table A3 *EU provisions and application of international law in Slovakian Constitution*

Amendments of 23 February 2001

1(2). The Slovak Republic recognises and honours general rules of international law, international treaties by which it is bound and its other international obligations.

7(2). The Slovak Republic may, by an international treaty ratified and promulgated as stipulated by law, or on the basis of such treaty, transfer the execution of a part of its rights to the European Communities and European Union.

Legally binding acts of the European Communities and European Union shall take precedence over the laws of the Slovak Republic. Undertaking of legally binding acts that require implementation shall be carried out by law or a statutory order pursuant to Article 120 Section 2.

7(3). The Slovak Republic may, with the aim of maintaining peace, security and democratic order, under the terms established by an international treaty, join an organisation of mutual collective security.

7(4). In order for any international treaties on human rights and fundamental freedoms, any international political treaties, international treaties of military nature, international treaties establishing the membership of the Slovak Republic in international organisations, international economic treaties of general nature, international treaties whose execution requires a statute and international treaties which directly constitute rights or obligations of natural persons or juridical persons to be valid, an approval of the National Council of the Slovak Republic will be required prior to their ratification.

7(5). International treaties on human rights and fundamental freedoms, international treaties whose execution does not require an act and international treaties which directly establish rights or obligations of natural persons or juridical persons and which were ratified and promulgated as required by law shall take precedence over the laws.

13(1). Duties can be imposed by . . . (b) international treaty pursuant to Article 7 section 4 which directly establishes rights and obligations of natural persons or juridical persons, or (c) government decree pursuant to Article 120 section 2.

30(1). Foreigners with a permanent residence on the territory of the Slovak Republic have the right to vote and be elected in the self-administration bodies of municipalities and self-administration bodies of superior territorial units.

84(3). In order to approve an international treaty stipulated in Article 7 sections 3 and 4 and adopt a bill returned by the President of the Slovak Republic pursuant to Article 102 letter (o), a consent of more than one-half of all deputies is needed.

84(4). The agreement of at least a three-fifths majority of all deputies is required to pass and amend the Constitution and constitutional laws, to adopt an international treaty stipulated in Article 7 section 2 . . . and to declare war on another state.

Table A3 (*cont.*)

86. The jurisdiction of the National Council of the Slovak Republic comprises, above all: . . . (d) expressing consent, prior to ratification, with the international treaties on human rights and fundamental freedoms, international political treaties, international treaties of military nature, international treaties establishing membership of the Slovak Republic in international organisations, international economic treaties of a general nature, international treaties whose execution requires the passing of a law, as well as with international treaties that directly establish rights or obligations of physical persons or juridical persons, and at the same time making determination if these are international treaties stipulated in Article 7 section 5.

87(4). . . . Details of promulgation of laws, international treaties and legally binding acts of an international organisation pursuant to Article 7 section 2 will be set out in a law.

120(2). If so stipulated by law, the government is authorised to issue decrees in order to execute the Europe Agreement establishing an association between the European Communities and their Member States, of the one part, and the Slovak Republic, of the other part, and to execute international treaties stipulated in Article 7 section 2.

125a(1). The Constitutional Court decides on compliance of the concluded international treaties for which consent of the National Council of the Slovak Republic is required with the Constitution or a constitutional law.

125a(2). The petition for a decision pursuant to section 1 may be filed with the Constitutional Court by the president of the Slovak Republic or the Government before submitting of the concluded international treaty for a deliberation to the National Council of the Slovak Republic.

125a(3). The Constitutional Court decides on the petition pursuant to section 2 within the period stipulated by law; if the Constitutional Court by its decision expresses that the international treaty is not in compliance with the Constitution or a constitutional law, such international treaty may not be ratified.

144(1). Judges are independent in execution of their function and bound solely by the Constitution, constitutional laws, international treaties stipulated in Article 7 section 2 and 5 and laws.

144(2). If the court is of the opinion that another generally binding legal regulation, its part or a particular provision related to the subject-matter of the proceeding contravenes the Constitution, constitutional laws, international treaties stipulated in Article 7 section 2 and 5 or laws, it will interrupt its deliberations and propose that a proceeding under Article 125 section 1 is initiated. The finding of the Constitutional Court of the Slovak Republic is binding for all courts.

Table A4 *EU provisions and application of international law in Czech Constitution*

Amendments of 18 October 2001

1(2). The Czech Republic observes the obligations issuing for it from international law.

10. Promulgated international agreements, the ratification of which has been approved by the Parliament and by which the Czech Republic is bound, constitute part of legislation; if an international agreement makes provision contrary to a statute, the international agreement is applied.

10a(1). Some powers of bodies of the Czech Republic may be transferred to an international organisation or institution under an international agreement.

10a(2). The approval of the Parliament is required to ratify an international agreement stipulated in subsection 1, unless constitutional law provides that approval awarded in a referendum is required for ratification.

10b(1). The Government informs the Parliament regularly and in advance of issues related to obligations issuing from the Czech Republic's membership of an international organisation or institution stipulated in section 10a.

10b(2). The Chambers of Parliament make statements on the decisions of such an international organisation or institution that are being prepared as provided by their rules of procedure.

10b(3). The act on the principles of conduct and relations of both Chambers mutually and in external relations may entrust the competence of the Chambers under subsection 2 to a joint body of the Chambers.

39(4). The approval of a three-fifths majority of all Deputies and a three-fifths majority of all Senators in attendance is required to pass a constitutional act and to approve the ratification of an international agreement stipulated in section 10a, subsection 1.

49. The approval of both Chambers of Parliament is required to ratify international agreements . . . (c) under which the Czech Republic assumes membership of an international organisation.

52. . . . The method of promulgating a law and international agreement is provided by the law.

87(2). A constitutional court also passes verdicts on the conformity of an international agreement under section 10a and section 49 with the constitutional order, such being before ratification thereof. Until such time as the Constitutional Court makes a decision an agreement cannot be ratified.

89(3). A decision of the Constitutional Court whereby, in accordance with section 87, subsection 2, non-conformity of an international agreement with the constitutional order is pronounced, prevents ratification until such time as the non-conformity is eliminated.

95. In his decision-making, a judge is bound by the law and any international agreement constituting part of legislation; he is entitled to assess the conformity of another legal regulation with the law or with such international agreement. Should a court conclude that the law that is to be applied in the settlement of a matter contravenes the constitutional order, it shall submit the matter to the Constitutional Court.

Table A5 *EU provisions and application of international law in Slovenian Constitution*

Amendments of 7 March 2001

3a(1). Pursuant to a treaty ratified by the National Assembly by a two-thirds majority vote of all deputies, Slovenia may transfer the exercise of part of its sovereign rights to international organisations which are based on respect for human rights and fundamental freedoms, democracy and the principles of the rule of law and may enter into a defence alliance with states which are based on respect for these values.

3a(2). Before ratifying an international treaty referred to in the preceding paragraph, the National Assembly may call a referendum. A proposal shall pass at the referendum if a majority of voters who have cast valid votes vote in favour of such proposal. The National Assembly is bound by the result of such referendum. If such referendum has been held, a referendum regarding the law on the ratification of the treaty concerned may not be called.

3a(3). Legal acts and decisions adopted within international organisations to which Slovenia has transferred the exercise of part of its sovereign rights shall be applied in Slovenia in accordance with the legal regulation of these organisations.

3a(4). In procedures for the adoption of legal acts and decisions in international organisations to which Slovenia has transferred the exercise of part of its sovereign rights, the Government shall promptly inform the National Assembly of proposals for such acts and decisions as well as of its own activities. The National Assembly may adopt positions thereon, which the Government shall take into consideration in its activities. The relationship between the National Assembly and the Government arising from this paragraph shall be regulated in detail by a law adopted by a two-thirds majority vote of deputies present.

47. No citizen of Slovenia may be extradited or surrendered unless such obligation to extradite or surrender arises from a treaty by which, in accordance with the provisions of the first paragraph of Article 3a, Slovenia has transferred the exercise of part of its sovereign rights to an international organisation.

68. Aliens may acquire ownership rights to real estate under conditions provided by law or a treaty ratified by the National Assembly.

Pre-existing provisions on application of international law

8. Laws and regulations must comply with generally accepted principles of international law and with treaties that are binding on Slovenia. Ratified and published treaties shall be applied directly.

153(2). Statutes must conform with generally accepted principles of international law and with international agreements currently in force and adopted by the National Assembly, and regulations and other legislative measures must also conform with other ratified international agreements.

Table A6 *EU provisions and application of international law in Polish Constitution*

New Constitution, 1997
90(1). The Republic of Poland may, by virtue of international agreements, delegate to an international organisation or international institution the competence of organs of State authority in relation to certain matters.
90(2). A statute, granting consent for ratification of an international agreement referred to in paragraph 1, shall be passed by the Sejm by a two-thirds majority vote in the presence of at least half of the statutory number of Deputies, and by the Senate by a two-thirds majority vote in the presence of at least half of the statutory number of Senators.
90(3). Granting of consent for ratification of such agreement may also be passed by a nationwide referendum in accordance with the provisions of article 125.
90(4). Any resolution in respect of the choice of procedure for granting consent to ratification shall be taken by the Sejm by an absolute majority vote taken in the presence of at least half of the statutory number of Deputies.
91(1). After promulgation thereof in the Journal of Laws of the Republic of Poland (*Dziennik Ustaw*), a ratified international agreement shall constitute part of the domestic legal order and shall be applied directly, unless its application depends on the enactment of a statute.
91(2). An international agreement ratified upon prior consent granted by statute shall have precedence over statutes if such an agreement cannot be reconciled with the provisions of such statutes.
91(3). If an agreement, ratified by the Republic of Poland, establishing an international organisation so provides, the laws established by it shall be applied directly and have precedence in the event of a conflict of laws.

Table A7 *EU provisions and application of international law in Hungarian Constitution*

Amendment of 17 December 2002
2A(1). The Republic of Hungary for the purpose of becoming a Member State in the EU through the conclusion of an international treaty – until the necessary degree in order to fulfil the obligations and to exercise the rights stemming from the founding Treaties establishing the EU and the European Communities – can exercise certain constitutional powers jointly with other Member States. This joint exercise can be conducted also separately through the institutions of the EU.

Table A7 (cont.)

2A(2). For the purpose of ratifying the international treaty stipulated in sub-section (1) above, the two-thirds majority of the MPs is required.

6(4) The Republic of Hungary shall participate in establishing European unity for the accomplishment of the freedom, welfare and safety of European peoples.

32/D(1)The National Bank of Hungary is the central bank of the Republic of Hungary. The National Bank of Hungary is responsible for monetary policy in such manner as specified by a separate law.

35(1)(k) [The Government shall] represent the Republic of Hungary in the institutions of the European Union functioning with government participation.

35A(1) A majority of two-thirds of the votes of the Members of Parliament in attendance is required to pass the law specifying the detailed rules governing . . . the obligation of the Government to provide information in affairs related to European integration.

35A(2) The Government shall send the Parliament all the proposals being on the agenda in the decision-making procedures of the institutions of the European Union functioning with government participation.

70(2) All adult Hungarian citizens residing in the territory of the Republic of Hungary and adult citizens of any other Member State of the European Union residing in the territory of the Republic of Hungary have the right to be elected and – provided that they are in the territory of the Republic of Hungary on the day of the election or referendum – to vote in local government elections of representatives and the Mayor, as well as to participate in local referenda and popular initiatives. . . .

70(4) All adult Hungarian citizens residing in the territory of the Republic of Hungary and adult citizens of any other Member State of the European Union residing in the territory of the Republic of Hungary have the right to be elected and to vote in European parliamentary elections.

79 A national ratification referendum shall be held regarding the accession of the Republic of Hungary to the European Union according to the treaty of accession. . . .

Pre-existing provisions on international law

7(1). The legal system of the Republic of Hungary accepts the generally recognised rules of international law, and shall further ensure the harmony between domestic law and the obligations assumed under international law.

Table A8 *EU provisions and application of international law in Estonian Constitution*

Act on Supplementing the Constitution of Estonia, 14 September 2003

1. Estonia may belong to the European Union, proceeding from the fundamental principles of the Constitution of the Republic of Estonia.

2. In case Estonia belongs to the European Union, the Constitution of the Republic of Estonia shall be applied taking into consideration the rights and obligations arising from the Accession Treaty.

3. The present Law can only be amended by referendum.

Pre-existing provisions on application of international law

3. Generally recognised principles and rules of international law are an inseparable part of the Estonian legal system.

123. The Republic of Estonia shall not conclude international treaties which are in conflict with the Constitution. If laws or other legislation of Estonia are in conflict with international treaties ratified by the Riigikogu, the provisions of the international treaty shall apply.

Table A9 *EU provisions and application of international law in Latvian Constitution*

Amendments of 8 May 2003

68(2). Upon entering into international agreements, Latvia, with the purpose of strengthening democracy, may delegate a part of its State institution competences to international institutions. International agreements in which a part of State institution competencies are delegated to international institutions may be ratified by the Saeima in sittings in which at least two-thirds of the members of the Saeima participate, and a two-thirds majority vote of the members present is necessary for ratification.

Membership of Latvia in the European Union shall be decided by a national referendum, which is proposed by the Saeima.

Substantial changes in the terms regarding the membership of Latvia in the European Union shall be decided by a national referendum if such referendum is requested by at least one-half of the members of the Saeima.

Table A9 *(cont.)*

79. A draft law, decision regarding membership of Latvia in the European Union or substantial changes in the terms regarding such membership submitted for national referendum shall be deemed adopted if the number of voters is at least half of the number of electors as participated in the previous Saeima election and if the majority has voted in favour of the draft law, membership of Latvia in the European Union or substantial changes in the terms regarding such membership.

Pre-existing provisions on international law
89. The State shall recognise and protect fundamental human rights in accordance with this Constitution, laws and international agreements binding upon Latvia.

Table A10 *EU provisions and application of international law in Lithuanian Constitution*

Amendment of 20 June 2002
119. Members of municipal boards shall be elected, for a four-year term of office as set forth in the law, from citizens of the Republic of Lithuania and other permanent residents of an administrative unit by citizens of the Republic of Lithuania and other permanent residents of an administrative unit exercising the universal, equal and direct right of election in a secret voting.

Amendment of 23 January 2003
47(3). In the Republic of Lithuania foreign entities may acquire the ownership of land, internal waters, forests and parks subsequent to a constitutional law.

Pre-existing provisions on international organisations and international law
135(1). In conducting foreign policy, the Republic of Lithuania shall pursue the universally recognised principles and norms of international law . . . and shall take part in the creation of sound international order based on law and justice.

136. The Republic of Lithuania shall participate in international organisations provided that they do not contradict the interests and independence of the State.

138(3). International agreements which are ratified by the Parliament of the Republic of Lithuania shall be the constituent part of the legal system of the Republic of Lithuania.

Table A11 *EU provisions and application of international law in Romanian Constitution*

Selected amendments of 19 October 2003

145.1(1). Romania's accession to the constituent treaties of the European Union, with a view to transferring certain powers to community institutions, as well as to exercising in common with the other Member States the abilities stipulated in such treaties, shall be carried out by means of a law adopted in the joint session of the Chamber of Deputies and the Senate, with a majority of two-thirds of the number of deputies and senators.

145.1(2). As a result of the accession, the provisions of the constituent treaties of the European Union, as well as the other mandatory community regulations shall take precedence over the opposite provisions of the national laws, in compliance with the provisions of the accession act.

145.1(3). The provisions of paragraphs (1) and (2) shall also apply accordingly for the accession to the acts revising the constituent treaties of the European Union.

145.1(4). The Parliament, the President of Romania, the Government and the judicial authority shall guarantee that the obligations resulting from the accession act and the provisions of paragraph (2) are implemented.

145.1(5). The Government shall send to the two Chambers of the Parliament the draft mandatory acts before they are submitted to the European Union institutions for approval.

145.2 Romania's accession to the North Atlantic Treaty shall take place by means of a law adopted in the joint session of the Chamber of Deputies and the Senate, with a majority of two-thirds of the number of deputies and senators.

11(3). If a treaty Romania is to become a party to comprises provisions contrary to the Constitution, its ratification shall only take place after the revision of the Constitution.

16(4). After Romania's accession to the European Union, the Union's citizens who comply with the requirements of the organic law have the right to elect and be elected in the local public administration bodies.

19(11). By derogation from the provisions of paragraph (1), Romanian citizens can be extradited based on the international agreements Romania is a party to, according to the law and on a mutual basis.

Table A11 *(cont.)*

20(2). Where any inconsistencies exist between the covenants and treaties on fundamental human rights Romania is a party to, and the national laws, the international regulations shall take precedence, unless the Constitution or national laws comprise more favourable provisions.
35.1 After Romania's accession to the European Union, Romanian citizens shall have the right to elect and be elected for the European Parliament.
41(2). . . . Foreign and stateless persons shall only acquire the right to private property of land under the terms resulting from Romania's accession to the European Union and other international treaties Romania is a party to, on a mutual basis, under the terms stipulated by an organic law, as well as a result of lawful inheritance.
136(2). Under the circumstances of Romania's accession to the European Union, the circulation and replacement of the national currency by that of the European Union may be acknowledged, by means of an organic law.

Table A12 *Application of international law in Bulgarian Constitution*

Pre-existing provisions on application of international law
5.4. Any international instruments which have been ratified by the constitutionally established procedure, promulgated, and come into force with respect to the Republic of Bulgaria, shall be considered part of the domestic legislation of the country. They shall supersede any domestic legislation stipulating otherwise.
85.2. Treaties ratified by the National Assembly may be amended or denounced only by their built-in procedure or in accordance with the universally acknowledged norms of international law.

INDEX